CAMBRIDGE LIBRARY COLLECTION

Books of enduring scholarly value

Women's Writing

The later twentieth century saw a huge wave of academic interest in women's writing, which led to the rediscovery of neglected works from a wide range of genres, periods and languages. Many books that were immensely popular and influential in their own day are now studied again, both for their own sake and for what they reveal about the social, political and cultural conditions of their time. A pioneering resource in this area is Orlando: Women's Writing in the British Isles from the Beginnings to the Present (http://orlando.cambridge.org), which provides entries on authors' lives and writing careers, contextual material, timelines, sets of internal links, and bibliographies. Its editors have made a major contribution to the selection of the works reissued in this series within the Cambridge Library Collection, which focuses on non-fiction publications by women on a wide range of subjects from astronomy to biography, music to political economy, and education to prison reform.

An Essay on Intuitive Morals

Frances Power Cobbe (1822–1904) was an Irish writer, social reformer and activist best known for her contributions to Victorian feminism and women's suffrage. After the death of her father in 1857, Cobbe travelled extensively across Europe before becoming a leader-writer addressing public issues for the London newspaper The Echo in 1868. She continued to publish on the topics of feminism, social problems and theology for the rest of her life. These volumes, first published anonymously in 1855, introduced Cobbe's theistic religious beliefs, which blend a belief in Divinity with Immanuel Kant's idea of freedom of will, in which a person's moral imperative is independent of outside authority and provides proof of the existence of God. Cobbe discusses Kant's moral philosophy, explaining the religious beliefs which formed the basis for her later discussions of Christianity. Volume 1 contains her ideas on the origin of morality. For more information on this author, see http://orlando.cambridge.org/public/svPeople?person_id=cobbfr

T0382405

Cambridge University Press has long been a pioneer in the reissuing of out-of-print titles from its own backlist, producing digital reprints of books that are still sought after by scholars and students but could not be reprinted economically using traditional technology. The Cambridge Library Collection extends this activity to a wider range of books which are still of importance to researchers and professionals, either for the source material they contain, or as landmarks in the history of their academic discipline.

Drawing from the world-renowned collections in the Cambridge University Library, and guided by the advice of experts in each subject area, Cambridge University Press is using state-of-the-art scanning machines in its own Printing House to capture the content of each book selected for inclusion. The files are processed to give a consistently clear, crisp image, and the books finished to the high quality standard for which the Press is recognised around the world. The latest print-on-demand technology ensures that the books will remain available indefinitely, and that orders for single or multiple copies can quickly be supplied.

The Cambridge Library Collection will bring back to life books of enduring scholarly value (including out-of-copyright works originally issued by other publishers) across a wide range of disciplines in the humanities and social sciences and in science and technology.

An Essay on
Intuitive Morals

Being an Attempt to Popularise Ethical Science

VOLUME 1: THEORY OF MORALS

FRANCES POWER COBBE

CAMBRIDGE
UNIVERSITY PRESS

CAMBRIDGE UNIVERSITY PRESS

Cambridge, New York, Melbourne, Madrid, Cape Town, Singapore,
São Paolo, Delhi, Dubai, Tokyo

Published in the United States of America by Cambridge University Press, New York

www.cambridge.org
Information on this title: www.cambridge.org/9781108020268

This edition first published 1855
This digitally printed version 2010

ISBN 978-1-108-02026-8 Paperback

AN

ESSAY

ON

INTUITIVE MORALS,

BEING

AN ATTEMPT TO POPULARISE ETHICAL
SCIENCE.

PART I.

THEORY OF MORALS.

LONDON:

LONGMAN, BROWN, GREEN, AND LONGMANS.

1855.

Londo n
A. and G. A. Spottiswoode,
New-street-Square.

ADVERTISEMENT.

THE present volume of this Essay treats solely of the Theory of Morals. It may perhaps be followed by another which shall develope the principles herein stated in their application to Practice. That branch of Ethics called Politics will not be taken into consideration in either volume.

PREFACE.

ERRATA.

Page 49., note *, for "The truth is, that they," read "The truth is, *not* that they."

„ 79., note ¶, for "Dial Tyr" read "Dial. Try."

„ 99., note, line 6., for "The Irishman Pelagius, who with Celestius the Briton," read "The Briton Pelagius, who with Celestius the Irishman."

„ 125., line 25., for "from we" read "for we."

„ 131., line 1., for "with, and filling the soul" read "with vital power, and filling the soul."

„ 170., NOTE. Since printing this Book I find that Robertson, Jortin, and White, as well as Hallam, have all availed themselves before me of this quotation of Mosheim from St. Eligius. It deserves to be reckoned among the curiosities of literature, since it has been proved to be, after all, a most nefarious garble of the original. In the sermon of the saintly Goldsmith the words extracted do *not* form a continuous and entire "description of a good Christian," but are simply fragments of a long and excellent delineation of a character holding the weightier matters of the law in quite as much reverence as those externals of which alone the quotation takes note. — *See* "Maitland's Dark Ages," p. 100. *et seq.*, and "D'Acheri Spicilegia," vol. ii. p. 96.

PREFACE.

No Preface would be needed by a book which should effectually supply a great want, or give adequate utterance to a great truth. Perhaps none will be able to plead the apology of an Essay which must fail to accomplish either of these noble aims.

It cannot surely be questioned but that we want a System of Morals better than any of those which are current amongst us. We want a system which shall neither be too shallow for the requirements of thinking men, nor too abstruse for popular acceptation; but which shall be based upon the ultimate grounds of philosophy, and be developed with such distinctness as to be understood by every one capable of studying the subject. We want a System of Morals which shall not entangle itself with sectarian creeds, nor imperil its authority with that of tottering Churches; but which shall be indissolubly blended with a Theology fulfilling all the demands of the Religious Sentiment,—a Theology forming a part, and the one living part, of all the theologies which ever have been or shall be.

We want a system which shall not degrade the
Law of the Eternal Right by announcing it as a
mere contrivance for the production of human Happiness, or by tracing our knowledge of it to the experience of the Senses, or by cajoling us into obeying
it as a matter of Expediency; but a system which
shall ascribe to that Law its own sublime office in
the universe, which shall recognise in man the faculties by which he obtains a supersensible knowledge
of it, and which shall inculcate obedience to it on
motives so pure and holy, that the mere statement of
them shall awaken in every breast that higher and
better Self which can never be aroused by the call of
Interest or Expediency.

It would be in itself a presumption for me to disclaim the ability necessary for supplying such a want
as this, nor have I ever contemplated it as possible
that I could do so.   In writing this book I have
aimed chiefly at two objects.   1st. I have sought to
unite into one homogeneous and self-consistent whole
the purest and most enlarged theories hitherto pro-
pounded on ethical science.   Especially I have endeavoured to popularise those of Kant, giving the
simplest possible presentation to his doctrines regarding the Freedom of the Will and the supersensible
source of our knowledge of all necessary Truths,
including those of Morals.   I do not claim, however,
even so far as regards these doctrines, to be an exact
exponent of Kant's opinions; neither do I profess in
giving the name of INTUITIVE to this Scheme of Morals
to apply the word in a strictly scientific sense according to any one psychological system.   For an avow-

edly Popular Treatise I have taken a word in itself popular, which yet seems to convey with sufficient accuracy the idea of that purely mental element or subjective factor of thought which is admitted universally by transcendental schools to form a constituent of all human knowledge, and to be both base and superstructure of deductive science. 2ndly. I have sought (and this has been my chief aim) to place for the first time, as the foundation of ethics, the great but neglected truth that the End of Creation is not the Happiness, but the Virtue of Rational Souls. I believe that this truth will be found to throw most valuable light not only upon the Theory, but upon all the details of Practical Morals. Nay, more, I believe that we must look to it for such a solution of the "Riddle of the World" as shall satisfy the demands of the Intellect while presenting to the Religious Sentiment that same God of perfect Justice and Goodness whose ideal it intuitively conceives and spontaneously adores. Only with *this* view of the Designs of God can we understand how His Moral attributes are consistent with the creation of a race which is indeed "groaning in sin" and "travailing in sorrow;" but by whose Freedom to sin and Trial of sorrow shall be worked out at last the most blessed End which Infinite Love could desire. With this clue we shall also see how (as the Virtue of each Individual must be produced by himself, and is the share committed to him in the grand end of creation) all Duties must necessarily range themselves accordingly—the Personal before the Social—in a sequence entirely different from that which is conformable with the hypothesis that Happiness is "our being's end and aim;" but which is, nevertheless, precisely the sequence in which Intuition has always peremptorily demanded that they should be arranged. We shall see how (as the bestowal of Happiness on man must always be postponed by God to the still more merciful aim of conducing to his Virtue) the greatest outward woes and trials, so far from inspiring us with doubts of His Goodness, must be taken as the strongest evidences of it, and of the glory of that End of Virtue to which they are subservient. We shall see how at this very hour while grief spreads a flood of tears over our land, while tens of thousands of noblest hearts lie cold in their Crimean graves, how God the Good One has permitted that all this woe should come upon his creatures, has left to its tyrant author the Freedom he has misused to work it, and has brought out, through sorrows and agonies untold, Love, Generosity, Fortitude, Patience, and Piety, such as without them neither we nor those noble sufferers would ever have known ; VIRTUES.which have hallowed this world, and which the Martyrs shall carry with them through all the worlds to come.

I cannot hope that I have succeeded in these two designs of producing a Self-consistent System of Ethics, and of setting forth the great doctrine of the true End of Creation. To digest and systematise an immense body of philosophy, such as that of Ethics, would require an extent of learning and a grasp of thought which no labour would enable me to attain. To explain popularly, and yet accurately, the Metaphysic of Morals would demand a lucidity of

expression after which, I fear, I have often striven
unsuccessfully. To speak in any way worthily of
the solemn themes of the Eternal Law, and of the
Designs of God, would ask for better gifts than learning or eloquence — gifts whose deficiency I must
much more deeply deplore. Yet, with the consciousness of all these imperfections, I have thought it well
to give such labour as was in my power to this particular work, and for this reason : — I do not believe
that the experience of any human mind is ever soli-
tary, but that the truths which have proved of vital
importance to one must be of value also to many.
I believe, therefore, that the solutions of my own
difficulties must be the solutions of the questionings
of other hearts no less anxious than was mine ere
those solutions were found. In a word, I have written
this book because, if it had been in my hands in youth,
it would have been to me a help such as I should account myself most blessed to be allowed to give to
one of my fellow-creatures.

I know that it will be said that it would be better
to have no help at all than such as this. My book
will be condemned by some for advancing new religious views, which *must* be false because we have
no evidence that the Apostles held them ; and it will
be condemned by others for going back to old meta-
physics, which *must* also be false because Fichte and
Schelling and Hegel have lived since Kant. What
can I say ? I admit, sincerely, that I am convinced
there must be many errors left behind in the large
field I have attempted to traverse. I am convinced
that (especially in the metaphysical part) there are

many errors of logic, and errors in comprehension of
the great masters whose views I have endeavoured to
explain. In the face of profound books like those
of the Germans, or of such English ones as those of
Hamilton or Mill, a book of this kind seems an im-
pertinence ; yet, as it is the very depth and greatness
of the really philosophic works which exclude them
from popular perusal, and as it is the main design of
this one to make Morals a *Popular* Science, perhaps
some indulgence will be shown to a superficiality
whose absence would neutralise the only utility it can
hope to achieve. I can but repeat what I said above
— This philosophy, these arguments, these meta-
physics, all imperfect though they be, have been of
true practical value to my own mind ; and, if so,
there must needs be many other minds not so far
different as to be incapable of deriving advantage
from them.

It would seem that there is an epoch in the life of
every thinking man in which the religious dogmas
learned in childhood, and with them all Religion and
Morality, are involved in temporary Scepticism. It is
well that it should be so ; for by such process only can
our Faith acquire the higher value of a possession
earned by our own toil over that which we inherit
without exertion.

" The road to Resolution lies through Doubt." *

The simple credence of the child, though so often

<hr>

* Quarles
Tennyson also says,

<blockquote>
" There is more Faith in honest Doubt,
Believe me, than in half the creeds."
</blockquote>

lauded and coveted, is useless, or at best hazardous, for the man. He must himself " hew out of the solid marble of life " a Faith which shall resist the summer's heat and winter's storm, while the snowy image of infancy melts away in the first beams of the sun. But, needful though it be, this transition through Scepticism, this "journey across the howling wilderness of Doubt to the new, firm lands of Faith beyond," * is a fearfully dangerous one. We cannot sit still in our libraries to work out the great problems of existence with calmness and security. During all the months and years of that dread task, we are compelled to *live*, to feel, and act, as well as to think and study. Nay, the work is commonly forced upon us at the very time when life is most vigorous within us, and the passions of youth are struggling to free themselves from every bond. At this crisis there is nothing we so much want as a sound Morality whose fetters no alchemy of sophistry can dissolve. We want to be assured that the Conscience which speaks to us is a real voice, and that it has a right to be heard. We want to ratify our Intuitions in the court of the Intellect, and to be convinced that there are other realities and a still surer knowledge than those which our strong senses can feel or teach. Till we have found some great Law which has a right to regulate our actions, we are in no condition for other inquiries. The slave of Impulse can never be the liege Servant of Truth, nor can any of our Mental faculties perform their functions aright while our Moral Nature is in a state of anarchy.

* T. Carlyle.

I hope that this book may in a measure meet the necessities of this solemn period of life; that there may be some whose doubts it may resolve, and whose confidence in the certainty of Moral Truths it may increase. I hope that there may be some who will bear from its perusal the conviction that Philosophy has no lesson more sure, nor Religion any doctrine of more Divine authority, than that Voice of INTUITION which ever speaks in their hearts of the Infinite Goodness of our Father in Heaven, and of the awful Sanctity of that Eternal Law which is impersonate in His righteous Will.

London, February, 1855.

AN

ESSAY ON INTUITIVE MORALS.

PART I.

THEORY OF MORALS.

THE Science of Intuitive Morals treats of the Theory and Practice of the Moral Law, deduced exclusively from certain necessary Truths possessed intuitively by the Human Mind.

The Theory of Intuitive Morals teaches —
    1st. What is the Moral Law.
    2nd. Where it is to be found.
    3rd. That it can be obeyed.
    4th. Why it is to be obeyed.

The Practice of Intuitive Morals teaches —
    1st. Social Duty.
    2nd. Personal Duty.
    3rd. Religious Duty.

CHAPTER I.

WHAT IS THE MORAL LAW.

<div align="center">~~~~~~~~~~</div>

. . . " ἄγραπτα κἀσφαλῆ θεῶν
νόμιμα. . . . . .
οὐ γάρ τι νῦν γε κἀχθές, ἀλλ᾽ ἀεί ποτε
ζῇ ταῦτα, κοὐδεὶς οἶδεν ἐξ ὅτου 'φάνη."

Σοφ. 'Αντιγ. 454.

THE Sentiments and Actions of all Rational Free Agents possess a certain character peculiar to them as such. All creatures, rational and irrational, experience sentiments and perform actions which may be properly qualified as strong or weak, durable or transient, useful or injurious. But it is exclusively to those of Rational free agents that we apply the terms Right or Wrong, Good or Evil, Virtuous or Vicious. The ideas symbolised by these words refer to the *moral* character of the sentiments or actions in question ; and this moral character (according to the universal sense of mankind) can only be attributed when the subject or agent is Rational, — that is, cognisant of such character in his sentiments and actions; and morally Free, — that is, capable of determining such character.

This moral character of good or evil is a real, universal, and eternal distinction, existing through all worlds and for ever, wherever there are rational creatures and free agents. As one kind of line is a straight line, and another a crooked line, and as no line can be both straight and crooked, so one kind of action or sentiment is right, and another is wrong, and no action or sentiment can be both right and wrong. And as the same line which is straight on this planet would be straight in Sirius or Alcyone, and what constitutes straightness in the nineteenth century will constitute straightness in the ninetieth millenium, so that sentiment or action, which is right in our world, is right in all worlds; and that which constitutes righteousness now will constitute righteousness through all eternity. And as the character of straightness belongs to the line, by whatsoever hand it may have been traced, so the character of righteousness belongs to the sentiment or action, by what rational free agent soever it may have been felt or performed.*

* "The distinction of right from wrong is discerned by reason, and as soon as these words are defined, it becomes evident that it would be a contradiction in terms to affirm that any power, human or divine, could change their nature, or, in other words, make the same acts to be just and unjust at the same time."—CUDWORTH *On Eternal and Immutable Morality.*

"La Justice est un rapport de convenance qui se trouve réellement entre deux choses; ce rapport est toujours le même quelque être qui le considère, soit que ce soit Dieu, soit que ce soit un ange, ou enfin que ce soit un homme."— MONTESQUIEU, *Lettres Persanes*, p. 83.

"All the relations of all things to all must have been always present to the Divine Mind, even before the things themselves existed. The eternal *different* relations of things involve a consequent fitness or unfitness in the application of things one to another, with a regard to which the will of God always chooses, and which also ought to determine the wills of all rational creatures. These eternal differences make it fit for the creatures so to act; they lay an obligation on them so to do, separate from the will of God, and antecedently to any prospect of advantage or reward. Nay, wilful wickedness is the same insolence and absurdity in morals, as it would be, in natural things, to pretend to alter the relations of numbers, or to take away the properties of mathematical figures."—MACKINTOSH'S *Abstract of the Doctrines of Clarke.* Both Mackintosh and Whewell remark the fallacy of the last assertion. Clarke overlooked the fact that into wilful wickedness there enters another element beside mere knowledge of right and wrong. To *say* that wrong is right is the same absurdity as to pretend to alter the relations of numbers; but to *do* wrong, knowing it to be wrong, is not an absurdity, but a sin. Absurdity is the error of the intellect,—wickedness, of the will. But it more concerns me here to remark that the terms used by Clarke of "fitness" and "unfitness," to characterise moral distinctions, are very exceptionable, and have tended somewhat to discredit the truth of that distinction on which I am insisting. The fact is that all analogies fail us, and only introduce confusion when we apply them to the distinction between moral good and moral evil, which is one entirely *sui generis*, and without parallel in the material world. Even the use of the term "right," — whose felicity of metaphor has caused it to be so consecrated to moral purposes by the universal consent of mankind that such use of it is more familiar to us than its primary signification of straightness,—even the use of this word has not been unproductive of error. In the last century we find Tucker (a moralist of some note, author of "The Light of Nature Pursued,") blundering as follows : — "Right belongs to lines, being the same as straight in opposition to curved or crooked. From hence it has been applied, by way of metaphor, to rules and actions which, lying in the line of our progress to any purpose we aim at, if they be wrong they will carry us aside, but if they conduct by the nearest way, we call them right. Therefore, the very expression of 'right in itself' is absurd; because things are rendered right by their tendency to some end; so that you must take something exterior into the account, in order to evince their rectitude." "It is curious," observes Whewell, "that his own illustration here did not at least cause some scruple in his mind, for in truth we do *not* 'take anything exterior into account' to determine whether a line be straight or crooked. Its reference to some given point may decide whether it be in the *right direction*, but it is straight in virtue of the necessary relations of space altogether independent of direction."— *Hist. of Moral Philosophy in England.*

Hooker is not altogether exempt from the same error :— "Goodness in actions is like unto straightness; wherefore that which is done well we call right.

And of this distinction language affords a reliable exponent. When we have designated one kind of figure by the word Circle, and another by the word Triangle, those terms, having become the names of the respective figures, cannot be transposed without transgression of the laws of language. Thus it would be absurd to argue that the figure we call a circle, may not be a circle; that a " plane figure, containing a point from which all right lines drawn to the circumference shall be equal," may not be a circle but a triangle. In like manner, when we have designated one kind of action as Right, and another as Wrong, it becomes an absurdity to say that the kind of actions we call Right may, perhaps, be Wrong. If a figure be not a Circle, according to *our sense* of the word, it is not a Circle at all, but an Ellipse, a Triangle, Trapezium, or something else. If an action be not Right, according to our sense of the word, it is not Right at all, but, according to the laws of language, must be called Wrong.

It is not maintained that we can commit no error in affixing the name of Circle to a particular figure, or of Right to a particular action. We may at a hasty glance pronounce an ellipse to be a circle; but when, with rule and compasses, we have proved the radii to be unequal, needs must we arrive at a better judgment. Our error was caused by our first haste and misjudgment, not by our inability to decide whether an object presented to us bears or does not bear a character to which we have agreed to affix a certain name. In like manner, from haste or prejudice, we may pronounce a faulty action to be Right; but when we have examined it in all its bearings, we ourselves are the first to call it Wrong. On this topic, of what, in moral judgments, is fallible and what possesses mathematical certainty, I shall have much to say hereafter. My object at present is to convince the reader

For as the straight way is most acceptable to him that travelleth, because by it he cometh soonest to his journey's end, so that in actions which do lie nearest between us and the end we desire, must needs be the fittest for our use. Besides which fitness for our use, there is also in rectitude, beauty ; as, contrariwise, in obliquity, deformity ; and that which is good in the actions of men doth not only delight as profitable, but as amiable also."—*Eccles. Pol.,* i.

Of the inadequacy of this popular simile of physical beauty to moral rectitude, I shall speak hereafter.

that, if he admit the grand postulate of the eternal moral
distinction of actions, he may carry into the future steps of
the inquiry concerning it, a security in the general meaning of
the terms of human language applied to that distinction.

But what is this distinction of Right and Wrong practically
considered? Is it not that of actions which are Right for a
Rational free agent to do, or wrong for him to do? When
we attempt to analyse the terms, we find that their essential
significance is that of *obligation* to do the right and refrain
from the wrong. We cannot sever the idea of such obligation from the distinctions, or think of the moral character of
actions as we can of the æsthetic or dynamic, with no concomitant sense of moral obligation. All the axioms of the
science of ethics translate themselves spontaneously into the
imperative mood : "It is right to speak truth" means " Speak
truth ;" " It is wrong to be cruel" means " Be not cruel."
All our terms for moral distinctions and moral obligations
are interchangeable. That which is " right " is what we
" ought" to do ; that which it is our "duty " to do, is what
is good or virtuous. And this idea of obligation not only
responds to, but exhausts the idea conveyed by the moral
distinction. When we have said that an action " ought " to
be performed, we have rendered to the full the meaning of
its appellation of Right, Good, or Virtuous. Any other characteristics it may possess are not moral, and are not involved
in these terms.

Thus, then, moral Distinctions resolve themselves into
moral Obligations, whereby all rational free agents are
bound in the nature of things to do and to feel those actions and sentiments which, according to these eternal distinctions, are right, and to refrain from those which are wrong.
This may also be proved negatively. If there were no moral
beings in existence, nothing could be right or wrong in any
world. Nothing could be done right, for there would be no
one to do it. Nothing could be known to be right, for there
would be no one to know it. But if, in a universe inhabited
only by brutes, moral distinctions could not exist, it is plain
that they now have their existence only in the moral natures
of God and his rational creatures. We here arrive at the

important conclusion that Right and Wrong are things in the minds of Moral Agents, and are eternal, because coeval with the existence of such beings, of whom God is chief.

Further : minds capable of being the subjects of moral distinctions assume their respective characters, inasmuch as their sentiments and actions correspond with one or the other. If they do and feel Right, they are Virtuous; if they do and feel Wrong, they are Vicious. Ultimately, then, all moral distinctions resolve themselves into the Virtue or Vice of Rational Free Agents.

This Obligation to do and feel all Right actions and sentiments, and to abstain from those of an opposite character, constitutes the Moral Law. It has been often represented as of a double nature, — declaratory and imperative ; teaching us what is right, and commanding us to do right. This distinction, however, becomes superfluous when we recognise the truth on which I have above insisted,—that the essential property of a right action is, *that it ought to be performed by a rational free agent,* and that there is no possibility of severing the idea of Right from that of Obligation. The Moral Law is the simplest of all things, It is the result solely of the nature of the action and the nature of the agent. These two terms being given, the obligation of the rational free agent to perform the right action results necessarily in the nature of things. We call this moral obligation the " law," and a law it truly is—the basis of all other laws; but it is needful to guard against the errors of applying to this underived law the analogies of human derived legislation. The authority of the human lawgivers, the rewards and punishments with which their codes are enforced, the end of utility at which they mostly aim, — none of these things belong to the simple Moral Law. That law is a bare obligation grounded on the nature of things, and standing out all the more grandly in its naked dignity when divested of extraneous authority, of a protective system of rewards and punishments, or of any end of utility whatever. Even the Virtue of rational beings, into which, as I have said, moral Right resolves itself in the last analysis, even this Virtue we must not regard as if it were the end for whose production the Moral Law might be considered as a contrivance.

That law is no system of technical rules for the attainment of a condition of purity, benevolence, and piety. If there were not an intrinsic excellence in those acts and sentiments, distinguished as morally right, there could be nothing excellent in the condition of soul uniting them all. It would be arguing in a vicious circle to affirm " the Moral Law is made to produce virtue," and " virtue consists in obedience to the law." The Moral Law is not *made* at all. It exists necessarily in the nature of things founded on distinctions properly belonging to the actions and sentiments of rational beings, as the distinctions of equality and inequality belong to numbers, and the distinctions of straightness and crookedness belong to lines. It is not the standard of Right, which is, or can be, shifted so as to conduce to our beatification ; it is our Virtue which must be fitted to meet that standard.

Human virtue, then, is the end of the Moral Law, only in the sense that it is its impersonation and fulfilment—the concrete form of its abstraction.

And this human virtue, like that eternal Right which it impersonates, is a real and positive thing—not a mere negation of vice. Both etymologically and philosophically, " wrong " means " wrung " from, " divergent from " the right. Right is the positive, wrong merely its negation. It is no less inaccurate to say, " Whatever is not wrong is right," than to say, " Whatever is not cold is heat." In each case we must say, "The negative of right is wrong;" " The negative of caloric is cold." It may seem that this distinction is merely a logical quibble ; but it has vast practical weight. So long as we look on right as the mere negation of wrong, we can never comprehend its affirmative importance, its energy, reality, and vitality. To " do no harm " becomes our aim, not to " do good and be good." The evil of the world lies on us like an incubus, for we think *it* the reality; and love, and truth, and purity merely the absence of hatred, falsehood, and corruption. Like the clown, who believes that cold and darkness are something positive, and not merely the negations of caloric and light, we give to evil an affirmative existence,— nay, a personified one. We believe that the universe contains not only One absolutely good, but also One absolutely evil; not only a God, but a

Devil. But these are visions of the night. The universe has indeed a Sun of light and heat, but it has no sun with rays of darkness and frost. "Evil," as saith the brave old oracle, "is more frail than nonentity."* It is evanescent, a negation ever dwindling before the growing reality. Human virtue is a real thing, the strength and goodness of an immortal spirit. Human vice is its temporary subtraction of weakness and evil. Virtue is the "plus," vice the "minus," of the great arithmetic of the world. The eternal Right is the true law of our being; to obey it is normal, to disobey it, abnormal. There is no "broad road to destruction," from which to keep our feet would make us virtuous. There is a "narrow way," the divergencies from which radiate in every direction and to every distance, and the first step in such divergency is Wrong.

Hitherto I have spoken of the obligation of man to obey the eternal Right, considering such obligation, as it is truly founded, simply on the nature of moral actions and moral agents. I have affirmed such obligation as the fundamental postulate of sound ethics, a necessary truth given in the nature of man, and incapable of demonstration as the axioms of geometry.

But though it be thus possible, and, for argumentative purposes, useful, to contemplate man standing alone in the universe with this bare abstract obligation to perform the right and eschew the wrong, it is, nevertheless, impossible to obtain a just idea of his moral condition, without taking into consideration that the abstract law of right is resumed in One righteous Will, towards whom he stands in all the complicated relations of creature to Creator.

We have seen that human virtue is the concrete of the abstract law. The question which next concerns us is: What relation does that virtue bear to the will of God?

Now, concerning the attributes of the Deity, from which

* Proc. de Prov., Cory's Fragments.

we must deduce the answer to this momentous inquiry, it is always difficult to speak. Whenever we attempt to dogmatise about the nature of the Supreme, our hearts sink within us, and we feel that it is indeed " dangerous for the feeble brain of man to wade far into the doings of the Most High, whom, although to know be life, and joy to make mention of His name, yet our soundest knowledge is to know that we know Him not as indeed He is, neither can know Him, and that our safest eloquence concerning him is our silence, whereby we confess, without confession, that His glory is inexplicable, His greatness beyond our capacity and reach." * In the infinite abysses of His being, the thoughts of man pale and falter. In the heights of His stupendous grandeur, even Adoration falls back from her soaring flight, to nestle amid the flowers of earth. Nor is it only the immensity of God, the eternal Past, the eternal Future, the infinite Within, the infinite Without, which thus bewilder us. All the conditions of dependent and caused existence disappear in the self-sustained First Cause. We have, in fact, no standing point on which to rest — not even an analogy to which we might cling.

It is no marvel that our dazzled sight should fail us, when gazing on this Light of Light. No marvel that we should confound the bounds of the possible and the self-contradictory, when we picture a Power which

" Spreads undivided, operates unspent, "

beyond the utmost horizon of finite vision. It seems as if He who built the heavens could know no limits of necessity; as if He could change the past †, and alter the relations of numbers, and make right wrong, and evil good. We ask, impatiently, What means necessity in the presence of God the Almighty? Did He not give to matter its laws? and, by His will alone, does not gravitation roll the suns? These things are hidden in night our feeble eyes can never pierce.

---

* Hooker, Eccles. Pol., b. i.
† " Wherefore Agathon rightly says, Of this only even God is deprived, the power of making things that are past not to have been."—ARISTOT. *Ethics*, b. vi. c. ii.

How came there to be an universe at all, — an island in the shoreless ocean of eternal Time and infinite Space? *How came there to be a God?* Then, prostrate in dismay and awe, fall our audacious spirits

> " Upon the great world's altar-stairs,
> Which lead through darkness up to God."

Yet — yet it is not *all* darkness. The Lord, before whose majesty our hearts fail within us, is the same Father by whose everlasting arms we have been supported all our life long. Yea, Father, Mother, All! Source of every joy, Teacher of every truth, Hearer of every prayer, Witness of every thought! Do we know nothing of a Being near to us as this? Has He been guiding us by His providence, speaking to us through conscience, blessing us, both with joys and punishments, from our cradle till this hour, when He stands close to our inmost hearts, and yet can we form no conception of His character?

The truth is, that it is neither right, nor even possible, for us to put aside inquiry into the attributes of God. The human mind inevitably returns, after every failure, to attempt afresh the solution of a problem on which something more than its happiness depends. The deepest want of the soul is an object for its adoration, and it can know no rest till the intellect has ratified its intuitive ascription to its Creator of that character which it spontaneously reveres and loves. And God, also, has shown us that He desires we should thus search out His attributes. In giving us moral natures, He has expressly founded His claim to our adoration on the veneration those natures feel for goodness and holiness, and which it is impossible for them to feel towards any being, howsoever great and powerful, in whom they do not recognise those attributes. In deigning to hold with us the awful communion of prayer, He has drawn us up from the position of criminals before our Judge to that of children at the feet of our Father. As " *our good Father*," then, are we bound to adore Him ; and just as the noblest filial piety would lead us to search out and vindicate with triumphant love the character of our earthly parent, so the truest piety towards

God will teach us to seek every evidence accessible to us of His glorious attributes.

It does not enter into the scope of a treatise on morals to discuss the evidences of natural theology. It will be enough if I here refer to the shortest and clearest of those arguments concerning the moral attributes of the Deity, which, being deduced from intuition, harmonise most perfectly with intuitive morality.

The distinction of right and wrong being a real distinction in the nature of the things which are right and wrong, it is clear that it must be the same distinction, whatsoever being regard it. To hold with Ockham*, that good and evil exist only in the mere pleasure of God, who, if He so willed it, could make all crime right and all virtue wrong, is to confound reason, and even to undermine the religion professedly exalted ; for if there be nothing real in goodness, independent of the will of God, it is altogether unmeaning to affirm that His will *is* good ; that truth, the most vital of all, becomes the senseless truism " God's will, is His will." There is no more place left for that which constitutes the essence of religion,—our reverence for His moral attributes ; their reality is sunk with the reality of the distinctions of the right which God loves, the wrong He abhors. We may still bow to His omnipotence, but there is an end of adoration of His goodness.†

Moreover, such an exercise of omnipotence as the transformation of right into wrong is altogether an absurd and fantastic notion, tending, not to exalt our ideas of God, but to involve Him in a haze of obscurity. When we endeavour to give a definite shape to such an assertion, we see that it is equivalent

* Brown seems to have held this error, which is, perhaps, derivable from that of the Moral Sense being the true foundation of Ethical Science. A *sense* gives us pleasure and pain *contingent* on the order of Providence ; an *intuition* of the pure reason teaches us a *necessary* truth. Chalmers exposes Brown's mistake in his Preface to his Lectures. The heresy, however, is a very common one, though more frequently latent in the minds of theologians and moralists than distinctly recognised. See it broadly avowed, however, *inter alia*, by Johnson: "I have heard him strongly maintain," says Boswell, "that what is right is *not* so from any natural fitness, but because God wills it to be right."—*Life of Johnson*, b. iv. p. 30. (3rd edit.)

† "If we make holiness, justice, and purity the mere result of God's commands, we can no longer find any force in the declaration that God is holy, just, and pure."—WHEWELL, *Hist. of Ethic. Phil.*, p. 59.

to one which should maintain God's power to make twice two to constitute five. The human mind must peremptorily reject absurdities like these, or suffer itself to sink into a hopeless fatuity. It must decide, once for all, to dwell in a cloud with neither sun above nor earth below, or it must hold fast that ground under its feet which was given by the Creator to be the basis of all thought, the belief in the stability of necessary truths. Now, as I have so often repeated, the distinctions of right and wrong are necessary, existing in the things which are right and wrong, as straightness and crookedness in lines, evenness and unevenness in numbers. God, who knows all things, must needs know this distinction. It must be perfectly clear to Him what kind of government of the universe would be right and what would be wrong; and if He be perfectly cognisant of those real distinctions, it is not hard for us to find evidence that his character is such that He will always do the right and never the wrong. For this purpose we need not have recourse to arguments of the necessary holiness of a pure Will, untrammelled by any lower nature; neither need we gather up from this beautiful and happy universe the proofs of the benefi- cence of its Creator; we have evidence of His character nearer and clearer even than these. These hearts of ours, which God has made, what is it which they are compelled by their nature to revere and love? Is it not justice, benevo- lence, purity, truth? Must not He, then, be *that* which He has made them adore? What is it that they spontaneously despise and scorn? Is it not injustice, malevolence, impurity, falsehood? Is it possible, then, that any action of His can partake, be it never so remotely, of those characteristics which He has forced us to contemn and abhor? *

In whatever way we envisage the moral attributes of God,

* Isaac Taylor has acutely remarked that even those unhappy persons who seem to hate God always deny his goodness before they can pretend to do so. "Thus does the Supreme Benevolence secure and receive the most implicit homage even from the most envenomed lips ; for why should the divine cha- racter be aspersed, if it were not that the fixed laws of the moral world — those very laws of which God is author — forbid hatred to exist at all, except on a pretext which is itself drawn from the maxims of goodness ? What proof can be more convincing than this, that these same maxims, the rules of virtue and benevolence, were actually the guiding principles of creation, and therefore belong as essential attributes to the Creator?"—*Hist. of Fanaticism.*

this blessed fact, that He is *our Creator*, meets us as the response to our questioning. Do we want to know whether the distinctions of right and wrong, as they appear to our puny intellects, are identical with the distinctions perceived by His omniscience? The answer is clear. That knowledge which *we* possess *He* gave. Our intuition is His tuition. The fundamental axioms of the reason were given by Him to afford us a basis of thought. Even the inductions of the understanding are all drawn by the mental machinery with which He has provided us, from the visible universe His hands have made. When, honestly and carefully, we have arrived at the conviction that "truth is right," we may confidently trace back that conviction to God. Our knowledge of the fact is a mere reflex of His knowledge, such as He has been pleased to give us. To suppose that it is fallacious, is to attribute to Him the most horrible deception. And fallacious it would be, if increased knowledge were to prove that what we thought right were wrong, or that what we thought wrong for us were right for others. The only difference which can exist between divine and human knowledge of moral distinctions is, that God knows *all* the goodness of good—*all* the evil of evil, and we know but a part of either. But *that* part we know truly. As we advance in knowledge throughout our immortality, we shall see more and more the goodness of justice and benevolence,—the evil of injustice and malevolence; we can never see less good in the first—less evil in the second. We contemplate an action of God now, and we know it to be good; hereafter we shall see tenfold more goodness in it. But it can never come to pass that when we behold all its bearings we shall find aught which in our heart of hearts we should call *less* than absolutely good.

Again: do we want to know whether, while He *beholds* the same moral distinctions as ourselves, He will always *choose* the right?—whether that awful self-sustained despotic Will which rules the heavens is always determined by the intrinsic rightfulness of every act? Here, again, as I have said, we are answered by the fact that it is He alone who has breathed into our hearts that reverence for the right which makes us restless till we see it throned in and with Him. It is He who has taught us to bow our souls only to that " sceptre of his kingdom which is a right sceptre," and to loathe and despise the most powerful of despots who should not determine his actions by the eternal law.

God, then, is absolutely Just and Benevolent in *our sense* of those words. He fulfils to the uttermost, and surpasses immeasurably, our ideas of those attributes. We shall continually learn that He is more *what we call* just and benevolent than we now think Him to be. We shall never find that He is in the remotest degree what, in the inmost recesses of our hearts, we should call less than perfectly just and perfectly benevolent.

Having reached these conclusions concerning the character of the Deity, we are now qualified to discuss the question with which we started, namely : What relation does human Virtue bear to the Will of God ? What share had its production in His designs when He created our race ?

Proceeding on our premises that the omnipotence of God is not to be supposed to include self-contradictions, we observe at the outset that (so far as we can understand subjects so transcendent) there were only, in a moral point of view, three orders of beings possible in the universe : —

1st. One Infinite Being. A Rational Free Agent, raised by the infinitude of his nature above the possibility of temptation. He is the only *Holy* Being.

2nd. Finite creatures who are Rational Free Agents, but exposed by the finity of their natures to continual temptations. These beings are either *Virtuous* or *Vicious*.

3rd. Finite creatures who are not rational nor morally free. These beings are *Un-moral*, and neither virtuous nor vicious.

Dismissing for the present the consideration of the first and third classes, I return to consider the second, which, in our planet, is occupied solely by the human race.

I have said that finite creatures who are rational free agents are exposed to temptation in consequence of their finite natures. This truth is commonly disputed. We are told of angels, of dwellers in the stars, and of the spirits of the departed, all of whom men have imagined to be beyond the

c

reach of temptation to sin. But surely a little reflection
might convince us that the attributes we give to such beings
mutually exclude one another, and that while we call them
finite, we are claiming for them the distinctions of infinity.
It is precisely the infinitude of God which enables us to
predicate His absolute holiness. His alone is that pure Will
which has no lower nature with blind instincts against which
to contend. Or (if it be objected that we cannot positively
assert that there be no created incorporeal beings) at least He
alone is omnipotent, absolutely happy, and self-sufficing, incapable of receiving addition to His happiness. But none of
this can apply to a finite creature. Short of infinity there
is always room for increase of happiness and consequently for
temptation. Short of omniscience and omnipotence there is
room for ignorance and weakness. In a word, short of perfection, there must be imperfection.

Now two infinite beings are, mathematically speaking, impossible, — One alone fills all space and time. Therefore in
creating a being, the decision (with reverence be it said) lies
solely between a moral fallible nature or an unmoral one,
such as belongs to the brutes. It is in vain that we dress
the phantom of our brains in the glorious plumes of an angel.
A created being who *could not* sin would be, not *above*, but
below humanity. With the liability to temptation he would
also lose the possibility of virtue without attaining any the
nearer to that holiness which results, not from the negation
of moral freedom, but from the positive Infinity of the Holy
One.* An impeccable finite being is a brute.

Were it otherwise, and were it within the scope of
Almighty Power to create beings morally free, yet morally
perfect, this world of trial and sin would, indeed, present a
riddle utterly insoluble. Could all that we learn in it be
miraculously imparted to us at our birth, this great school of

---

* " Evil is not out of (*ex*) God, nor co-eternal with God, but evil arose out
of the free-will of our rational nature, which was created good by Him who is
good; but man's goodness is not equal to the goodness of his Creator, since he
is not of his nature (as the Manichees taught), but his workmanship ; *therefore
he was under the possibility*, not the necessity, of sinning. But he had not even
been under the possibility had he had the nature of God, who neither wills to be
able, nor is able, to will to sin."—St. AUGUSTINE, *Op. Imp. Julian. Pelag.*,
iv. 5.

souls would be a superfluity, a pleonasm in creation. Were righteousness something external to the soul, wherewith it might be " clothed " at any moment, and not rather a strength and agility to be acquired by our own exercise, — were it a wealth like that of gold, to be " imputed " to us in a bank-book, and not rather the riches of the mind to be earned by our own study, — *then*, indeed, we might vainly ask, why a God all good and holy has pained by trial, and left struggling with sin, creatures whom, by a word, He could have made absolutely happy and absolutely virtuous. But in truth a circular triangle, a square ellipse, a cubical pyramid, are not more surd and senseless notions than a Sinless Creature, an Infinite Finite, a Perfect Imperfect being.

Now it appears that God has seen fit to create beings occupying this second grade in the universe. Our own planet not only swarms with irrational creatures, — beasts, birds, fishes, and insects, on whom, so far as we may judge, no moral freedom has been bestowed, — but it is also peopled by men. We are rational and morally free. We are fallible and imperfect, capable of virtue and capable also of vice. The precise rank which we hold among other orders of rational free agents, the degree of our moral strength and moral weakness, we must, of course, consider to be that appointed for us by the wisdom of our Creator. We are at liberty to believe that, as among the individuals of our own race, these conditions vary considerably, and men are to be found in all stages of moral progress, from that of the cannibal to that of the martyr, so among the innumerable orders of intelligences throughout the thousand clusters of suns, these conditions and the stages of progress vary still more vastly, even to an extent which might appear to us infinite. But (as I have endeavoured to demonstrate) that we and they must ever be *fallible* and *imperfect*, is as much a necessity as that a number not being equal must be unequal.

God having actually created such free and fallible moral beings, it remains to consider what end He can have had in view in their creation. Did he make us for His own sake, or for the sake of any other beings in the universe, or for our own sakes?

It is strange that a question like this should need formal response; yet how often do we hear the phrase, "God does so and so for His own glory," used in a manner which reveals the speaker's conviction that the act in question does actually enhance the "glory" of the Supreme; and that the said "glory" is something desirable to Him! Now, when we attempt to analyse the idea conveyed by this ambiguous word, we find that it presents two different impressions, according as we use it respective or irrespective of witnesses. Apart from the admiration or cognisance of any intelligent being, "glory" can mean nothing but intrinsic wisdom, justice, or goodness. To say, then, in this sense of the word, that God does an act for " His glory," only means that He does it because it is wise, just, or good ; and the perfection and felicity of God being absolute and incapable of receiving addition, it is manifest that the wisdom, justice, and goodness of His acts can have reference only to the creatures towards whom they are exercised, and in no degree to His own character.

But if we understand "glory" with reference to the witnesses of glorious things, and talk of the "glory of God" as consisting in the reverence, admiration, and homage of intelligent beings, then to say that "He acts for the sake of such glory " is not, as in the former case, to use a vague and inaccurate phraseology, but fearfully to derogate from the Divine character. What! shall we despise a man who acts justly or benevolently merely for the sake of admiration, and shall we dare to attribute such a motive to the infinitely Pure? Shall we contemn a man (a *man* who has equals for admirers) if he build an almshouse for sake of applause, — and shall we venture to affirm that He whose ineffable happiness could not be increased by the united hallelujahs of the created universe, has yet designed and built the starry heavens for no more noble a purpose?

And if not for His "glory," neither can it be for "free pleasure," nor " arbitrary preterition," that God could have made man. We have no ground to believe there is room for such things in His nature. Whatever is good and just, that we know to be the pleasure and choice of God; but to attribute to Him any other pleasure or choice is gross anthropomorphism. Goodness is the nature of God, and God is personified essential goodness. We know of Him nothing more.

If God did not make us for His own sake, still less could He have made us for the sake of any other order of beings in the universe. So far as we are aware there is no class of beings above ourselves to whose welfare we contribute; and it would be absurd to suppose us made for the advantage of the lower animals, — the greater for the less. Even were it otherwise, with respect to beings above or below us, and we had reason to believe ourselves of essential consequence to their happiness, still it could never be admitted that any sentient, far less intelligent, link in the chain was made solely for the sake of the rest; if so, why the whole chain?

Man, then, was created for his own sake, — that is, for some end proper to himself. His Creator being just and good, but two such ends could be designed — either his Virtue or his Happiness.

It is common for moralists of that school which I shall call Euthumists, to blend as much as possible these two terms. As I conceive that such amalgamation is illogical, and that the indiscriminate use of the words is, to the highest degree, mischievous to sound ethics, I shall preface my attempt to demonstrate which end must be primary in the great design of our Creator, by endeavouring to define the terms, so as best to distinguish their significance.

Happiness is the gratification of *all* the desires of our nature. So long as any desire natural to man is unfulfilled, so long it is impossible to describe him as perfectly happy. He has bodily senses which crave their proper gratifications, æsthetic tastes desiring the beautiful, intellectual faculties for ever stretching after knowledge and truth, social affections yearning to love and be beloved in all the various relationships of humanity, a religious sentiment continually soaring up restlessly till it recognise the fit object for its adoration on the throne of the universe, a moral nature for ever ordering him to obey the eternal Right, and desiring that joy (altogether unique and *sui generis*) to be found in such obedience.

To be perfectly happy, man must, then, have sensual and æsthetic gratifications, knowledge, love, religion, and virtue. The *absence* of any of these joys is the *negation* of happiness, so far as that part of our nature is concerned in which pleasure is absent. *Pain* is more than this negation of happiness, it is a *minus* in the sum. It is manifest that in our complex natures an immense variety of conditions, as respects happiness, are possible to us without taking into consideration the infinite degrees of the various pains and pleasures up to that highest possible gratification of all our desires simultaneously which would constitute absolute happiness, and which it is not to be supposed we shall ever enjoy. Let a be moral pleasure, b intellectual, c affectional, and d sensual. The martyr's sum of happiness is, perhaps, $a + c - d$; the voluptuary's is $d + b - c - a$. Any one joy, or any one pain, may be so great as for the time to render the part of our nature which experiences it predominant over all the other parts which are not in an equal state of excitement. Excessive pain arising from our affections will commonly render us obtuse to any intellectual or sensual pleasure whatever; and, on the other hand, the sensual pains of the stake and the rack have been almost unfelt in the moral rapture which has flooded the soul of the virtuous sufferer. This fact, that the extreme excitement of any one part of our nature renders it for the time so completely dominant that we seem to be *only* moral, or *only* sensual creatures, has given colour to all the debates of ancient philosophy as to the true essence of happiness, from the Ἡδονή of Aristippus to the Εὐθυμία of Democritus. But though any one pleasure may be so great as to render us *partially* insensible to any other; yet, as all the other parts of our nature have a real existence, and are capable of gratifications each of which would be an addition to the sum of happiness, we can never accurately calculate that sum while ignoring these items, however small they may be compared to the larger ones. To affirm, then, that moral pleasures can constitute *absolute* happiness, is to affirm that the part is equal to the whole. It is true that they form, rightly, the grandest integer in its sum, and therefore to mistake them for the whole is far less erroneous than to give such im-

portance to any other pleasures. Moreover, their present
preponderance is undoubtedly less than that which they will
obtain hereafter. In the normal development of man the
moral nature tends continually to engross a larger share of
his being; and precisely as the affections of youth supersede
(though they do not suspend) the infant's gratifications of
sense, so in the full grown soul the joys of virtue and religion
will be fully recognised as the sweetest and grandest of which
humanity is capable. Still, however great these joys may
grow, so long as we have any other natures beside the moral,
so long as we are intellectual, affectional, and sensual beings
(and this must surely be always), so long the fit gratifications
of the desires of intellect, affections, and senses must form a
necessary part of our happiness. Let the moral joys swell to
never so vast an amount, and let the lesser gratifications even
remain at their present value (which is every way improbable), still they must ever remain in the sum of human
happiness real and appreciable items.

But of this multiform nature of happiness moralists have
commonly taken little heed; thereby inducing endless confusion into their treatment of the subject. While some of
them have quite excluded the joy peculiar to virtue from
their account of what a Benthamite denominates a " lot of
pleasures," others have put forward that joy as the sole *bonâ
fide* constituent of happiness, and have argued, with Cicero,
that "virtue alone is sufficient for a happy life." Thus,
when the question is put, "Whether happiness be the end of
creation?" we shall find two parties answering it in the
affirmative; one of them implying that God made man that
he might enjoy knowledge, love, beauty, and sensual pleasures; and the other that He made him that he might find
everlasting bliss in the peculiar joy of virtue and religion.
And, again, when it is asked whether we ought to do right
for the sake of happiness, the same two parties answer, "Yes."
But one means, "Do right that you or you and all your
fellow-creatures may be healthy, peaceful, rich, and re-
spected;" the other means, "Do right that you may enjoy
the blessedness of a *mens conscia recti.*" I shall endeavour,
presently, to show that both these parties are in error in

giving any affirmative reply to the supposed question; but
it is needful to bear in mind the very different senses in which
they make it, lest, while combating the one, we leave the
other unassailed. Now, it is manifest that *virtue* is a very
different thing from this " gratification of all the desires of
our nature." The moral distinctions of good and evil actions
and sentiments existing in the nature of things, the obligations
founded thereon are Necessary, and their agreement with, or
contradiction of, the contingent actions and sentiments which
gratify our contingent desires, must be in every way Contingent. Virtue is the voluntary and disinterested obedience of
a free agent to that eternal law which embodies all moral
obligations. The obligations being necessary, and the law
necessary, so also must be the virtue, which must be sub-
stantially the same in all intelligences in the universe. But
the desires of such intelligences vary infinitely, as do their
physical constitutions ; and as the gratifications of their
desires are various, so various are the constituents of their
happiness. The Necessary law, therefore, must continually
intersect the endless Contingent constituents of happiness in
all intelligent beings. To obey that law they must, then,
frequently renounce those constituents of happiness, or, in
other words, to be virtuous they must often relinquish
pleasure and accept pain. Here we find an antagonism between Happiness and Virtue. Happiness is the gratification
of all the desires of our nature ; Virtue is the renunciation of
such of them as are forbidden by the moral law. Thus, if
that peculiar pleasure felt in virtue which constitutes the
gratification of the desire of the moral part of our nature, is,
in that sense, to be taken as an item *plus* in the sum of our
happiness, it is on the other hand frequently obtainable only
by the sacrifice of some other gratification of the lower parts
of our nature, and is then a *minus* in the sum of happiness of
some lower pleasure, at the same time that it is a *plus* of the
higher.

But to this view of the case it is objected, that Virtue
cannot be counted as antagonistic of Happiness, because
the providence of God has so arranged the world that
it is precisely by obedience to the Moral Law that the

largest share of all forms of happiness is to be acquired, — that
benevolence, honesty, truth, and temperance are the only
paths to health, wealth, and honour. Therefore (it is argued),
the man who obeys the law which orders him to renounce a
certain constituent of his happiness does not thereby at all
diminish the sum total of his happiness; but, on the contrary, secures to himself a larger share than he could possibly
do by snatching at the forbidden pleasure. And, as this is
affirmed without reference to the moral pleasure taken in the
virtuous act, it follows that virtue, instead of being the anti-
thesis of happiness, is simply the *guide* to it — not the
narrow way which is hedged up on both sides lest we stray
from it to pluck forbidden fruit, but simply the shortest path
to the orchard where the largest quantity of the best fruit
may be obtained.

Now it must be confessed that if the definition of Virtue
included nothing but obedience to the law, if it were only a
legal and not also a moral thing, it would be impossible to find
an answer to the above arguments. If we could be *virtuous*
while merely following a set of rules to which Providence has
so adapted the condition of the world that their adoption shall
produce our greatest Happiness, then it would be idle to set
up any dilemma between virtue and happiness, or inquire
for which end God could have created us, unless indeed we
were to dispute the proposition that in *all* cases virtue does
produce the happiness of our lower natures. But this, though
open to argument, would still leave the undeniable fact that
in the *majority* of cases it does so, and that therefore it is with
the best *chance* of increasing the sum of his happiness that a
man obeys the law commanding him to relinquish individual
items of it.

The real answer is very different from this. Virtue is not
only "voluntary obedience to the law," but "*disinterested*"
obedience to it. To *be* virtue it must be an obedience motived
by reverence for the inherent right of the law. On this subject I shall have much to say in the 4th chapter. For the
present I can only pursue the demonstration that virtue as
truly defined is perfectly antithetic to happiness. The sacrifice which the virtuous man makes of his gratification to the

law is wholly unconditional on a future increase of happiness
to be gained thereby. His surrender is complete, and grounded
solely on the right of the law so to command him. If he be
tempted to act from desire of future happiness, his action
ceases to be virtuous; if he act without any prospect or chance
of future happiness, his action becomes more and more virtuous
as such happiness recedes from his prospects. Thus, again,
we arrive at an antithesis between virtue and happiness; an
antithesis subjectively and in the present absolute and complete, though we may have some reason to believe that objectively and in the future it will be done away. The
virtuous man *now* renounces his happiness unconditionally on
any restoration of it, and purely from obedience to the law.
His act and motive will not have been less complete and pure,
if hereafter God, seeing him to have reached that virtue which
can only be gained through trial, bestows on him "sevenfold
more" for all he has sacrificed.

Further. It is of the very essence of Virtue that this anti-
thesis and dilemma between itself and Happiness should exist
and present itself to the virtuous soul. Were the whole law
precisely conterminous with our desires, so that we might
fully gratify them all while obeying it to the utmost (an
hypothesis which is self-contradictory as regards a finite
being), virtue would then lose its essential character, its
merit.

The free obedience which constitutes the virtue implies a
choice. The moral freedom to obey requires not only a knowledge of both good and evil, but a choice between them.
Now choice can only exist where there is a measure of desir-
ability in both objects, a dilemma, however unequal. There
must be a possibility of choosing either way, and this possibility requires no less the internal *motive* of choice than the
external power of causation. If we had no sort of motive
whatever to disobey the law, *i. e.*, no desire to gratify by our
disobedience, we could not be strictly said to *obey* it, but only
not to disobey. Our state might be called one of "innocence;"
but it could never be called one of "virtue."

Now the actual condition of humanity permits of both
innocent happiness and virtuous renunciation of happiness.

The law coincides in thousands of cases with our natural desires. It orders us to feed and protect our bodies from mutilation and destruction; and the desires of food, warmth, ease, and life fall in so perfectly with duty that we never dream of claiming merit for our obedience. The law also ordains love of benevolence towards all our fellow-creatures, and the affectional part of our natures has already given to many of them that love of complacency which includes and outruns benevolence. No husband claims merit for loving his bride; no mother calls it virtue to " wish well " to her child. In these and thousands of cases our actions and sentiments are perfectly *innocent;* but no one can esteem them *virtuous,* being done without *choice, i. e.,* without motive of choice. But, on the other hand, when the law does contradict our natural desires,—when it bids us be mild, chaste, and temperate, while our irascible and sensual passions are clamouring for their gratification,—when it bids us suffer hunger and cold that we may feed and clothe the starving and perishing, — when it bids us

> " Give an enemy
> Our plank, and plunge aside to die,"—

then there is struck out from the clashing law and desire the divine flame of true virtue, then the freedom of the moral agent comes into play, and the glory of the finite creature is achieved. In the soul's coercion of the lower nature its energies can alone be exerted and its valour displayed. And this use of its powers is also that by which alone they can grow. The progress of the soul takes place, not by Innocence, but by Virtue. Each step must be won by an effort, a conquest. We stand still when there is no trial; we advance regularly by the ordinary difficulties of life; we may leap onward with giant strides when Providence sends us extraordinary trials.

Antithetic, then, in the highest degree, must be Virtue and Happiness, if the one can only be manifested by the abnegation of the other, and grows precisely in the ratio of the deductions it makes from it.

Now to our question.

Of Happiness thus defined and Virtue thus defined, which must be the one chosen by an all-just and all-good God for

the end of His creation of rational souls ?   To put the question thus is to answer it.   What is justice ?   Is it not the
maintenance of virtue, the punishment of vice, regardless of
every other consideration ?   Is not its watchword

" Fiat justitia, ruat cœlum ? "

To suppose for a moment that a just and holy Being could
have any object prior in His design to the virtue of His
creatures, is a self-contradictory hypothesis.   Few indeed
have been the minds so benighted as to deny that God does
actually "rule the world in righteousness," that He rewards
virtue and punishes vice in accordance with absolute justice,
though one school of moralists believe that He maintains such
a system of rewards and punishments as the best method of
producing happiness*, and another that He does so out of
regard to the abstract principles of right.   With whatever
errors men entangle their intuitions, the belief of mankind
remains that God does govern us with absolute rectitude.
Nor can we imagine Him postponing that absolute Right
to any end whatsoever, were it even the salvation of a
world.   Half the traditional creeds of mankind are only
schemes for preserving this idea of God's Justice unimpaired
while reconciling it with that of His Goodness, before the
human mind has grasped the truth that these two attributes
are in absolute harmony while aiming at that justice which is
the perfection of goodness, and at that goodness which is the
perfection of justice.

But it is not only the Justice, it is the Goodness of God, which
makes Virtue and not Happiness the primary end of creation.
Those who have believed that this happiness is His sole aim
have rested exclusively on this attribute of goodness.   But
has love *indeed* nothing better to desire for its object than the
gratifications of intellect, affection, and sense ?   It seems to
me that there is something more precious than these that it
would far rather bestow.   Who that has loved deeply, nobly,

---

* This is truly a strange inversion.   Happiness is a *contingent* accumulation
of desires, and their gratifications ; Virtue, obedience to a law as *necessary*
as those of numbers ; yet it is affirmed that the fixed is a system contrived to
produce the mutable, and necessary truths mere adaptations to those which
are contingent !

worthily, does not know that the honour, goodness, purity, truth of our friend is dearer to us than his enjoyment of all the pleasures of life, fondly as we would pour them also at his feet? How base would be the love which should regard our friend's virtue with indifference, and, while praying for his worldly prosperity, breathe no aspiration for his moral perfection? They were *mothers* who have said "I would rather have seen my son in the grave, than prosperous in iniquity."

But if this be so with *us*, —if poor short-sighted human love, so often dazzled with the glitter of earthly happiness, so in-capable of comprehending the true grandeur of virtue, can yet choose that virtue before all things for the one beloved,— what must be the choice of that divine love which from heaven looks down to see happiness a grain of dust in the balance against virtue?

It is hard for us who strive so little after it to comprehend in any measure what virtue really is, even the virtue attain-able in this infant stage of our being. The difference be-tween a soul which voluntarily obeys the great law of the universe, and one which disobeys and rejects it, is a differ-ence so great that all analogies fail us to express it. A good soul and a bad soul do not differ from one another as light from darkness, beauty from deformity. They differ as the God-like from that which can only find its parallel in the likeness of the visionary fiend. A virtuous mind filled with benevolent affections; unsusceptible of malice, wrath, jealousy, or envy; pure, so as to shrink from every contaminating thought; true, so as to think, look, speak, and be absolutely sincere; content, so as to bear within a peace passing all understanding: such a mind may in-deed be of the same *nature* as one wallowing in pollution; but its *condition* affords a stronger contrast than anything the material world can offer as comparison. Even then, were there only in question the Happiness of earth and the Virtue of earth, there could be no hesitation but infinite love must choose Virtue as the best boon to bestow on its object. But in truth the concerns of this life, though they occupy so large a space in the field of our vision, can be in

the eyes of God only the first short stage of an endless
journey. The virtue to which the noblest of us can attain
in our three score years and ten, is the virtue of a child compared to that glorious manhood to which we shall grow
through the ages of our immortality. The law of spirit is,
that virtue shall thus for ever gain fresh strength in every
fresh victory. We know not whether the resistance of the
lower nature must always remain a fixed quantity, but we
find that even here the higher is continually acquiring greater
force, and thus more and more perfectly mastering it. This
law, guiding spirit up its everlasting ascent, is as patent as
that law which forces matter to gravitate. It is not more
the nature of matter to attract, than that of a soul to grow.
Each step towards goodness leads to and facilitates subsequent
advance, just as the force of attraction increases in the in-
verse ratio of the squares of the distance. The nearer the
stronger is the law for both. At the beginning of the moral
life, when we make our first steps towards virtue, all seems
weakness, doubt, and hesitation. At the climax of mortal
goodness we see that the saint's footing stands secure on the
angel's ladder, whose summit is lost in heaven's splendours.
Though the clouds of death roll between us, we know that
he is ascending still beyond our straining sight.

Nor can there be any end to this ascension of the immortal
soul. There is no reason whatever to doubt that the virtue
of finite intelligences, being never capable of attaining absolute
perfection, is infinitely progressive toward it. Through the
infinite number of grades which divide the soul from such
perfection, there is nothing to arrest its journey, but one
degree must for ever facilitate the attainment of the next
with ever-growing security and rapidity. As in mathematics
so in morals, there is an infinite approximation, an asymptote
which as it is produced approaches continually yet never
reaches the hyperbola. When the soul now grovelling in
sin should have struggled up to better life, when the sinner
should have become a saint, and the saint should have passed
through all the gradations of excellence our imaginations attribute to the seraphic ranks of the noblest created spirits,
at the highest pinnacle of the spiritual universe, he would not

have reached perfection—he would still see infinity between himself and the holiness of God.

If we believe in this unbounded power of growth in the human soul, its capacity for endless progress, we cannot I think fail to recognise such capacity as the most important attribute of a finite intelligence.   In comparison of the ideas of Godlike goodness, ineffable peace, purity, and magnanimity which thus open to us as possible for us, all the delights of this life, the kingdoms of the world and the glory of them, seem unworthy of a thought.   We feel that the one thing real in this world of shadows is the state of the soul, its progress towards or its retrogression from this glorious bourn. And God, who sees even now down the far-off cycles of the future the blessed virtue to which the child of clay may, aye *shall*, assuredly attain, must not *He* set forth that consummation so prominently as the end of his creation that in comparison thereof the pleasures of this life shall be accounted but as the toys of an infant to the throne he shall inherit hereafter?   Who will say Goodness seeks but the Happiness of the creature?   It would not be goodness, but direst cruelty, which should set our happiness on earth before our virtue through all eternity.

Goodness and Justice then, as we conceive of them, both distinctly point to human Virtue as the end of human existence; and (as I have already stated) God's goodness and justice are only the absolute perfection of those ideals of them which He has placed in our hearts.

And that this beneficent and righteous end is indeed the grand object of our Creator's will may be deduced most clearly from that very condition of imperfection and suffering in which we find the world, and which has given cause for so many doubts and fears. *Happiness*, as I have said, is only the gratification of the desires of our nature.   There is nothing in such contingent accumulation of desires and their proper gratifications (so far as we can perceive) beyond the donation of Omnipotence.   It is possible, indeed, that absolute and perfect happiness may be beyond the limitations of a finite creature, and possible also that some degree of unhappiness may be necessary to secure to us the utmost possible degree of happiness, as we must consider is the case with respect to the pain suffered by the brutes for the evident purpose of preserving their lives and the integrity of their bodies. The subject is a very obscure one, but the principle on which I have so often insisted must not be lost sight of, namely, that Almighty Power is never to be understood to include contradictions. It is perfectly credible that a being can no more be at the same time finite and perfectly happy than a number can be at the same time equal and unequal. Still, making every allowance, it must be manifest to every dispassionate observer, that the eudaimonist optimists have failed to make good their ground. Whatever degree of unhappiness *must* have existed in the world to produce the "utmost possible happiness," it is clear there is an immensely *larger* proportion actually to be found in it than can be so accounted for. We are all optimists as regards the joyous birds, and beasts, and insects; but which of us can believe that Omnipotence could not have made *man* happier than he is? If then, in creating us, God desired primarily our happiness, why are we *not* happy? This is the question on which Atheists rest so triumphantly,—those saddest Atheists who doubt our Father's goodness rather than his power. All shame be to the low philosophy which can leave such stone of stumbling in their path!

But *virtue* is not an accumulation of joys at the disposal of God. It is not a thing which Omnipotence itself can *make*. It is the *free* obedience to the eternal law by a free intelligence. God must *conduce* to this obedience in a thousand ways; but it is a contradiction in terms to say He can *produce* it. That is exclusively in the power of the creature who wills or does not will to be virtuous. Now sad experience proves to us how little the best of us do thus will to be virtuous; and thus we see how, though God may desire our virtue before all things, the world is yet "groaning in sin." Not even Almighty Power could make it otherwise unless He were to withdraw from us rationality and moral freedom, and reduce us to brutes.*

* Of course I do not mean that there was a necessity why we should occupy that precise rank we hold among intelligences, with precisely so much

And on the same hypothesis that God desires primarily
our virtue, it is no less clear why our world is not a perfectly
happy one.   The virtue to which God desires to conduce, is,
as I have already shown, the free obedience to Right when
Wrong has some claim to option — the choice of Good, while
Evil still offers temptation.   In a state of happiness no such
temptation could take place.   Trial is the necessary condition of the virtue of finite beings.   But a state of trial is
precisely that in which we find that God has actually placed
us.   The presumption then is enormous that He has done so,
because our Virtue is the primary end of our creation.   The
more we study the condition of the world, the more will this
presumption force itself on us.   True, every advance in physical science tends to point out more clearly the solicitude of
the Creator for the Happiness of man, a solicitude often par-
taking no less of a mother's tenderness than of a father's care.
To doubt God's will to make us happy is to show a callousness
which no benefits can win.   Yet we are *not* happy, though the
Almighty could so easily fill our little cups to the brim, if not
to overflowing!   We must find some clue to the anomaly,
some other end at which His benevolent will is aiming, while
He withholds the joys we crave so beseechingly.

If we seek this clue either in our inward or outward natures, we find, collaterally with the evidences of care for our
enjoyment, another series of providential arrangements tending
no less manifestly to the encouragement of virtue.   The system of rewards and punishments which obtains among all the
circumstances surrounding us points everywhere to a design in
which our lower propensities (the necessary machinery of our
moral life) shall gradually be subdued in a course of unending
progress towards virtue.   Nor could this system be pushed
further than it is without compromising the very end at which
it aims.   Were any outward prosperity invariably attached to
virtue, or any physical evil instantly and inevitably consequent
on vice, the motives for the pursuit of virtue would be debased
to mere prudence.

moral light and power, and so much weight of the lower nature.   We must
trust Infinite Love that the position chosen for us is best for us, and not sigh
that He had made our task to battle amid the clouds instead of to toil through
the mire.

D

Thus, as the world is actually constituted, instead of presenting the insoluble riddle which it confessedly does to the philosopher who looks to *happiness* as " our being's end and aim," we find it on the contrary to accord in all its general outlines with that in which we should have predicted that a just and benevolent God would place the creatures whose *virtue* was the end for which he called them into existence. *

Nay, the very magnitude of the evil in our present condition becomes an argument on our side. For let us remember what stupendous result is that immortal Virtue at which God is aiming! Could such an end as *that* be attainable by trifling means, by trifling trials, trifling sorrows? Could the bounds of freedom be made narrow when by that freedom alone we can rise to the virtue of the martyr, as well as sink to the crime of the persecutor? Could that retribution which the Eternal Law demands, and of which the Lord of the heavens is the executioner, be a thing of small account, so

---

* There is a very singular argument often brought forward against doctrines of this kind. It amounts to this : " That it is useless for man to attempt to solve any of the larger problems of theology by the light of his own reason, because it is, *à priori*, highly improbable that a being of such narrow faculties should ever be able to form a right apprehension of the character or providence of God, and that it is audacious to attempt it." Now, to this line of argument, which is most suspiciously favoured by a certain class of reasoners, I answer,— 1st, That I can discover no *à priori* improbability that through the reason He has given them God permits and intends that His children shall seek and obtain continually more and more correct apprehensions of those infinite perfections in His character and providence on which, in giving them a moral nature, He has expressly founded His claims to their adoration and obedience. 2nd, That I can discover no audacity in pushing to the last generalisation those inductions concerning the beneficent designs of God whose study has ever been deemed one of the noblest tasks of piety ; and that it does not seem to me more audacious to affirm that God made our souls and all the material universe for the sake of virtue, than that He made our eyes for the purpose that we might see, and protected them by eyelids and eyelashes for the preservation of sight. 3rd, That I can find no force in the logic that because God is so much above us, we are therefore to calculate on His nature and dealings being altogether different from and opposite to the conceptions of them which we frame from the intuitions He has given us ; or, in other words, that the more our theological conclusions seem *probable,* the more we are bound to consider them *improbable.* It does not seem to me either reasonable or reverent to suppose that God has constructed our intellectual faculties with such a curious inversion of veracity as that the more clearly we seem to trace our deductions from His intuitions, the more likely we are to be wandering into error. Were this the case, the converse, of course, would hold equally good, and the more *improbable* any creed appeared, the more powerful would be its *à priori* claims on our credence. A spacious field would be here opened for debate between the rival pretensions to unlikelihood of Brahminism, Odin-worship, Fetishism, &c.

that for much sin we might expect to find little sorrow ? Not so. There *must* be great evil now, if there is to be great good hereafter. The extent of human crime and human woe is the earnest to us of the future greatness of human virtue and human happiness. The depth of the foundation shows how high the Master-builder will carry his temple, aye, till every spire thereof reaches to heaven !

And this theory regarding the design of creation, not only solves many of the mysteries of our present condition, but affords us a glimpse of a scheme of Divine government far less unworthy of its assumed Author than any which can be accommodated with the opposite hypothesis.

The Moral Law is resumed in the holy will of God. God must, consequently, desire that that law should reach fulfilment in the Virtue which is the highest manifestation (so far as finite creatures are concerned) it can receive. For this virtue He has created our spirits, and clothed them with the bodies so " fearfully and wonderfully made." And, as a means to the same end, He must have created the whole material universe, which is but a habitation meaningless, unless intended for its inhabitants. All the " hundred million spheres " revealed to the astronomer, all the unimaginable worlds in the infinite beyond, are but the schools of God's rational creatures, the palace-homes of His immortal children. It is true that He has also replenished those worlds with the myriad tribes of irrational living beings, to fill up with their innocent happiness the complement of His measureless bounty.* But not for them, not for the poor dumb slaves

---

* " For the sustenance of the vital spirits, Brahma created all this animal and vegetable system, and all that is moveable or immoveable."—*Institutes of Menu,* c. v., v. 28. It is not possible for us, in our ignorance of ultra-mundane things, to decide dogmatically that there is no ultimate destiny for " the soul of the beast which goeth downward." Through what stages life and consciousness and self-consciousness may *possibly* be evolved, and what may be the true " Natural History of the Creation," both of minds and bodies, it is, perhaps, equally unphilosophical to hazard our groundless conjectures, or to pronounce those conjectures false. All that I desire to insist on in the text is, that the brutes in their present condition, and so far as we know of their destination, can only be considered as the complement of creation. To speak more accurately, their happiness is the end of *their* creation, our virtue not only of *our's,* but of the *whole.* Most absurd, however, is the old notion that the *primary* end of the existence of any sentient creature could be the benefit of another, and that the brutes are made expressly for the service of man. It is true that their existence

who throng their lower courts, were built these glorious
mansions of planets, with their libraries of wisdom, their
galleries of beauty, inappreciable to beast and bird.   For us,
for all God's rational offspring, were launched into space
those mighty orbs whose creations and cataclysms are less
momentous than the lapses and regenerations of our deathless spirits.

Nor does God abandon His work when He has called us
into being, and prepared for us these sumptuous abodes.
That law which His own Will resumes He graves on the
" fleshy tablet of our hearts," — nay, welds indissolubly into
the very substance of our inmost being.   Over that primal
germ of our moral nature His spirit for ever broods; and,
ever present, ever active, strengthens and vivifies it.   And,
jointly with His Spirit within, works His Providence without.
The woof He fixes wherein our freewill may work its warp,
is fitted with absolute precision to our moral wants.   The
trials, the encouragements, the punishments we require, all
come to us with unerring exactitude.   All the elements and
all the creatures are God's ministers, and inevitably work in
each individual case precisely as He has from all eternity
foreseen that the innumerable contingencies of the lives of
free intelligences would require them to work to forward the
design of creation.   We are each of us the centre of a stupendous machine, ever grinding its complicated wheels to
evolve at last the virtue of our souls.

Further: while thus working for the completion of His

as well as our own, while fulfilling the main beneficent design of God, ever
serves
> " To second, too, some other use."

And of a large portion of this secondary service of some tribes of animals we are
the inheritors.   But, as Buckland observes (*Geol.*, vol. i. p. 101.), " With regard
to the lower animals, there are comparatively but very few, amid their countless
multitudes, that minister either to the wants or luxuries of the human race.
Even could it be proved that all existing species are serviceable to man, no such
inference could be drawn with respect to those numerous extinct animals which
geology shows to have ceased to live long before our race appeared upon the
earth.   It is surely more consistent with sound philosophy, and with all the information that is vouchsafed to us, respecting the attributes of the Deity, to
consider each animal as having been created first for its own sake, to receive its
portion of that enjoyment which the Universal Parent is pleased to impart to
every creature that has life ; and, secondly, to bear its share in the maintenance
of the general system of co-ordinate relations, whereby all families of living
beings are reciprocally subservient to the use and benefit of one another.   Under
this head only can we include their relations to man."

blessed design, God is simultaneously executing continually that perfect Justice which the law exacts. As absolute Lord of His creation, God necessarily holds the "Justitia rectoria" of the universe. It is to Him it pertains to give to the abstract Law a real potentiality, to make Justice an infinite and eternal Fact, to apportion to crime its punishment with the wisdom of Omniscience, and inflict the same with the might of Omnipotence.

Justice, as we apprehend it (and, as I have shown, our intuition of it is God's tuition), demands that no infraction of the moral law shall pass unexpiated by a corresponding amount of suffering. Benevolence is, indeed, free to bestow happiness as a free gift (and not as a *reward*) on *innocent*, though unmeritorious beings. It is to fulfil the law as regards Benevolence, and not to infringe it as regards Justice, to do so. But Justice requires that towards the *guilty* He who holds its "balance and rod" shall withhold happiness and inflict punishment in exact proportion to the guilt. To man, indeed, the *measure* of suffering which effects this retribution is unknown. The intuition of it is not given to him; and for this plain reason, that he can never know the measure of the guilt to be punished, the infinite variety of circumstances which enhance or palliate it. But it is given to him to feel that there *is* such a principle as Retribution in the eternal law. In every page of human history he involuntarily seeks for its manifestations; in every ideal of a future state it occupies the foreground of his imagination; in every conception of the character of God he trembles before His avenging Justice, before he learns to adore His infinite Love.

One thing only is granted to us to know concerning this Retribution, beside the fact of its existence, — namely, that it is *finite*. The sins of finite creatures, though never so multiplied in number, never so aggravated in character, are still always to be predicated with mathematical certainty as finite also. The finite cannot sin infinitely; nor can any degree of graduated crime be infinite; nor can any multiplication of finite crimes amount to infinity. Neither does our intuition of retribution (such as it is) at all point to infinite punishment. Our sense of what actually constitutes it is but a vague approximation; but we feel clearly enough that there *are* limits to just retribution. Though we cannot tell *affirmatively* what punishment would justly expiate an angry word, we can tell *negatively* that it would far exceed justice and become injustice to break the offender on the wheel. But, if *any* earthly (*i. e.* finite) punishment* would be too great for any, even the smallest, sin, then eternal (*i.e.* infinite) punishment would be too great for any multiplication or aggravation of sins, which, to be of infinite guilt, must each be of infinite and not of graduated ill desert.

---

* For some other arguments respecting the eternity of future punishments see Chap. III. The subject, however, cannot properly be discussed in a treatise not professedly polemical, because the hypothesis that such a thing exists rests solely (so far as it has any foundations whatever) on traditional grounds, with which the mere philosophic moralist has nothing to do. As I have above demonstrated the common intuitions of mankind, so far from pointing to an infinite retribution for sin, most distinctly affirm the existence of its limits ; and as I shall hereafter show, the gift of moral freedom by an All-good and All-foreseeing God is ample pledge that its eventual results will be the virtue of all on whom it has been bestowed. Nevertheless, it is precisely with the aid of this dogma, which is exclusively their own assumption, that certain controversialists have chosen to attack those who hesitate to accept their theological system. They begin by assuming that sin deserves eternal punishment, and that God is pledged by His justice to inflict it on the sinner, and then they triumphantly ask, "How can you hope for salvation ?" As well might we ask the repentant child, sobbing at its mother's knee, "What pledge have you that your mother will not cast you on the fire ?" And, again, by a circular sort of argument, it is attempted to be shown that philosophical systems of theology and morals are necessarily imperfect, because they offer no provision to meet a want which they do not recognise. If God's justice demand that every sinner shall expiate his sins in endless torment, then, it is said, we must have some scheme by which God can be shown to be "just and yet the Justifier of the wicked." (See, for one instance out of thousands, this argument set forth in the concluding chapter of Chalmers' *Bridgewater Treatise.*) But *who* affirms that God's justice demands any such everlasting sacrifice — who, save the very persons who put forth the scheme of escape ? It is the same physician who gives us this disease of terror, and then comes forward with his cure. *We* hold that sin deserves *finite* retribution, and that that finite retribution God's justice will assuredly inflict in absolute harmony with His goodness, which, by the same punishment, will affect the correction of the sinner. From this finite correction and retribution it would not be a mercy, but a cruelty, to relieve us. Of the nature of the punishments of the future life we can form no more conception than the unborn infant can imagine the conditions of our life on earth. The tremendous sufferings, however, which we sometimes witness *here*, may well impress us with the most awful ideas of what may be endured hereafter, when the demands of the offended law of the universe must be paid "to the uttermost farthing." That any world or state of existence is *wholly* penal, seems, however, an hypothesis unsupported by any analogy in the Divine government, so far as we are acquainted with it. All worlds are, indeed, Purgatories,—places for the purification of souls. But it is as a School, more or less severe, that we find this planet fulfils the design of the Universal Father, and it is no unwarrantable presumption, that in some analogous mode (of course under infinitely diverse circumstances), the same design will be carried on for ever.

This just, but finite, retribution God will undoubtedly inflict, here or hereafter, on all the sins of His creatures.

Beside the Retribution which we thus expect God to inflict in His character of Executor of eternal Justice, we look to Him also for Correction of sin in His character of Father of the sinner. The aim of Retribution is to fulfil the demands of the law : the aim of Correction is to conduce to the result of the law. The first accomplishes the behests of abstract Justice: the second conduces to the growth of concrete Virtue. In this light, the pains inflicted on us by God as the punishment of our sins are intended to reform us through the purifying influence of suffering. There is, of course, every reason to suppose that such Correction, which displays the Divine benevolence as Retribution displays the Divine justice, will never cease its merciful ministration in this life or the next, till the sufferings of the prodigal drive him back to his Father's feet.

Thus, on the hypothesis that it is not *happiness* which God primarily designs in our creation, but that *virtue* which is the result of the law He resumes in his own nature, we find the unhappiness of human life accounted for, by the two great forms and reasons of punishment, namely, Retribution and Correction.

Does God inflict pain *only* as a punishment for sin, whether retributively, or correctively? We cannot affirm it. It does not seem as if St. Augustine were justified in his sweeping assertion, " Evil is of two sorts; one which a man doth, the other which he suffers. What he doth is sin; what he suffereth, punishment." * Intuition by no means teaches us that it would be an injustice towards any creature for its master to cause it to endure suffering which he should know with unerring certainty were necessary for the production of some good overbalancing (to the creature itself) the evil of the suffering. Experience goes still further, and affords us vast presumption that God does exercise His just Mastership in this manner. We find, as I have already had occasion to notice, that the brutes con-

* St. Aug., c. Adim., c. xxvi.

tinually endure pain (which, of course, can be neither retributive nor morally corrective), for the obvious purpose
of securing their lives and the integrity of their bodies. In
other words, they suffer some Pain for the sake of their
general Happiness, which, as we have seen, is the highest
end of their existence. *A fortiori*, then, we may suppose
that God causes human beings to suffer pain which is neither
retributive, nor corrective; but intended not merely to secure
Happiness, but to conduce to their higher end of Virtue, to
which the conditions of Happiness are always postponed.
The "uses of adversity" are, indeed, manifold. No one who
has known them can doubt how true it is that

> " The energies, too stern for mirth,
>   The reach of thought, the strength of will,
>   'Mid cloud and tempest have their birth,
>   Through blight and blast their course fulfil."

The storms which God causes to sweep over us are but intended to speed us with redoubled swiftness to our haven,
and will ever do so, if we but turn our prow as He would
have us.

Suffering, then, in whatever way our Creator inflicts it
upon us, is absolutely JUST. That is to say, it is just if a
punishment for past sin, and just if an aid to future virtue.
And suffering is absolutely GOOD. It is good if a punishment which shall heal our sin, and good if an aid to that
virtue which is better than happiness. Were God less just,
He would be less good; for He would do less for our best
interests. Were He less good, He would be less just; for
He would less perfectly fulfil the behests of everlasting Right.

The question of this Chapter has now been answered.

The Moral Law is the resumption of the eternal necessary
Obligation of all Rational Free Agents to do and feel those
actions and sentiments which are Right. The identification
of this law with His will constitutes the Holiness of the
infinite God. Voluntary and disinterested obedience to this
law constitutes the Virtue of all finite creatures. Virtue is
capable of infinite growth, of endless approach to the Divine
nature, and to perfect conformity with the law. God has
made all rational free agents for virtue, and all worlds for

rational free agents. The Moral Law, therefore, not only
reigns throughout His creation (all its behests being enforced therein by His omnipotence), but is itself the reason
why that creation exists. The material universe, with all its
laws, and all the events which result therefrom, has but one
great purpose, and tends to one great end. It is that end
which infinite Love has designed, and which infinite Power
shall accomplish—the everlasting approximation of all created
souls to goodness and to God.

CHAPTER II.

WHERE THE MORAL LAW IS FOUND.

"Another point which is also demonstrative of God's providence, is, that when God formed man, He implanted within him from the beginning a natural law. And what, then, was this natural law? He gave utterance to conscience within us, and made the knowledge of good things, and of those which were the contrary, to be self-taught. They say that there is no self-evident law placed in our consciences, and that God hath not implanted this in our nature. But, if so, whence is it, I ask, that legislators have written those laws concerning marriages, murders, trusts, of not encroaching on one another, and a thousand other things? Did such persons, perchance, learn them from their elders, and they from those who were before them, and these again from those beyond? From whom did those learn who were the first originators and first enactors of those laws? It is evident that it was from conscience; for they cannot say they held communication with Moses, or that they heard the prophets. How could they, when they were Gentiles? But it is evident, from the very law which God placed in man when He formed him, that from the beginning laws were laid down."—St. CHRYSOSTOM, *The Statues, Hom.* xii.

THE results of the most advanced inquiries into the nature and origin of human knowledge may be briefly indicated somewhat as follows : —

All sciences are either Exact or Physical, or are applications of Exact to Physical sciences.

Exact sciences are deduced from axiomatic necessary*

* To some of my readers a brief explanation of the terms " necessary" and " contingent," as used technically by metaphysicians, may not be unacceptable. "Necessary truths," says Whewell (quoted by Lewes, *Hist. of Phil.*, iv. p. 123), " are those in which we not only learn that the proposition *is* true, but see that it *must* be true; in which the negation is not only false, but impossible; in which we cannot, even by an effort of the imagination, or in a supposition, conceive the reverse of that which is asserted. That there are such truths cannot be doubted. We may take, for example, all relations of number. Three and two make five. We cannot conceive it otherwise. We cannot by any freak of thought imagine three and two to make seven."

Contingent truths, on the contrary, are those which, without doing violence to reason, we may conceive to be otherwise. If I say, "grass is green," "Socrates was a philosopher," "the sun will rise to-morrow," "London is a great city," I assert propositions which *are* true, but *need* not have been so; no absurdity is involved, no violent effort of imagination is required to suppose them false. It might have pleased the Creator to make grass blue; Socrates might never have lived; if the rotatory motion of the earth were stopped, the sun would not rise; London may be at this hour engulphed by an earthquake.

Axiomatic necessary truths (as I have said in the text) are the grounds of the Exact sciences. These are such as are simplest and at the base of our knowledge, so that we cannot descend beneath them, or give them any demonstration, but must inevitably receive them with absolute conviction ; *e. g.*, the axioms that " the whole is greater than its part," that " things which are equal to the same thing are equal to one another." From such axiomatic necessary truths as these the exact sciences are deduced, and result in universal propositions which are all necessary truths; *e. g.*, from the axioms of geometry we deduce, through a series of consecutive demonstrations, that, " If two right lines cut one another, the angles vertically opposite are equal to one another." This proposition is Necessary and Universal. It must hold good of all such angles in all worlds for ever; and no sooner has the mind apprehended that it *is* true, than it perceives that it *must* be true, and by no freak of imagination can it conceive it otherwise.

Experimental contingent truths are the grounds of the Physical sciences, which induce from them general propositions which are all contingent truths; *e. g.*, from investigating the anatomy of animals we obtain a multitude of contingent truths (all of which might have been otherwise without absurdity) ; and from these we induce the general proposition, that " all vertebrate animals have red blood." This proposition is neither Necessary nor Universal. It might not

Truths, and result in Universal propositions, each of which is a Necessary Truth.

Physical sciences are induced from Experimental Contingent Truths, and result in General propositions, each of which is a Contingent Truth.

We obtain our knowledge of the Experimental Contingent Truths on which Physical science is induced by the united action of our bodily senses and of our minds themselves, which must both in each case contribute their proper quota to make knowledge possible. Every *perception* necessitates this double element of *sensation* and *intuition*,*—the objective and subjective factor in combination.

We obtain our knowledge of the axiomatic Necessary Truths from which Exact science is deduced by the *à priori* operation of the mind alone, and (*quoad* the exact science in question) without the aid of sensation. Not, indeed, by the *à priori* operation of a mind which has *never* worked with sensation, for such a mind would be altogether barren†; but of one which has reached normal development under normal conditions, which conditions involve the continual united action productive of perceptions of contingent truths.‡

have been true of any vertebrate animal, for they might all have had white blood, and it may not now hold good of species yet to be discovered, or in the whole fauna of another planet.

* " Space and time are intuitions *à priori*. To convert a representation into *knowledge* demands a notion and an intuition welded together into one perception ; but from the *à priori* singulars are derived all the notions of the configurations of space and of the combination of number. . . . . Physical science consists of the continuous synthesis of singulars with universals. But in physics the notions alone are *à priori;* the phenomena to which categories are applied are given only in experience."—SEMPLE's *Introd. Kant's Met. Eth.*, lvi.

† " If we were placed in a universe of *thought*, where nothing around us suggested extension or figure, we have no reason to suppose that any such conceptions would ever be formed in the mind."—MORELL's *Psychology*, pp. 290-1.

‡ The great argument on which is founded the assertion that we acquire necessary truths by the mind's own operation, is this : that on the opposite hypothesis (namely, that we acquire them as we do contingent truths, by the joint action of sensation and intuition, which constitutes perception, the sum of which perceptions constitute experience) it is impossible to account for our consciousness that, as regards necessary truths, the knowledge will hold good where that experience is wanting, *i. e.,* for our consciousness of the *universality* over and above the *generality* of a proposition. " When it is asserted (deduced from the necessary truths of geometry) that the asymptote and hyperbola continually approach yet without ever meeting, a position is advanced obviously transcending the possibility of experience ; and the evidence and certainty of it cannot be sought in the inductive method, plainly falling short of its extent. In like manner, when it is asserted that the hypothenuse squared is equal to the sum of the square of the sides, the proposition is seen to be of *necessity* true and of *uni-*

In this distinction between the sources of our knowledge lies the most important discovery of philosophy. Into what-

versal extent, and to embrace every right-angled triangle whatever, although there are many possible triangles which have not fallen under the scope of the geometer's investigation. It cannot, therefore, be from experimenting upon figures that the geometer arrives at the universality of his conclusions, nor is that certainly increased by successive observations."—Semple's *Introd. to Kant*, p. 30.

The objections urged to this argument are these: 1st, That our ideas of necessary truths do not *begin* by a knowledge of the axiom which includes them. We induce (not deduce) in childhood that a candle burns, and that effects must have causes. "The fundamental idea of causality," says Lewes's *Hist. of Phil.*, vol. ii. chap. v., "is a generalisation. Now, of course, the general includes the particulars ; but, though it *includes*, it does not *precede* them ; and the error is in supposing that it must and does precede them. A boy, as Locke says, knows that his whole body is larger than his finger, but he knows this from the perceptions of the two, and not from any knowledge of the axiom that the whole is greater than its part. Whewell would say that he could not have such knowledge unless he had the fundamental idea; whereas we side with Locke in asserting that the mind never *begins* with generalisations, but *ends* with them, and to say that because the general axiom includes the particular instance, or that the particular instance implies the general axiom, that therefore the axiom is independent of experience, is to cheat oneself with words."

Now, to all this it is answered, that it is perfectly true that we do begin with the instance and end with the generality in all the ordinary conclusions of the mind, and it is by this process only (as above insisted on in the text) that the mind attains its development, the *union* of the two elements of sensation and intuition being necessary to every perception, and a multiplicity of perceptions being indispensable to the education of the mind. The child grows up to be a man, watching candles burn, and observing the parts of other things besides his own body less than the wholes to which they belong, before he says to himself, "It is a contingent truth that candles burn and that fingers are less than the whole body ; but it is a necessary truth that all phenomena must have causes, and that the part of every thing must be less than the whole." All this we are ready to grant to the sensationalist. But what then ? Does it justify him in jumping to the conclusion that the knowledge of necessary truths possessed by the *matured* mind comes from no higher source than the perceptions of contingent truths ? If so, let him account for that one mark by which we trace its supersensible descent — *our consciousness of its universality and necessity.* The truth seems to be that we can never trace the pedigree of any one thought in a fully grown mind,— all we can do is to analyse it as we find it. By this process we arrive at the discovery that our thoughts are of two perfectly distinct characters,—that between the Dioscuri, which at first seemed perfectly alike, there exists all the difference between the mortal and the immortal, the contingent truth with every mark of mutability, the necessary truth for which we can imagine no possibility of change. A distinction so vital as this must be accounted for by the experimentalist before he can fairly pretend to trace all our knowledge to perception. How do we obtain *that* knowledge of the Universality and Necessity of the truths over and above that Generality which is all his Experience can assume to teach? How do we know it with a degree of clearness so remarkable, that no event in a man's mental history is comparable to his first appreciation of the nature of a mathematical demonstration ? The Kantist is not bound to the old stake of innate ideas, to be baited thereat by the Lockist. It need be no concern of *his* how we come, through the joint action of our double nature, to apprehend at first those truths which, when apprehended, he knows to be necessary. The metaphysician has only to constate such facts ; it is the business of the psychologist to explain them. The Kantist's thesis is simply this, that when we *have* apprehended necessary truth, we know that it *is* necessary. How dost thou account

soever knowledge the element of Sensation necessarily enters
as a constituent part, therein there can be no absolute certainty of truth ; the fallibility of sensation being recognised
on all hands, and neutralising the certainty of the pure

for that, oh Experimentalist? 2nd, A second argument urged against the theory
that the axioms derived solely from the operation of the mind are infallibly
true, is this — that there are some accepted axioms placed most conspicuously
in the Kantian philosophy, which are *not* true. It is said that the supposed
axiom — " Every effect must have a cause "—must be false in one case if there
be a First Cause, and false in millions of cases if man's will be a free cause. I
answer that the formula, as it stands, is undoubtedly defective, and has only
been called an axiom in its present form by those who, thinking solely of a
world of phenomena, applied it only to such a world *in which it is true.* No one
believing either in an infinite or in finite spirits ever deemed them ruled by the
same necessity of causation, or that the world of noumena is bound by the
same chain as the world of sense. I conceive that the true axiom which every
competent mind will recognise as necessary truth, is this: — " Every *phenomenon*
must have a cause." This cause, if noumenal, is primary; if phenomenal,
secondary.

It neither enters within the scope of this little work, nor of my ability, to
pursue to its profound basis the greatest controversy of philosophy. It is surely,
however, no presumption to foretel, that while the mere dialectic subtleties of
the schools of Schelling and Hegel can afford no final resting place (if such
were desirable) for the human intellect, the philosophy of coming time must
bear much nearer affinity to the *true* German transcendentalism of Kant
than to the bare experimentalism of England in the last century of doubt.
Locke professed himself unable to account for our idea of substance (b. ii.
c. 22., and b. i. c. 4.), thereby leaving all philosophy without a basis. Hume,
by proving that the idea of causation could not be legitimately derived from
experience, believed that he had undermined the throne of the Great First
Cause ! Surely it was time to take into honoured place in our councils the
noblest powers of our nature, when excluding them led to such disastrous results! It is a popular error, however, to place the Scotch school of philosophy
in such entire opposition to the German as is usually done. All its great
leaders have admitted the existence of certain fundamental ideas, below which
we cannot proceed, and which are given in the constitution of our minds.
These ultimate and universal facts correspond perfectly with our definition of
necessary truths; and regarding them they admit change to be incogitable.
Not to swell this note too much, I will only quote the following:—Reid maintains " that the expectation we feel of the continuance of the laws of nature is
an original principle of our constitution, which does not admit of any explanation, and which, therefore, is to be ranked among those general and ultimate
facts beyond which philosophy is unable to proceed." Dugald Stewart adopts
the opinion which Condorcet tells us that Turgot held of, the regularity of
cause and effect:—" Nous avons la conscience d'avoir observé cette constance et
un sentiment involontaire nous force de croire qu'elle continuera de subsister."
—*Vie de Turgot,* p. 11. Stewart further condemns, as the grossest absurdity,
" the idea that the mind is only a receptacle which is gradually furnished from
without by materials introduced by the channels of the senses."—*Elements,* c. i.
p. 4. Of some moral and religious truths he beautifully says, " They are
so incorporated and identified with our nature, that they reconcile us even to
the absurdities and contradictions with which we suppose them to be inseparably
connected.   The histories of human imbecility are, in truth, the strongest
testimonies which can be produced to prove how wonderful is the influence of
the fundamental principles of morality over the belief, when they are able to
sanctify, in the apprehension of mankind, every extravagant opinion and every
unmeaning ceremony which early education has taught us to associate with
them.—*Elements of the Philosophy of the Human Mind,* pp. 34. and 205. " The

mental element.* But when we discover an order of sciences which, without aid from sensation, are deduced by the mind's own operation from those necessary truths which (however we may have happened originally to *apprehend* them) we actually *hold* on a tenure marking indelibly their distinction from all contingent truths whatsoever, then we obtain footing in a new realm. The fallibility which adhered so tenaciously to all our physical science is left behind, and we enter on a domain of thought wherein we have to deal only with truths which carry with them not only *de facto* a conviction from which we should vainly endeavour to free ourselves, but also *de jure* a philosophic title to credence which could never be possessed by truths revealed by the aid of the senses, let their evidences be never so multiplied. †

To determine, then, to which order of sciences any one science belongs is, in fact, not only to decide its proper mode of logical treatment, whether deductive or inductive, but to determine its value in point of reliability, its inherent claims on our credence. If the science prove to belong to the order of phys cal sciences, we shall give it the share of belief which experience warrants us to bestow on its contingent truths. If the science prove to belong to the order of exact sciences, we shall pay it that implicit credence which the constitution of our nature forces us to give to all necessary truths.

In the ensuing pages I shall endeavour to demonstrate that

belief in God, so indelible in the human mind, has been well compared to that image of himself which Phidias wished to perpetuate by stamping it so deeply on the shield of his Minerva, — "Ut nemo delere posset aut divellere qui totam statuam non imminueret."—JOHN SMITH's *Essays.*

* It is not necessary for proof of this to have recourse to the well-known instances of the deceptions to which light, hearing, taste, smell, and touch are at all times subject. The truth is, that they are *sometimes* false exponents of the qualities of their objects, but that we cannot tell that they are *ever* true." There is not the slightest reason for believing that what we call the *sensible qualities* of the object are a type of anything inherent in itself, or bear any affinity to its own nature. A cause does not, as such, resemble its effects; an east wind is not like the feeling of cold, nor is heat like the steam of boiling water; why, then, should matter resemble our sensations?"—MILL's *Logic,* vol. i. p. 80.

† The English mind seems to have a natural antipathy to supersensible evidence and a rooted prejudice in favour of the testimony of Eyes and Ears, even when it has been transmitted for centuries through Tongues and Pens. Yet Oersted defined well the true Infidelity as " the tendency to reject all those immediate truths which do not proceed from the impressions of the senses, and to found its entire faith on these and on the decisions of the logical understanding." — *Soul in Nature,* p. 60.

E

the science of Morals is properly an exact and not a physical
science, and that it has consequently a right to that conviction wherewith we hold the truths of arithmetic and
geometry.

This task has, indeed, been already accomplished by Kant
in his splendid " Grundlegung zur Metaphysik der Sitten,"
and " Kritik der Praktischen Vernunft," works which it would
be presumption in me even to disclaim the ambition of following up. Nevertheless, as Kant himself foretold that a time
would arrive when the strict science to which he confined
himself might be given a popular form, and thus rendered
more commonly useful, I venture to attempt the task, pre-
mising that I aim confessedly thus to *popularise* morals, and
not to carry them out into new paths with scientific rigidity.

Instead, therefore, of repeating Kant's demonstration of
the validity of our consciousness of moral freedom, and following him in deducing thence consecutively the autonomy
of the will, the " law fit for law universal," which alone the
freewill can self-legislate, and the identity of this "law fit
for law universal" with the moral law ; instead, I say, of thus
deducing our knowledge of the moral law from the fundamental idea, Freedom, I shall venture to take a shorter path
which, though less rigid, seems more suited for popular
service. The idea Freedom may be indeed theoretically the
ultimate axiom, the undermost substratum of our consciousness. But the idea Duty, the idea of Obligation, to do and
feel those actions and sentiments which, according to the
eternal necessary distinction, are Right,—this idea is one whose
deduction from the idea Freedom is so spontaneous, that
probably not one man in a million has ever been cognisant of
the mental process of such deduction ; and the consequence
of such spontaneity of deduction is, that we can treat the
idea Duty as if it were the fundamental idea itself. We
can equally apply to it the test of a necessary truth, which,
though proper to *all* necessary truths, can yet be only safely
applied to deduced propositions when their deduction from
the original axiom has been recognised by the mind as a
mathematical demonstration. This test, which forms the
grand postulate of the Kantian philosophy, is as follows : —

What truth soever is necessary and of universal extent " is derived by the mind from its own operation, and does not rest on observation or experience ; as, conversely, what truth or perception soever is present to the mind with a consciousness, not of its necessity, but of its contingency, is ascribable not to the original agency of the mind itself, but derives its origin from observation and experience." (Of course from an experience combined of the sensational and purely mental elements)

The *consciousness* of the Contingency, or the *consciousness* of Necessity (*i. e.*, the consciousness that the truth *cannot* be contingent, but must hold good in all worlds for ever), these consciousnesses are to be relied on, for they have their origin in and are the marks of the different elements from which they have been derived.   We may apply them to the fundamental truths of any science, and by observing whether the reception of such truths into our minds is accompanied by the consciousness of Necessity or of Contingency, we may decide whether the science be rightfully Exact or Physical, deductive or inductive.

For example, we take the axioms of arithmetic and geometry, and we find that we have distinct consciousness that the truths, " A number which is not equal must be unequal," " two right lines cannot inclose space," are Necessary truths. The sciences, then, which are deduced from these and similar axioms are Exact sciences.

Again : we take the ultimate facts of geology and astronomy, and we find that we have distinct consciousness that the truths, " Saurians existed in the secondary formation," and " there are about 20,000,000 suns in our cluster," are Contingent truths.   The sciences, then, which are induced from these and similar facts are *not* Exact Sciences.

If, then, morals can be shown to bear this test equally with mathematics—if there be any fundamental truths of morals holding in our minds the status of those axioms of geometry and arithmetic of whose Necessity we are conscious, then these fundamental truths of morals are entitled to be made the basis of an Exact science whose subsequent theorems must all be deduced from them.   It is true that this method of proving the veracity of morals must rest directly on the veracity of the human consciousness; *more* directly than other forms of argument. But it has been a thousand times demonstrated that on this veracity of consciousness must ultimately depend *all* human knowledge whatsoever; therefore, I conceive, that in building *immediately* upon it the only thing needful is to ascertain that it is really and actually the *true* consciousness on which we build—that it is that normal consciousness common to us all, and clear and distinct in all minds which have reached a certain point of development. This, I apprehend, we may ascertain by keeping in view the parallel with mathematics in which the consciousness of certain truths is common to all minds at a certain point of development. If the SAME consciousness, then, accompanies some moral as accompanies some mathematical truths, surely the argument is, for all practical purposes, at an end. If we need not doubt our moral consciousness till we doubt our mathematical consciousness — if we need not doubt that " benevolence is right," and " falsehood is wrong," till we doubt that " two and one make three," and that " two right lines cannot enclose space,"—we may surely rest content with the degree of certainty pertaining to our moral science.

I may, however, be permitted to record here my conviction that this Cartesian doctrine of the veracity of consciousness*, though philosophically correct, can only be brought into play with any degree of fairness where Morals are concerned, where another part of our nature adds its voice to the mere intellectual consciousness. The science of morals stands alone in this respect, that it is the perpetual antagonist of our desires—that each of its propositions is a check upon some passion or interest. Accordingly the mental effort necessary to *attend* to our moral consciousness and to develope it into the complete science requires another motive than the mere curiosity for abstract or desire for useful knowledge which is the sufficient inducement to the study of other sciences. Hobbes declared that " Men would doubt the demonstrations of Euclid did they interfere with their interests;" and if we smile at the assertion,

---

* " Quicquid tam clarè ac distinctè percipitur quàm istud verum est."— DESCARTES, *Princip. Phil.*, iv.

we must at least admit that if the theorems of geometry were
actually so many checks upon our passions, a degree of can-
dour different from the present would be needful for their due
appreciation. The truth is that, were there no ally within the
citadel of our thoughts, the truths of morals would hardly find
an entrance—the consciousness even of the plainest axioms
would remain latent and unnoticed. But such an ally they
possess, nay, he is the rightful sovereign of the place. The
pure Will, the true Self of man, ever self-legislates the right.
Whenever its voice is heard, it is in the solemn imperative:
" Let the law be obeyed;" and it is this deep voice which alone
makes fully audible the voice of the Intellect: " There is a
Moral Law." All that the Intellect can do is to recognise
the abstract obligation under which lie all moral agents, to do
and to feel those actions which, according to an eternal necessary distinction, are right. This obligation the Will (as I
shall hereafter show) by its nature accepts and self-legislates. *
Its Willing is a Willing to do and feel the right, and, though
often overpowered by the blind instincts of the lower nature,
it is never perverted by them, but whenever its voice is heard
at all, it is the same, " Let the right be done." The exertion,
then, of the pure Will, the *raising of its voice* above the
clamour of the passions, is necessary, not only to give practical effect, but any degree of clearness and audibility, to
the assertion of the Intellect. The experience of every one
must corroborate the truth of this. Our consciousness of
the Moral distinctions between any actions presented for our
choice increases in lucidity to an extent we cannot fail to
notice in proportion as it is accompanied by the strong resolution of the Will to do the right when we shall have discovered it. "Let the Will," says Fichte, " only be firmly
directed towards the Good, and the understanding will of
itself apprehend the True." †

To return; the endeavour to establish morals in the rank
of an exact science is one commonly regarded with so much
distrust, and " geometric ethics "‡ have been spoken of so often

---

* See Chap. III.   † Bestimmung des Menschen. b. iii.
‡ Mill maintains that it is more to Astronomy than to Geometry that all
social sciences ought to be assimilated. Of the upholders of the Geometric
Method of studying, he says, " These thinkers perceive (what the partisans

as a sort of metaphysical " squaring of the circle," that before
commencing an attempt to show their true position, it will
be proper to take this prejudice into consideration.   It will
be found, I conceive, to rest partly on a popular error which
need not disturb our progress, and partly on a philosophic
truth, which must for ever limit the assimilation of morals
and geometry.*

The popular error is this — that moral consciousness must
be a consciousness of *all* moral truths. Ignorance is herein
displayed of the distinction between a fundamental truth—an
Axiom which, so far as we can trace, is not deduced from any
other truth, but is itself the basis of thought — and a Proposition logically deduced from such axiom.   Both axioms and
propositions are indeed Necessary truths.   It is no less necessarily true that " the superficies of a sphere is equal to four
great circles of the sphere," than that " things which are
equal to the same thing are equal to one another."   But our
consciousness of necessary truth can apply only in the first
place to the axiom, and then subsequently to the proposition,
when we have found the deduction thereof from the fundamental axiom to be perfectly demonstrated.   We only know
the proposition to be true at all in virtue of this deduction;
and if the steps of it be unknown to a man, he cannot have
any consciousness of its necessary truth.   If we ask an illiterate person whether he have a consciousness that it is a
necessary truth that " things which are equal to the same
thing are equal to one another," he will answer, that he
has such consciousness.   But if we ask him whether he have
a consciousness that it is a truth that " the superficies of a
sphere is equal to four great circles of the sphere," he will
answer, that he has no such consciousness.

Precisely the same results follow when it is attempted to
apply the test of consciousness to the propositions instead of to
the axioms * of Morals. The whole validity of the proposition

of the chemical or experimental theory do not), that the philosophy of society
is a deductive science.   But geometry affords no room for what so constantly
occurs in mechanics and its applications, the case of conflicting forces.   In the
geometrical theory of society, it is supposed that each social phenomenon results
always from one force, one single property of human nature." — MILL's *Logic*,
vol. ii. p. 490.
    * " I must say, that a very baseless objection has been urged against the ap-

must of necessity rest on the logical accuracy of its deduction from the axiom; which deduction ninety-nine persons in a hundred have never so much as thought of, far less verified. The consequence is, that the answers required from consciousness do not come from it at all, and moral Science is taunted with an uncertainty which arises from the ignorance of the inquirer. If we ask a person who has never studied morals, whether he have a consciousness that it is a necessary truth, that "honesty and veracity are right," he will say, that he has such consciousness. But if we ask him whether he have a consciousness that it is a necessary truth that "nothing can justify a lie," he will probably answer, that he has no such consciousness.

Yet, as the *geometer* is no less sure of the remotest proposition of his science than of its axiom, though the illiterate person is conscious only of the truth of the axiom, neither need the *moralist* be disheartened because the man who has never studied morals is conscious only of the veracity of the rudimentary truths of his science, and falls into the most egregious errors when he *guesses* at the more advanced propositions. I conceive that this popular error, which, by confounding together axioms and propositions, confounds *what it is* which consciousness ought to teach us, has been the origin of the larger part of the discredit thrown on the whole science of morals. Conscience is absurdly represented as a sort of priestess, bound to mount her tripod and deliver oracular response to every question in the remotest degree connected with ethics, and an outcry is raised over the contradictions in answers which she never made nor could make. Men like Hume traverse the history of our race, to collect all the piteous instances of aberrations which

plication of the word *axiom* to the fundamental principles of morality. It has been said that the moral precepts, "Be truthful," "be just," "be kind," cannot be called axioms, inasmuch as they are not propositions at all, but commands. Now, this distinction overlooks altogether the peculiar and distinctive character of morality. To say that "*It is right* to be kind," is to say to man's moral ear, "Be kind." When the ideas of rightness, of duty, of virtue, of a law of our nature, are once apprehended, it is seen they involve an obligation to act. Moral principles are preceptive in their nature. They are necessarily imperative even when they are merely assertions. The categorical form involves an epitactic meaning."—WHEWELL's *Elements*, Pref. xvi.

have resulted from neglect or imperfect study of the
moral consciousness; and then they cry, "Behold what it
teaches!" Yet I suppose that it will be admitted that man
is an animal capable of knowing geometry; though, if we
were to go up and down the world, asking rich and poor,
Englishman and Esquimaux, what are the ratios of solidity
and superficies of a sphere, a right cylinder and an equilateral
cone circumscribed about it, there are sundry chances that we
should hear of other ratios beside the sesquialterate.*

He who should argue that because *people ignorant of
geometry* did not know the sesquialterate ratio of the sphere,
cylinder, and cone, therefore *no man* could know it, or that
because they *disputed* it, that therefore it was *uncertain*,
would argue no more absurdly than he who urges the divergencies of half-civilised and barbarian nations as a reason
why no man could know, or know with certainty, the higher
propositions of morals. But the *axioms* — Who has questioned these? Let the sceptic seek again through history,
and find a fresh cloud of witnesses to depose that, to their consciousness, Truth, Justice, and Benevolence are wrong, and
Falsehood, Injustice, and Malevolence right!† Could all that
men have thought and felt since our race began lie written out
before our gaze, surely we should find less tokens of such moral
blindness, than in the statistics of physical sight we should
find instances of darkness to the light of the sun? Moral
blindness, if it really exist at all, is a phenomenon far too rare
to be taken into account in the psychology of our race. The
goître is, indeed, a melancholy evidence of the evil results of
depressing physical conditions; the Chinese woman's foot
displays, remarkably, the power of bad training: but the

---

* "As it is the object of the geometric sense to originate a geometric axiom
from which reason may deduce a scientific geometry, so it is the office of the
moral sense to originate a moral axiom from which reason may deduce a
scientific morality. The geometric sense is not the science of geometry, nor the
moral sense the science of morals."— *Social Statics*, by HERBERT SPENCER.

For the accurate meaning of the words "moral sense" according to Kant,
see Chap. IV.

† After that saddest of all *jeux d'esprit*, in which Hume sets forth the moral
heresies of the nations, he candidly adds, "Yet in how many circumstances would
an Athenian and Frenchman of merit certainly resemble one another? Fidelity,
truth, justice, courage, temperance, constancy, dignity of mind; these you have
all omitted, only to insist on the points in which they may by accident differ."
A Dialogue, p. 483., HUME's *Essays and Treatises* (4to edit.).

anatomist of healthy humanity does not describe goîtres and club-feet as our normal condition. Even this estimate, however, of the importance of diseased manifestations of our Moral nature is too high. Those few exceptional beings whom we have (for argument sake) supposed to question the axioms of morals, should be classed, not with the blind, deformed, and crippled, but with idiots such as are unable to recognise the relations of numbers.* Man is a Rational being, though there may be irrational idiots of his race. Man is a Moral being, and possesses a consciousness of moral axioms, though there should be found such a thing as a moral idiot without such consciousness.

The philosophic ground of the objection to all attempts to assimilate morals to geometry is this : — That it is impossible ever to give to morals a terminology to be compared for accuracy to that of mathematics. In mathematics we treat of definite numbers, definite dimensions. Having once defined the meaning of the words " circle," " triangle," " cone," " cylinder," there is no chance of error in the use of the terms, for no other figures will answer the definition, and any mind capable of apprehending our propositions at all, must perforce apprehend them rightly. In a science, on the contrary, which treats of human sentiments, the case is reversed,— Sentiments cannot be defined by any accurate terms, for they " vary with every fresh condition of humanity." † In each person's mind each sentiment acquires a peculiar character, corresponding to that of the mind in which it dwells, and this character changes, *visibly* every year, *actually* every hour of life. We

---

* The same was said long ago of men devoid of the religious sentiment :— " Notwithstanding the great varieties of opinion which have existed concerning the nature of God, yet the law and reason of every country are harmonious that there is a God, the King and Father of all, and that the many are but co-rulers under God. But if there have been, since the beginning of time, two or three atheistical, senseless individuals, whose eyes and ears deceive them, and who are maimed in their very souls, an irrational, barren species, as monstrous as a lion without courage, an ox without horns ; yet out of these you will be able to understand something of God."—MAXIMUS TYRIENSIS.

† MORELL's *Psychology*, p. 197. It is not needful for my present purpose to enter more deeply into the profound subject of the philosophy of language or point out that even in mathematical definition there is latitude for more or less clear apprehension of the nature of figures. What I have desired to insist on is, that mathematical language *is* sufficient, and moral language *cannot* be made sufficient, for the purposes of rigid mathematical deduction. I may, how-

should require a language for every individual, and for every hour of his life, were we to define love and hatred, gratitude and resentment, as they exist in the souls of the virtuous or vicious, magnanimous or base, sanguine or phlegmatic, happy or miserable ; and even then the word which would express his own sentiment to a man's own apprehension would fail to convey a just apprehension of it to another whose mental experience was different. And were we to exclude the consideration of Sentiments, and limit our study of morals to moral Actions, we should still find that the circumstances under which they take place modify them so entirely, that, short of a *description of the circumstances*, no term can be invented to define any one action. The difficulties in the way of defining those criminal actions wherewith penal jurisprudence is concerned, have produced enormously voluminous codes, and yet compelled all legislatures to leave great latitude to the judgment of magistrates in each individual case.

If, then, a strict terminology of the objects wherewith Moral Science has to deal be unattainable, it is manifest that to attempt to compete with the geometer in framing a series of consecutively deduced propositions is altogether presump-

---

ever, be allowed to quote these admirable observations of Morell : — "Words have no *absolute* meaning, but can only signify to any individual what he is able to convey into them from the results of his own inward life. In points where the mental experiences or intuitions of mankind, in every age or country, have been well nigh identical, the corresponding words will be so much the more synonymous. Such are the primary properties of the material world. On the other hand, when we go into those regions of mental experience which vary with every fresh condition of humanity, then we see at once how diverse, both in the character and intensity of their meaning, will be the terms in which those varied developments of mind have embodied themselves. It is this which renders it *impossible* to reproduce perfectly the meaning of words which grow up in a state of civilisation and moral development wholly different from our own ; and this we may likewise add, which renders it philosophically certain, that human words can never be the ultimate measure of absolute and infallible truth."— For Inductive science language is always an imperfect and often a deceptive instrument. "Common language (says HERSCHEL) is a mass of metaphor grounded not on philosophical resemblances, but on loose, fanciful, and often most mistaken analogies. From studying such language as the representative of nature no pure classification of facts can result." "In Aristotle (says WHEWEL) we have the consummation of this mode of speculation. The usual point from which he starts in his inquiries is that *we say* thus or thus in common language. Hence the doctrine of contrarieties — a most fertile source of Aristotelian confusion; thus for example *light* came to be considered as the opposite of *heavy*, not as its inferior degree, to the utter vitiation of the Aristotelian statics and dynamics."— *Quart. Rev.* vol. 68., p. 190. — *See ante* Chap. I. for similar error regarding the positive nature of Wrong.

tuous. The world laughed at Hobbes when, in his philosophical discussions, he affirmed that " the *space* occupied by one *point* was *large* enough to include another point," which his antagonist had demonstrated could not coincide with the first. Moral arguments pretending to the rigid form of geometric deduction are open to the same ridicule. The whole value of such geometric deduction depends on the absolute accuracy of the definitions, and Hobbes was guilty of no greater absurdity than the moralist who should use the forms of mathematical argument with a terminology impressed with all the laxity of colloquial phraseology.

The only method open to the moralist is to choose among the necessary truths of morals those which most nearly approach the character of axioms, and deduce from them, logically indeed, but not with the pretension of a chain of consecutive propositions, the principles of morality. But of this more will be said hereafter. My object, at present, has been to meet the philosophic opponent to " geometric ethics " by a candid confession that the science of morals cannot, in the nature of things, be ever placed on a par with the science of geometry.* At the same time I contend, that the reason of this is not because the truths of the one are one whit less true than those of the other, but simply because *we* have not, and never can have, an equally accurate organ wherewith to define them. *The truths are there.* There *are* axioms of morals, that is to say, fundamental principles of right; and there are propositions of morals, that is to say, subordinate principles deducible from the axioms. But, as the Iliad, or the Dialogues of Plato, could never be rendered into the language of the Hottentot or the Samoïede, neither can these thoughts of God be translated into poor human speech, and given therein adequate expression.

Having thus, as I trust, dismissed the first objection to the

---

* It will be observed that these concessions do not affect what I affirmed in Chap. I., that language affords a reliable exponent of moral *distinctions*. The immutable Necessary distinctions of Right and Wrong are conveyed to our minds by their proper terms precisely as the Necessary distinctions of Straightness and Crookedness are conveyed by their proper terms. This has nothing to do with the fact that we have no perfect medium for conveying to each other an absolutely correct conception of the particular Contingent Actions or Sentiments which our common Intuitions are to recognise as Right or Wrong.

attempt to make morals a deductive science, by showing the
objection to be founded on a misconception, and having
admitted the validity of the second objection, but shown that
it only extends to assumptions which I have no intention to
make, I now proceed to apply the Kantian test to the truths
of morals, by which test must be decided whether they be
Necessary or Contingent, and the science deductive or inductive.

I have shown, in answering the first objection, that it is
only to an *axiom,* and not to a proposition, that the test of
consciousness of necessary truth can be applied. Every
rational mind will be conscious of the necessary truth of the
axioms that " the part is less than the whole," " things which
are equal to the same thing are equal to one another," and so
on. But only a mind which has traced the consecutive deductions of the geometer is conscious of the necessary truth
of the propositions, that circles are to one another as the
squares of their diameters, and that spheres have to one
another the triplicate ratio of that which their diameters have.
If, then, we would apply the test of consciousness to a
moral truth, we must choose an axiomatic, and not a remotely
deduced truth for our purpose. To discover accurately and
scientifically what are actually the *ultimate* truths of morals,
the axioms below which no further descent is possible, would
require vast machinery. As I have already remarked, Kant
has made the Freedom of the Will the basis of his splendid
fabric ; but for an erection more purely popular, truths immediately and spontaneously deduced from the idea Duty may
be sufficient. In the second and practical part of this Essay
I purpose to range all duties, social, personal, and religious,
as deductions from the sublime canons of him who, by best
fulfilling them all, met most perfectly the conditions under
which moral and religious inspiration is granted to man.
The Canons are,—

Thou shalt love thy neighbour as thyself.

Be perfect as thy Father who is in heaven is perfect.

Love the Lord thy God with all thine heart.

Let us try how these truths stand the test of consciousness. What sense accompanies their reception into the mind?

Does it seem that the Love of our neighbour, Benevolence, as we call it, is right or wrong? And if right, is it right necessarily, immutably, universally, or only in some cases and contingently? Is it right for one man and wrong for another, right in England and wrong in New Zealand, right two thousand years ago and wrong now? And, as regards being Perfect, are Purity, Veracity, Temperance, Fortitude, and so on, right at all times, or sometimes right and sometimes wrong? Will unchastity be right in the next century? Was lying right in the days of Cheops? Let us stretch our imaginations beyond our world, and picture ourselves visitants to an unseen planet revolving round some sun whose ray reaches human sight after a journey of a thousand years. Analogies to aught our senses have revealed to us on earth have disappeared; old things have passed away; all things are new. Rational creatures, indeed, there are around us, but likeness to human form or the circumstances of human life we trace not. Yet they live in a social state, though all its relationships are different from our own; they hold communion with one another, though no crimson lips mould their language, and no marvellous ears convey sounds to the brain. Let us bethink us. In this social state of theirs, is it wrong to love our neighbour? Is malevolence, perchance, the right sentiment in this far-off world? Must this unknown mode of communication, in order to be right, be the medium of falsehood? To a thousand questions like these we should always be compelled to return the same replies. At the bounds of space and time goodness and truth will still be good and true; we cannot by any artifice picture it otherwise. *We have a consciousness that these moral truths are necessary truths and of universal extent.*

Now this consciousness, as I have said, is worthy of our implicit reliance. Our knowledge of such necessary truths is the result of the à *priori* operation of the mind itself, without admixture of (though not antecedently to) the sensation by which we obtain knowledge of contingent truths. To this knowledge, then, of Moral truth, which is identical in origin and nature with our knowledge of Mathematical truth, I shall henceforth in this Essay give the name of

INTUITIVE. I do not profess to apply the word in a strictly scientific sense according to any one psychological system, but for a popular treatise; I have taken a word in itself popular, which yet appears to convey with sufficient accuracy the idea of that purely mental element or subjective factor of thought which is admitted by all transcendental schools to form a constituent of *all* human knowledge, and to be both base and superstructure of deductive science. Of the theological aspect of Intuition I shall speak at the end of this Chapter.*

I now return to the demonstration that moral truths are Necessary, and moral science properly deductive. We have seen the affirmative side of the argument, namely, the consciousness we feel of their Necessity. The negative will serve our purpose equally well. We have assumed that morals form an exact science possessing axioms, and these axioms were recognised by our consciousness as necessary truths. Let us now, for argument sake, assume that morals may form an experimental science; and let us seek for those ultimate facts which make the basis of such a science, and apply to them the same test of consciousness, whereby to prove their necessity or contingency.

In the first place, we observe that it is impossible to obtain

---

* The schoolmen divided all knowledge into " cognitio intuitiva " (that which we gain by immediate presentation of the real individual object) and " cognitio abstractiva " (that which we gain and hold by the medium of a general term). Kant used the word intuition (*Anschauung*) in two senses,— empiric intuition being the *cognitio intuitiva* of the schoolmen, and pure intuition that which determines the formal and *à priori* conditions of all our perceptive knowledge (space and time). Morell defines intuition to be " that precise attitude of the soul in which it sees the various relationships of the universe presented to it spontaneously as an immediate objective reality. Perceptions, according to his view, involve intuitions of material properties, and are the *species* of which intuitions are the *genus*, being the spontaneous form of intelligence in its *universal* application to all human truth," moral and religious truth included. — See *Psychology*, pp. 161. 145. 147. 157.

Be it remembered, that in claiming for our knowledge of the necessary truths of morals the position of intuitive *à priori* operations of the mind, and making the ideas of duty fundamental ideas, I do not insist on their chronological antecedency, nor of that of any *idea* whatever, to that moral *sense* of pleasure in right and pain in wrong, which, as I shall hereafter show, is the peculiar interest attached to the mandates of the pure Will. As I affirmed at starting, the indispensable condition of the growth of our souls is the combined action of the sensational and intuitional elements from infancy; and long before the stage of abstract ideas has been reached through the training of perceptions, a considerable degree of moral sense has generally been developed in a rudimentary form.

by the experience of the senses anything that can be properly designated as an ultimate *moral fact;* we cannot hear, see, or feel whether an action be Right or Wrong; we may hear that a voice speaks loudly or softly, harshly or harmoniously; we may see and feel that a man's arm strikes a blow, which may be strong or weak, heavy or light: but whether it be Right to say what the voice says, or Wrong to do what the arm does, we cannot hear, see, or feel. Yet, by bringing into play certain intellectual (not *moral*) powers,—such as memory, comparison, and judgment, or, as Locke expresses it, by applying reflection to our sensations,—we may obtain the further result that words we have heard were English or Latin, in prose or verse, in accordance with fact or contradictory of it. Also, that the blow we have seen or felt was dealt cleverly (that is, so as to produce the desired result) or stupidly, that it was graceful or awkward, that it constituted or did not constitute a legal " assault and battery." But all these characteristics of words and actions lie exclusively in the region of the Intellect, and have no more to do with the Moral distinction of right and wrong than the thickness or strength of an iron bar has to do with its straightness or crookedness.

Nevertheless, the senses have yet another office beside that of informing us of the abstract properties of the objects of which they take cognisance; they are also inlets of pleasure and pain, according as these objects are suitable or unsuitable. This we may call, for convenience, the sense of well or ill-being; and it is in the revelations of *this* sense that experimental moralists profess to find the ultimate facts of their science. The pleasure and pain we ourselves experience, and that which (as man is able to convey his impressions by voice and otherwise) we perceive others to experience, afford a basis of facts from which reflection draws inductions respecting the pleasurable or painful results of classes of actions on the well or ill-being of individuals and of the community. These results being arrived at, it is assumed that those classes of actions which are found to produce well-being are to be held lawful, and those which produce ill-being unlawful. The former are *called* Right; the latter, Wrong.

Now, in the first place, these ultimate facts are confessedly
Contingent truths. No one pretends to have a consciousness
that his pleasurable or painful sensations received from certain
objects or actions must of necessity hold good for all time to
all sentient creatures. There is no absurdity in imagining that
the Creator might have made the objects which now gratify our
senses painful to them, or that he may do so for other creatures,
or for ourselves at another period of life. But not only are
these ultimate facts avowedly contingent, and so fit only to be
the basis of an inductive science suited to this planet, and
this epoch only ; they are not only theoretically mutable, but
practically subject to incessant change ; not only God might
without self-contradiction alter them, but He actually *has* made
them naturally fluctuating. As Hartley showed, the same
sensation which at one degree is pleasure, is at a degree more
intense positive pain ; and the sensation which at first gave
pain diminishes by use till it reach the degree of pleasure,
while the pleasant sensation dwindles to indifference. We see
this clearly in the sense of taste, in which our choicest luxuries
are things uncongenial to an untutored palate. Habit, and
not only habit but constitution, health, and strength regulate
the quantum of our sensations, on which depends their pleasure
or their pain. To take, then, any statement of the pleasurable
or painful results of an action as an ultimate fact of science,
is to give the science a very tottering basis indeed ; for not
only have we that absence of consciousness of its Necessary
truth which places it *à priori* in the category of Contingencies,
not only do we perceive that it might have pleased the Creator
to have reversed all our sensations, and that there is no absurdity or self-contradiction in supposing them to be at any
time so changed ; we also see that *actually* the Creator has
made sensation a matter continually shifting, not only between different creatures, but in one and the same creature.
Thus, at best, the facts at the base of Experimental Morals
are Contingent truths, of a character even more than usually
mutable.

But we must further ask?—Are they *moral* facts at all ?
Let it be admitted that we can arrive at true conclusions
regarding the influence of different actions on our well-being,

that such well-being constitutes the whole Happiness of man, and that we can from these premises obtain a series of general propositions forming a code of laws enforcing the beneficent class of actions and condemning the maleficent. Admitting even all this, still I ask, —

What will make laws so obtained *moral?*

Of two things one must hold,—either these laws aim at the Happiness of the Individual only (the inductions having only been drawn from his sensations of the actions which experience shows will on the whole make them the more pleasurable or painful), or the laws aim at the Happiness of the whole Community (the inductions having been drawn from the well-being of all of the actions found to tend towards the common happiness). The system which sets forth the happiness of the individual I shall call Private Eudaimonism, and that which sets forth the happiness of the community, Public Eudaimonism.

Now, in the first case, supposing the laws assume only to teach me how best to obtain my own happiness, entirely regardless of that of any one else, except so far as it may tend to my own, — I admit, indeed, at once, that there is logic in the matter, the science is neither more nor less than that of Prudence. It teaches me how I can make the best bargain with my senses, how I can clutch the largest possible quantity of pleasures for myself with the smallest possible danger to my health, wealth, or reputation.

Now, a code of laws such as this, among all the follies of humanity, has never yet been constructed. If some Aristippus were bold enough to put it forth, it must still be believed that no one would have the presumption to call it *moral.* Nor let it be said, that I have misrepresented the nature of laws framed only to promote the Happiness of the Individual. It is a gross fallacy to imagine that a science based only on our sense of well-being could lead of itself, and strictly carried out by induction, to any doctrines like those of universal justice, benevolence, truth, and purity. Studying only our own happiness with no *à priori* guide, we might indeed obtain rules of *general* honesty, *general* temperance. The world is actually so constructed, that as a *general* rule the maintenance

F

of the lower virtues is repaid in happiness. The connection is easy to trace, and prudential ethics can construct good rules upon it; but for the higher, nobler virtues, and even for the *universal*, over and above the *general* authority of the lower duties, it can say nothing; nay, it must point the wrong way. Take, for example, the virtue of Truthfulness. The Private Eudaimonist has perceived that a liar is never trusted, and that it is exceedingly inconvenient and unpleasant not to be trusted. Accordingly he says, " Speak the truth, for by so doing you will obtain approbation and escape distrust." So far so good. As a general rule these considerations of approbation and distrust will have sufficient weight to determine me in favour of truth. But, suppose that I am questioned respecting an offence which I have committed, will the same considerations lead to the same decision? Quite the contrary. If I desire approbation, I shall tell as many lies as may suffice to conceal my offence. If I fear distrust, I shall take good care not to show I have committed a dishonesty, a cruelty, or a deceit. Again, supposing that a wicked parent or tyrannical master order me to conceal his misdeeds by a lie, and threaten me with punishment on my refusal, will the moralist tell *me* (a helpless child or starving dependant) that *prudence* recommends truth? His notion of prudence must be stretched to the grossest *imprudence* ere it can do so. The distant and contingent advantages of virtue in this world (we shall consider those of a future state hereafter) are nothing compared with impending punishment and destitution. The regimen which such physicians prescribe for the chronic evils of life are ridiculous in the presence of the acute diseases of agony and desperation. Nor are the cases I have supposed exceptional ones. If urged by the Love of Approbation, our virtues will correspond, not with the eternal law of rectitude, but with the standard, low at the best, and, it may be, utterly depraved, of the society in which we move: nay more ; as it is only an outward and not an inward virtue, which can compete for such approbation, the temptation to adopt a course of hypocrisy and duplicity is almost inevitable. If, on the contrary, the Fear of our fellow-creatures be our motive, this will as often lead us wrong as right. In a low state of civilisation, and in the inferior grades of civilised society, oppression manifests itself most frequently by requiring the violation of duty; and if we were to take human rewards and punishments for a standard it would depend only on the chance whether we happened to have a good or a bad parent or master, whether virtue consisted in every good or in every evil deed. Thus, so far as this world is concerned, the principle " Do right that you may prosper " is manifestly deficient in many cases, and absurd in those numerous ones wherein the formula to hold good should rather be, " Do wrong, and you will prosper."

But I shall be told, that though the adherents of Private Eudaimonism start from the ultimate facts of our sensations on earth, and make their inductions from the results here experienced of human actions, their doctrine embraces a far wider scope than this, and is essentially modified by the considerations offered by religion. I shall be told that we are under the government of a God supremely just, and that we may accordingly be assured that, in this world or the next, virtue will be rewarded and vice punished with unerring rectitude. Truly I believe it from my soul! In the belief that Justice is not only rightful, but real " sovereign of the world *," I find a creed more joyous than the expectation of a Paradise, even as the doubt thereof is far more grievous to bear than that of our own immortality. And I admit more; I admit that if we could so impress this truth on the minds of men as to exclude from them all consideration of temporary advantage or disadvantage—if we could teach the child, the serf, the worldling, to behold with unwavering faith the hand of God for ever guiding with unerring justice the events of mortal life—then indeed we should impress on them a principle of action which would correspond absolutely in the *form*, though not in the *spirit*, of its manifestation with that of true intuitive morals.

But now, I ask, whence come these religious considerations which are so completely to modify our Eudaimonistic ethics, that the sin which Prudence might before have recommended, it now forbids because God will punish it?

It is no easy question, whether, on the grounds of the Expe-

---

* " Justice is rightful sovereign of the world."—PINDAR.

rimental Philosophy alone, we could ever have arrived at the
belief in a God. It seems that the doctrine of a First Cause,
which is commonly supposed to be the result of arguments on
the basis of Sensation, is yet indebted to Intuition for that precise notion of Causality on which it hinges. Hume has clearly
demonstrated that we cannot obtain through the senses the
conviction we possess that every effect must have had a cause.
And if we even appeal to traditional revelation for manifestations of God to the senses, those who accept the evidence
of such events in their most literal interpretation must
acknowledge that the whole value of the assertion made by
a voice from the sky that God would reward virtue and
punish vice, must depend on our possessing the assurance that
the voice of God must speak truth. Now, this assurance must
come from some other source than any such miraculous manifestation; for it is the trustworthiness of the being who manifests himself of which we want to be assured; and his own
assertion would be of no avail, had we not a testimony elsewhere that the character of the Being who could thus address
us is absolute Truth. This testimony, this assurance, we do
in fact possess ; and if some primitive prophet were able to
persuade his people that God had actually spoken to him,
that people would never dream of questioning whether God
had deceived the prophet.* It follows, then, that we have some
knowledge of God antecedent to any *miraculous* revelation,
just as we have an idea of Causation on which the inductive
argument of *Natural* Theology must rest. In both cases
the ideas can only be Intuitions, *à priori* operations of the
mind.†

Vast as are the *à posteriori* evidences of the existence and
holiness of our Creator, it thus appears that their whole
validity rests on Intuitions. Religion, then, can by no means
be claimed as part of the Inductive Science of Morals.‡ The

---

* See BLANCO WHITE, *Life.*

† See LEIBNITZ, *Nouveaux Essais*, liv. iv. c. xviii.

‡ Kant remarque ici que nous n'avons pas le droit de partir de l'idée de Dieu
pour en dériver les idées morales car ce sont précisément les idées morales qui
nous conduisent à reconnaitre un Etre suprême qui soit le modèle de toute
sainteté; par conséquent on ne peut considerer les lois morales comme fortuites
et résultant de la simple volonté de Dieu. La vertu n'est pas obligatoire par
la seule raison qu'elle est une ordre de Dieu ; mais elle ne nous parait un ordre
de Dieu que parce qu'elle nous oblige intérieurement." — VICTOR COUSIN,
Cours d'Histoire de la Philosophie Morale, en 18iéme *Siecle,* p. 318.

advocate of Prudence must not tell us that it is prudent to speak truth *because* God will punish a lie. We reply that he cannot prove that God will do so without appealing to Intuition; and to do this he must abjure his science; for, if there be such a power as Intuition revealing to us any truths, it certainly reveals Moral truths no less authoritatively; and one of these moral truths which it reveals is, that prudence is *not* the motive of virtue. And, driven from religion, the experimentalist is also driven from the doctrine of the rewards and punishments of a future state. The existence of such a state is pre-eminently a truth of Intuition; and even could we find, among the phenomena of mortality, grounds for the induction that the soul of man survives his body, still we should assuredly be at a loss to find, in that "undiscovered country" whither it goes, a basis for the belief that there the crimes of earth will meet their chastisement and its virtues their recompense.

Thus we see that the adherent of Private Eudaimonism is logically bound to confine his reasoning to those consequences of pleasure or pain which are visibly attached in this life to good and evil actions. We have already remarked, that if such a science were ever elaborated, and its rules stated, there would not be found any man bold enough to call it a System of MORALS.

But it is the Public, far more than the Private Eudaimonist, with whom the advocate of Intuition has to contend. Those who have given to Inductive Morals their vast importance in the world, are those who have held that it is *not* our own individual and exclusive happiness at which we ought to aim, but the "greatest happiness of the greatest number" of our fellow-creatures.

Of this system we shall have much to say hereafter, when we come to speak of the question, "Why the Moral Law ought to be obeyed?" For our present purpose of demonstrating that morals are properly an intuitive, and not an inductive science, it will be enough to show that utilitarianism itself rests on an Intuition.

Let it be assumed that we *can*, by induction, arrive at the rules, by following which we shall produce the "greatest

happiness of the greatest number," I ask, *why* are we to seek
that object?

If there be no such thing as an Intuition that Benevolence
is Right, or that we ought to do Right, — nay, no Intuition
of Duty at all, —what motive remains to induce us to sacrifice
the very smallest of our pleasures to procure thereby the happiness of the whole human race?

It cannot be because the happiness of our brethren will
reflectively produce our own, for this is to recur to the Private
Eudaimonism, whose fallacy we have exposed. And, moreover, if we have no Intuitive Moral Conscience, the production of the happiness of our fellows will procure for us no
applause of conscience, nor will they (having a similar deficiency) display towards us any more gratitude than they may
find it their interest to pay.

Neither can it be because God orders us to seek the happiness of our neighbours, and will punish us for not doing so.
We have already seen that he who takes his stand solely on
Experience has no reasonable ground for asserting *anything*
respecting God or His government.

But if we are neither to be made happy by our neighbour's
happiness, nor to be punished for neglecting to make him so,
what possible reason can there be for us as individuals to
give up one iota of gratification within our reach for the sake
of another?   Let it be remembered we do not ask why the
community is to make laws for securing this "greatest happiness of the greatest number," and affix penalties for breach of
the same.   That is another affair.   I ask only why the *individual* in those million cases to which no human laws can
reach, should sacrifice his own smallest convenience for the
lives of thousands of men?   There is no use reiterating that
it is selfish, hateful, wicked, to refuse to make others happy,
or that it is generous, noble, admirable, to make them so.
Unless these epithets find an echo in his breast, such as the
mere senses can never supply, they are altogether powerless
and unmeaning.

I conceive that, by resting the controversy respecting the
existence of Intuition on this simple fact, that our sense of
the obligation of Beneficence requires to be accounted for, I

am not only doing fairly by the utilitarian argument, but even allowing it a much greater force than it deserves. I might demur to its assumption, that it *can* teach us the right means of producing the " greatest happiness of the greatest number," without reference to a clue which the mercy of our Creator has afforded* to guide us through the labyrinths of political and social economy. Of all inductive sciences, these are the most abstruse, and require the largest groundwork of statistical facts ; and of all inductive sciences their results are the most unsatisfactory, inasmuch as all the signs of external well-being, of which alone they can take cognisance, do *not* constitute the Happiness which is aimed at, but often a most delusive shadow of it.

I might cavil also at the Public Eudaimonist's further assumption, that to aim at the greatest happiness of the greatest number constitutes not merely a part, but the *whole* of human virtue. I might appeal to his own consciousness whether he did not feel that certain personal virtues, such as Purity and Temperance, had a higher value than can be attached to their slight influence over the happiness of the

---

* "The well-being of mankind must necessarily be carried on in one of two ways, either without the injunction of any certain rules of morality, only by obliging every one on each particular occasion to consult the public good ; or, secondly, by enjoining the observance of determinate established laws which have, from the nature of things, an essential fitness to procure the well-being of mankind. Against the former of these methods lie several strong objections : first, to calculate the events of each particular action is impossible. Secondly, if that method be observed, we can have no standard to which, comparing the actions of another, we may pronounce them good or bad. It follows, therefore, that the great end to which God requires the concurrence of human actions must, of necessity, be carried on by the second method proposed, namely, the observation of certain universal determinate rules, which, in their own nature, have a necessary tendency to promote the well-being of the *sum* of mankind, taking in all nations and ages, from the beginning to the end of the world." (Bishop Berkeley's *Sermon on Passive Obedience*, viii.—x.) Now, the question is, whether these universal rules, which Berkeley and Bentham hold to be the result of Induction, *can* be so obtained. Whewell says, " The reason why I do not erect my system on the fact that happiness is the supreme object of human action, is simply that I *cannot*. I cannot from that principle obtain definite rules of action by any proofs which appear to me at all satisfactory or intelligible. I can discover no such definition, measure, or analysis of happiness as shall put this in my power." Whewell's *Systematic Morality*, sec. vi.

Mackintosh, in abridging the above passage of Berkeley, leaves the impression that he was a deductive moralist ; but the sequel of that unfortunate Discourse on Passive Obedience shows him to have considered the general rules for whose maintenance he argues to be discoverable by Induction. For an admirable satire on the views of passive obedience of a party when dominant and when oppressed, see Macaulay, *Hist. of England*, vol. ii. p. 392.

mass of mankind. If he feels this, he must account for such
consciousness otherwise than by the maxims of his own science.
But I am content to leave both these demurrers in abeyance.
Let it be granted that we can find the way to produce
" the greatest happiness of the greatest number," and that
to produce it includes all human duty, still I ask, —

Why is *it* a Duty?

It appears to me that it is impossible to answer this question without avowing that there is in man a power transcending his senses, or aught which the understanding can
draw from their teaching — a faculty of some kind or other, by
which he gains the idea of Duty in the abstract, and of the
fact that Beneficence is a Duty.

But, if this be so, our inquiry has terminated. We have
seen that the fundamental principles of morals, when tried
affirmatively, fully answer the test of Necessary truths, and
so constitute the science of which they form the basis an
Exact Science. And we found that, on the other hand, there
are no Ultimate Facts at all which can properly form the
ground of an Inductive Science of Morals, and that those which
claim to be so are not only Contingent, but actually in a state
of continual variation. Finally, that the attempts to construct an Inductive Science of Morals are futile, because it
must necessarily aim at either private or public happiness
exclusively. If it aim at that which belongs only to the
Individual, it becomes so base that no one can presume to call
it a Moral System, unless it bring to its aid considerations of
religion and immortality which it has robbed from Intuitive
Science.   And if it aim at Public Happiness, it must rest its
entire force of operation on the idea that it is the Duty of
man to make his fellow happy ; which idea is strictly Intuitive.

Is there, or is there not, then, in the world such an idea
extant as that of the Duty of Beneficence, wholly separate
from all concomitant ideas of benefit to ourselves ? Is not
this idea something greater than can be treated as fantastic
or exceptional?   Is it not the commonest of all ideas, and as
much a part of the human mind as the heart is of the human
body ? Has it not been embodied in every religion, assumed
by the laws of every state ? But, if this idea of Duty be

a real thing, a great thing, if we have demonstrated that we could not have obtained this idea through the senses, but must have gained it by Intuition, then Intuition must be given its natural position as the basis of the only veritable System of Ethics. The question with which this Chapter started has now been answered — The Truths of Morals are Necessary Truths. The origin of our knowledge of them is Intuitive, and their proper treatment is Deductive.*

* The whole doctrine of Necessary Truths as herein stated has been attacked in a very powerful manner by MILL. — (*Logic*, b. 2. c. 5.) He considers that Whewell's arguments in its defence amount only to the assertion " that propositions the negation of which is inconceivable, or in other words, which we cannot figure to ourselves, being false, must rest upon evidence of a higher and more cogent description than any which experience can afford." MILL replies to this by recalling the multiplicity of experiments by which the axioms of geometry have from infancy been fixed in our minds, insomuch that the association of ideas becomes indissoluble. He then proceeds to cite cases in which the contingent truths of the existence of antipodes and the power of gravitation were rejected as *absurd*. (*Logic*, vol. i. p. 313, *et seq*.) " Now (he adds) in the case of a geometric axiom, such for example, as that two straight lines cannot enclose a space, a truth which is testified to us by our very earliest impressions of the external world — how, is it possible that the reverse of the proposition *can* be otherwise than inconceivable to us ? Will it be really contended that the inconceivableness of the thing under such circumstances proves anything against the experimental origin of the conviction ? "—(Vol. i. p. 318.) These and other arguments to the same purpose are stated by Mr. MILL in a manner so masterly that it would be a presumption for me to attempt to dispose of them in a few paragraphs, and for an elaborate refutation I have no space, and doubtless no ability. Nevertheless, I must appeal to the consciousness of my reader whether all the arguments which MILL has brought forward have really satisfied him that the truth " twice two make four," occupies in his mind the same place as any contingent truth whatever, even such an one as the experience of his own senses has taught him with even greater reiteration since the hour of his birth. VICTOR COUSIN says : " Kant remarque avec raison qu'il est impossible de réduire cette notion de nécessité [that of the existence of a cause for every effect] à une habitude née d'une liaison constante: c'est là détruire et non pas expliquer le principe de causalité qui pour agir, n'attend pas l'habitude. L'idée de la nécessité ne se forme pas par morceaux et en détail; elle s'introduit pleine et entiere dans l'intelligence. Mille et mille généralisations ne l'engendrent pas elle en différe d'une absolue différence."—VICTOR COUSIN, *Cours d'Histoire de la Philosophie Morale au* 18*iéme Siecle*, vol. i. p. 47.
    Late physiological researches seem to have tended more and more to disprove the doctrine of Sensationalism as opposed to that of the transcendental source of a part of human knowledge. A writer in the *Quarterly Review*, No. cxci., observes. " The law of externality has also a very important bearing on some of the most vexed questions in Metaphysics, — that one, for example, of Locke, and especially of Condillac, that all our ideas are derived from sensations, and that the mind is a *tabula rasa*. The physiologist proves beyond all cavil that the so-called transformations of our sensations into ideas do not exist. On the contrary, he shows that as soon as the organs of sense begin to be acted on there is already a mind to *attend* to the nerve excitation, to receive and to perceive it, and to add to it the *idea* of space by giving that sensation a local habitation; without these mental acts no sensation is possible. The readers of Kant and

The further method of this treatment may require explanation.

I have already observed, that as it is in the nature of things impossible to give to Morals a terminology of any degree of accuracy, it is absurd to imitate that geometric method of demonstration by a consecutive chain of deductions, all whose value depends on the precision of the definitions employed. The only rational course open to the Moralist is to deduce his propositions logically, but not with pretensions to mathematical accuracy or sequence, from those fundamental canons of whose necessary truth he has consciousness. When this has been done, and the process of deduction carried to its full extent, then, and only then, must the exact science be *applied.* Then must experience be called in, to teach us how to apply to actual life with best effect the propositions of our abstract science.

The nature of all exact science is to teach us *abstract* universal principles. It cannot possibly descend below these to practical applications. By geometry I learn that a triangle is equal to half a rectangle under the same base and altitude; but no geometry can teach me whether one of my fields be a triangle with equal base and altitude with the adjoining rectangle. To know this, I must see and measure them; and then geometry will teach me that the one contains half as many acres as the other. Likewise, in morals, Intuition will teach me that I must love my neighbour, and reflection will thence deduce that I am bound to relieve the wants of the poor to the best of my ability. But Intuitive Morals cannot teach me what are the wants of A. B., or whether I

Leibnitz will need no further development of cognate ideas."—P. 110. Another *Review* to which I have lost my reference, thus describes the defect of the Sensational Philosophy, " Sharp and logical as Locke's intellect was, he erred in not penetrating deep enough. He began with the first story of Metaphysical inquiry, instead of the basement. It is the information of the mind he invites us to consider, and not the mind itself. His Essay assumes that ideas which at best do but furnish or stimulate our mental capacity, are more than that capacity they minister to. As reasonably might an anatomist pretend to explain human structure, by showing how food is converted into digested blood, muscle, bone, and nerve. We admit the importance of meat and drink to sustain life, but we deny that they explain the mystery of life. A steam-engine is motionless till water is put into the boiler, and fuel in the grate; but who in considering the beautiful and complicated workmanship would set the water and fuel above the mechanism?"

shall best relieve them by giving him alms or by providing him with employment. Experience must teach me which way will most effectually benefit him, and then Intuition will teach me that whichever does so it is my duty to pursue. Experience must collect the facts to which Intuitive science is to be applied, and a large and glorious field, a whole science of itself, is thereby opened to it. Without Experience, without that aggregate experience of millions which statistics afford us, our best efforts are aimed in the dark. *We* indeed benefit by them, for "every man is warmed by the fire of his own self-sacrifice;" but the objects of our ill-directed endeavours are as often injured as aided. In old times, when experience was never applied to such subjects, the mischiefs arising from the indiscriminate bounties inculcated by the Church were incalculable. Scarcely less were the evils resulting from blind efforts to correct personal vice by asceticism, regardless of the evidence that the supposed cure produced worse disease. Even in our own day there is an immensity for the experimentalist still to do, both in the collection of facts concerning human want and sin, and in drawing inductions of their most efficacious remedies.

But here let him stop! The office of experience goes no further; its wand must break on the threshold of that Intuition which reveals to us the necessary truths of the Eternal Right. Because Experience has shown us *how* to obey the Moral Law, how to put it's mandates most effectually into execution, it must not therefore be authorised to question those mandates themselves. Because it has aided us to fulfil the duty of conferring temporal Happiness on our neighbour, it must not set up that Happiness as the sole end of morality. Because it has advised our Benevolence what is Expedient, it must not make Benevolence a matter of Expediency. Let the experimentalist, by all means, show us how to improve the physical condition of the masses; but let him not question the expediency of raising MEN from the mire. Let him show us how we are to educate the poor, but not dare to ask the Utility of enlarging the capacity for virtue in rational souls. Let him teach us how to emancipate the slave, but not demur whether restoring one-sixth of a community to the rights of manhood will conduce to the " greatest happiness of the greatest number!" In a word, the moment Intuition has proved an action to be *Right*, Experience must no longer ask whether it be also *expedient*. Whether it be so or not, it is still THE RIGHT.

Thus we see that Intuition has its own allotted part in Moral Science, which must be stretched to its utmost limits, and into whose domain the inferior science may not enter. And Experience has also its part, in which there is yet much to be done, though not in the way of invading the domain of the exact science, yet in that of extending our knowledge of the facts to which it is to be applied. Where the deductive science of the Intuitionist stops there the inductive science of the Experimentalist meets it, and, by a process which modern logicians have happily named " Traduction," we pass from one order of reasoning to the other, and complete a Science of Ethics practically applicable to every detail of life.

Enough, I trust, has now been said concerning the *nature* and *method* of Moral Science, and also to convince the reader that the certainty of its deductions from Intuition is only inferior to those of mathematics, because it is unprovided with a language wherewith to define the subjects with which it deals with sufficient accuracy. Yet this deficiency of language, though extremely injurious in the case of all *written* treatises, wherein the terms used by the author in one sense may be understood by the reader in another, is of far less importance in that personal inquiry into the truth of each proposition which it is the office of the Moralist to urge, and the pride of the Intuitionist to place within the reach of every human mind. For it is to no learned works, no statistical tables, he refers his reader for judgment on the necessary truths which he enounces. He bids him only descend into his own consciousness, and observe what he finds there. He tells him that, if he even finds his guide to be in error, the result need not disturb him. He has but to clear away from his mind the figures which may have been scribbled over it, and then to work the sum for himself. If he find that another arithmetician have stated it falsely, he will not thereby lose confidence in the truth of arithmetic !

Now, of the *nature* of this Intuition which we hope to have proved to be a primary source of human knowledge, it is most difficult to speak. All the powers of our minds are mysterious; few more so than the commonest, Memory, Comparison, the Association of Ideas. Still darker seems the source of a power whereby we can say of a truth " That is Necessary and Eternal. It holds good in worlds we have never visited, it was the same milleniums ere our being commenced." All that we can say of such power is, that we have it, that none but our Creator could have given it to us, and that we must therefore treat it as the ground of thought He has mercifully placed in our minds; for without it we should be driven hopelessly through the world of Unreason without possibility of rest. It has been common, among a certain class of philosophers, to make light of the few axioms on which geometry and logic have been erected, when they have been quoted as affording a basis for Morals and Religion. It is said, that it is " staving out the ocean with a bulrush " to attempt to stem the torrent of scepticism by such truths as that " Things cannot at the same time be and not be," " The part is less than the whole," " Things which are equal to the same thing are equal to one another," and so on. May we not say rather, that when we feel the immutable nature of these truths we touch ground with our feet, and thereby gain courage to struggle on a little longer through the surf and the darkness? Surely, surely there is an Island of the Blessed even now at hand! We could never be doomed to feel certainty in such humble truths as these, and yet to find no rest at last in the haven of Virtue and Religion.*

In a practical point of view, so as we admit the *existence* of Intuition, it matters little what we think of its *origin*. Like Cato, we may think —

> "From God derived, to God by nature joined,
> We act the dictates of His mighty mind.
> And though the priests were mute, the temples still,
> God wants no oracle to speak His will.
> When first we from the teeming womb were brought,
> With *inborn precepts* were our spirits fraught." †

* " The spirit of true science discovered that it was only amongst a few of the simplest elements of human thought that it could find a sure and steady footing. This solid basis it obtained, first of all, amongst the relations of number and space. This step was secured. . . . A platform was laid on which reason could take its stand."—J. D. MORELL's *Psychology*, Pref. vii.

† " Hæremus cuncti superis, temploque tacente
Nil facimus non sponte Dei : nec vocibus ullis
Numen egit : dixitque semel nascentibus auctor
Quicquid scire licet."—LUCAN's *Pharsalia*, lib. ix. 573.

A more modern creed it is that "man's soul is at first one unvaried blank till it have received the impressions of external experience; yet has this blank been already touched by a celestial Hand, and, when plunged in the colours which surround it, it takes not its tinge from accident but design, and comes out covered with a glorious pattern." *

Oldest, and yet newest of all, is the faith of the world's noblest sons, that the voice of Conscience in their hearts was that of the ever-present God, the normal action of the Infinite Spirit on the finite spirits He has made. We shall find this doctrine everywhere, under every clime, in every age, blended into every system of religion. The Hindoo lawgiver, three milleniums ago, exclaimed : † "Oh friend of virtue! That Supreme Spirit which thou believest one with thyself resides in thy bosom perpetually, and is an all-knowing Inspector of thy goodness or thy wickedness."

After a thousand years Seneca seemed but his echo:—"There is a Holy Spirit throned within us, of our good and evil deeds the Guardian and the Observer. As we draw nigh to Him, so He draws nigh to us." ‡

Marcus Antoninus reiterates the same : — " There is that within thee which savours of the Divinity, which agitates thee quite otherwise than wires do a puppet. Is it fear, lust, jealousy ? No !§ Be not more desirous to breathe than to conform to the Intelligence which surrounds all things. The Spirit of God is everywhere, and not less willing to commune with man than the air is to enter his breast. ‖ He dwells with God who does as the God-given soul within would have him.¶ Nothing is more wretched than the condition of that man who moves in a perpetual whirl after knowledge, forgetting all the while that it is sufficient to keep inseparably near to that One Deity who dwells within us."**

Says Pythagoras :—" Those things which are agreeable to God cannot be known unless a man hear God himself; but

---

* Sedgwick.
† Institutes of Menu, viii. 91.
‡ " Sacer intra nos Spiritus sedet bonorum malorumque Observator et Custos. Hic prout a nobis tractatus est ita nos ipse tractat."—Ep. 41.
§ Meditations, b. xii.   ‖ B. viii.   ¶ B. v.
** B. ii.

having overcome, then thou shalt know of the indwelling of immortal God in mortal man."

Says his disciple Timæus: — " The most excellent thing to which the soul is awakened is her Guide or Good Genius; but if she be rebellious to it, it will prove her demon and tormentor."

The old oracles are full of like doctrine. The Chaldæan oracles of Zoroaster taught: — " The soul will in a manner clasp God to herself. Having nothing mortal she is wholly inebriated from God."* The Theurgists held: — " The more powerful souls *receive truth through themselves.* Such souls are saved through their own strength." † Menander sung: — " God is with mortals by conscience."‡ By the Greeks such συνείδησις was commonly spoken of as " the household guardian," " the domestic god," " the spirit of the place."

Nor was the creed of the Fathers averse to this view of conscience. The greatest of them all (St. Chrysostom) lays down the whole doctrine of Intuitive Morals: — " Another point, which is also demonstrative of God's Providence, is that, when God formed man, He implanted within him from the beginning a natural law. He gave utterance to conscience within us, and made the knowledge of good things and of those which are the contrary to be self-taught."§ " It should be known," says St. Gregory, " that the Divine mode of speaking is in two ways. For either the Lord speaks by Himself, or His words are adapted to us by means of an angelic creature. But when He speaks by Himself the heart is instructed. It is a discourse without sound, which both opens the ears, and yet knows not to utter a sound."‖ Says St. Bernard: — " Conscientia candor est lucis æterna et speculum sine macula Dei majestatis et imago bonitatis illius." And before him Tatian had said :— " Conscience and God are one." ¶

---

* Psell. xvii., Cory's Fragments.

† Proc. in 1 Alc., ibid. (a singularly Kantian phrase).

‡ Βροτοῖς ἀπάσι συνείδησις θεὸς . . . . οἰκεῖος φύλαξ, ἔνοικος θεὸς, ἐπίτροπος δαίμων.

§ St. Chrysost., Hom. xii , The Statues.

‖ St. Gregory the Great, Morals on Job, b. xxviii.

¶ Μόνον εἶναι συνείδησιν θεόν. JUSTIN MARTYR, *Dial. Tyr.* s.70., says, " The *evil* spirits have contrived to have the precepts concerning that which is just and

Fénélon's splendid " Traité de l'Existence de Dieu " follows
so completely the Transcendental Philosophy, that we are not
surprised to find him give to Conscience the highest rank which
its most reverent followers have claimed for it :—" Il n'y a
point encore eu d'homme sur la terre qui ait pu gagner, ni
sur les autres ni sur lui même d'établir dans le monde qu'il
est plus estimable d'être trompeur que d'être sincère, d'être
emporté et malfaisant que d'être modéré et de faire du bien.
Le *Maître* intérieur et universel dit donc toujours et partout
les mêmes verités.   Voilà donc deux raisons que je trouve en
moi : l'une est moi-même, l'autre est au dessus de moi.   Celle
qui est moi est très imparfaite, l'autre est commune à tous les
hommes, superieure à eux ; elle est parfaite, éternelle, immuable.
Où est elle, cette raison parfaite qui est si près et si différente
de moi ?   N'est elle pas le Dieu que je cherche ? " *
    The highest names in the English Church are on the same
side.   Jeremy Taylor affirmed that God's " laws are put into
a man's soul or mind as into a treasure or repository, *some in
his very nature,* some in after actions, by education and positive sanction." †   Hooker, after saying that " there are two
ways of discerning goodness,—the one the knowledge of the
causes by which it is made such, the other the observation of
those signs and tokens which are always annexed unto goodness,"—adds, " the most certain token of evident goodness is, if
the general persuasion of all mankind do so allow it.   For that
which all men have at all times learned, nature herself must
needs have taught ; and God being the Author of Nature, her
voice is but His instrument.   By her from Him we receive
whatever in such sort we learn." ‡
    Finally, there are a multitude of passages, in both the Old
and New Testaments, which, if we could divest ourselves of
certain associations, would appear to be the noblest asser-

---

right taught even to the priests of Mithra."   Such ·perversity was not confined
to the second century.   " The Rev. George Burroughs was executed at Salem,
Mass., in 1692, for witchcraft, in consequence of his unusual bodily strength.
On the scaffold he uttered so beautiful a prayer as to draw forth from Cotton
Mather the remark, ' No one could make such a prayer without the assistance of
the *Devil.*' "—HUTCHINSON'S *Essay on Witchcraft.*
    * Œuvres Spirituelles, Traité, &c., iii.
    † Jeremy Taylor's Ductor Dubitantium.
    ‡ Hooker's Eccles. Pol., b. i.

tions of the immanence of God in the conscience of man
But so many of these we have been accustomed to connect
exclusively with a miraculous inspiration, that (to avoid controversy) I shall only cite what St. Paul affirms of the Gentiles,
that they " who have not the law (of Moses) do by nature
the things contained in the law ; these having not the law,
are a law unto themselves, which show the works of the
law *written in their hearts*, their conscience also bearing
witness."

Yet it must be admitted that this wide-spread doctrine,
that conscience is the voice of God, is not free from difficulties.
It has hitherto been our endeavour to show the *certainty* of
its revelations of right and wrong, by demonstrating the
identity of nature between our Moral Intuitions and those
on which we have erected the mathematical sciences, which
we commonly look on as the impregnable citadels of human
knowledge.   But now, if our aim be to show the *Divinity* of
Conscience, this identity between it and the source of mere
secular knowledge may to some prove a stumbling-block.
Many will be ready to admit that our Maker may directly
teach us religious and moral truths, who will yet hesitate to
attribute to such special instruction the fundamental axioms
of profane science.

But are not all objections such as these founded on narrow
and imperfect ideas of the relation of the creature to Him in
whom he "lives, and moves, and has his being ?" Philosophers
of the Malebranche school have held that we " see all things
in God," that He is the Speculum on whose infinite surface
our minds behold all that they can perceive.   More natural
seems the belief that Necessary truths alone are divinely
taught, while the bodily senses are the inlets of those which
are contingent.   Still another creed there is, that Intuition is
a natural faculty of the human mind, whereby we obtain no
less moral than geometric truths without that more special
instruction from God called Inspiration, which He vouchsafes
only to faithful souls, and on religious and moral topics.
Lastly, there is the largest faith of all in numbers of its adherents, the smallest in the extent of the truth it holds, — the

G

supra-naturalist creed that God is not near to us, inspiring and guiding us *now*, but only that He did so inspire men in the dim perspective of the shadow-peopled past. I will not argue on these solemn topics, — I will only briefly state the convictions at which I have myself arrived, and which will be found to influence many views in this book.

When we say that " God is a Spirit, that He is omnipresent and omni-active," it seems to me that it is but a scholium of our proposition that " He is always present and always active in the *souls* of His creatures." " Can it be, as so many tell us, that God, transcending time and space, immanent in *matter*, has forsaken *man;* retreated from the Shekinah in the holy of holies to the court of the Gentiles?" * It is not only our bodies which live by the bread He daily gives, but our spirits also, which must be in ceaseless dependence on His aid. The higher our powers, the nearer are they to Him, the more capable of contact with Him; our bodies first, then our intellects, then our moral and religious affections, rising up purer and higher, till at last the contact becomes conscious in

---

* *Discourses of Religion*, by THEODORE PARKER, p. 174. The author's obligations to the writings of this great and brave man will be visible everywnere in this little work to those acquainted with them — too mucn so to require continual reference. The doctrine of Inspiration as stated by him is the keystone of a grander Theology than the world has yet beheld. I can only quote a few passages: — " Spiritualism teaches that there is a natural supply for spiritual as well as for corporeal wants; that there is a connection between God and the soul, as between light and the eye, sound and the ear, truth and the intellect. It teaches that the world is not nearer to our bodies than God to the soul. As we have bodily senses to lay hold on matter and supply bodily wants, so we have spiritual faculties to lay hold on God and supply spiritual wants. We have direct access to God through reason, conscience, the religious sentiment. Through these channels, and by means of a law, certain, regular, and universal as gravitation, God inspires men, makes revelation of truth. It is not a rare condescension of God, but a universal uplifting of man. To obtain a knowledge of duty, man is not sent away outside of himself to ancient documents for the only rule of faith and practice; the Word is very nigh him, even in his heart; and by this Word he is to try all documents whatever. Inspiration, like God's omnipresence, is not limited to the few writers claimed by Jews, Christians, and Mahometans, but is co-extensive with the race. As God fills all space, so all spirit. As he influences and constrains unconscious and necessitated matter, so he inspires and helps free and conscious man. There can be but one *kind* of Inspiration. It is the direct and intuitive perception of some truth, either of thought or of sentiment. There can be but one *mode* of Inspiration; it is the action of the Highest within the soul, the Divine presence imparting light, in the form of truth through the reason, of right through the conscience, of love and faith through the affections and religious sentiment. Is Inspiration confined to theological matters alone? . . . Most surely not. The *degree* of Inspiration must depend on the man's quantity of being and quantity of obedience. Universal and infallible Inspiration is not possible to man."—B. ii. c. vii.

the awful communion of intensest prayer. All this is natural, normal; it is not a miracle that the Omnipresent is close to us, that the Omni-active moves our hearts; it is not strange that the Infinite Father who bears us in His everlasting arms, should supply the highest cravings of our immortal souls, while He feeds the ravens and gives the young lions their prey. It *would* be a miracle, it would be as strange as terrible, were it otherwise. The law by which we are thus moved by God is certain, regular, and universal as gravitation; and, like gravitation, the amount of its force depends on the nearness, and on what we may call the "mass" of the soul to be drawn. "As we draw nigh to Him, so He draws nigh to us," said Seneca. As the soul is large by nature and education so large is its Inspiration. " The cup of ocean is filled as full as the harebell."

But while all spirits receive a portion of this Divine aid, and the larger and more pious spirits multiply their five talents to ten; still none can be infallibly, universally, absolutely inspired. Perfect inspiration could be received only by perfect beings fulfilling absolutely all the laws of mind and morals. In man there must always remain somewhat merely human, personal, fallible; the light which comes pure from the Sun of Truth is refracted as it enters the atmosphere of our thoughts, and receives from it colours of all kinds. There is somewhat of Divine and somewhat of human in the noblest thoughts and words of man. Commonly in what we call genius, even religious genius, the human is pre-eminent, the Divine merely a spark glimmering through the mist and darkness. But there have been saints on earth, in all whose words and works the Divine shone out with such glorious lustre, that our dazzled sight refuses the ungrateful task of seeking out the spots which must mark their humanity.

If these views be true, it is superfluous to debate where lies the boundary between Intuition and Inspiration, or how far the Divine influence descends among our intellectual as distinct from our moral faculties. Everything in our nature is continually influenced by God, the body by His material laws, the soul by His spiritual laws. This wondrous house of flesh,

" with bones for its rafters and beams, with nerves and tendons for cords, with muscles and blood for mortar * ," He laid its foundations in the womb of our mother, and has built it up year by year ever since, till it is all a monument of His skill.   By our senses we look out on the external universe, and behold the curtained sky and radiant earth, the visible " garb of God."†   We can feel nothing He has not made us feel, see nothing which is not His work.   Shall we say, then, our Bodies receive no Divine influence?   Higher is the destiny of our Intellects, which, starting from the grounds of thought He has provided, can soar up on the wings of the reason and memory He supports, and gather in every star throughout His infinite domain fresh incense for the altar of adoration. Who will say there is no Divine influence on the Intellect? But there are nobler powers still in our nature; Virtue is better than Knowledge, to Love God better than to study His greatness.   It is only in the moral and religious sentiments that humanity culminates, and in them, therefore, does it most nearly approach to God.   Everywhere, the world over, men have thought that duty and religion were taught us differently from other learning; that other science was the lesson our Father wrote for us on earth and sea, but that *this* His own voice whispered in the depths of our hearts.   Everywhere, also, men have believed in the possibility of communion with God, *not* through the intellect, but through conscience and piety.   They have not believed amiss.   Our contact with God, unconscious in the body and the mere intellect, becomes conscious when our wills come into perfect harmony with His Will; and loving Goodness we love Him who is supremely Good.   Of this communion, this contact of the Infinite and Finite Spirit, it is not well to speak much; the holiest fane in all the material world is less holy and solemn than it.

If these views of the nature of moral Intuitions be correct, it will follow that the most religious and obedient soul will receive the highest and purest Intuitions.   The law of Spirit is, that light and strength are bestowed by God on man as

---

* Institutes of Menu, vi. 76.
† " 'Tis thus at the roaring loom of time I ply,
    And weave for God the garb thou seest Him by."— GOETHE.

the latter places himself further from or nearer to their source. The plant which is sickly, weak, and white, growing in the darkness, acquires health, strength, and verdure when we bring it into the sunshine. " The magnetic bar which has lost its power, regains it when we hang it in the line of the meridian." There is no miracle in all this. It is true that when we pray to God that the rain may fall on our fields, we either pray for something which will surely take place whether we ask or no, or we pray that the laws of meteorology be set aside to suit our interest. But when we implore our Father to enlighten our consciences and purify our hearts, we do not ask him to *set aside* His laws, but to *fulfil them.* We bring our pale, faded souls within the rays of His warmth, and we say with confidence, " Heal us, oh Father, for we *know* that it is Thy will !"

And not only for that highest influence when the contact becomes conscious (a bliss too supreme to be often felt on earth), but for all spiritual and moral influences, for the week-day as well as the Sabbath of life, it is of the greatest importance that our hearts be always *turned towards* God, and open to receive His light. We ought never* to contemplate the solemn topics of virtue and religion in other than a reverential spirit, and with a remembrance of the presence of God looking on our thoughts. It is not hard to do this; by an act of the mind, readily understood, we raise and retain in the soul the idea, or rather the sense, that He, the Holy One, is at hand, while the intellect simultaneously and uninterruptedly exerts itself to define its Intuitions and apply them to its duties. Now, when our ideal of the Divine Holiness is subjectively true—that is to say, when it is the very highest which our minds at the stage they have arrived at can apprehend,—then is this Religious Method of studying Morals of invaluable service. A false creed may teach a man that in his special dealings with His creatures God has sanctioned crime. Then the intertwined sentiments of religion and

---

* " God is never so much turned away from any man as when he attempts to ascend to the most divine speculations or works in a confused or disordered manner, and, as the oracle adds, with unhallowed lips or unwashed feet. For of those who are thus negligent the progressions are imperfect, the impulses are vain, and the paths are dark."— *Chaldean Oracles of* ZOROASTER (Cory, 277.).

morals are all disordered, and the unfortunate believer, instead of feeling the presence of his Creator to be an atmosphere of purity and love, is driven to seek in prayer the strength to burn his brother! * But if no blasphemous dogmas have deluded the filial instinct of the man,—if God be to him the embodiment of all his highest conceptions of goodness, justice, truth,—then does the thought of Him light up the soul like the morning sun. Every spot and stain and dusty mote, unperceived before, stands instantly revealed. Conscience starts from her dreamy rest, and bows in penitent worship as the holy light streams upon her eyes, and then the soul sallies forth to its labour of the day with the gladsome chaunt " Thou God, seest me ! "

Now it is impossible that any man can thus seek to learn his duty, "not in the clouds of casuistry, but in the light of the Presence of the Holiest †," without doing so, pre-determined in his will to obey that duty when discovered. Thus we arrive at what may be called the more strictly *moral* method,—namely, that of seeking the law of right in such hearty sort that each does not ask " What is *allowable* for me to do ? " but " What is the *very best* and most virtuous thing I can possibly do ? " It appears to be a law that the state of

---

* Wherever anything in its nature odious and abominable is by Religion advanced as the supposed Will or Pleasure of a Supreme Deity, if in the eye of the believer it appears not indeed in any respect the less ill or odious on that account, then must the Deity of necessity bear the blame, and be considered as a Being naturally ill and odious, however courted and solicited through mistrust and fear. But this is what religion in the main forbids us to imagine. Whensoever, therefore, it teaches the love and admiration of a Deity who has any apparent character of ill, it teaches at the same time a love and admiration of that ill, and causes that to be taken for good and amiable, which is in itself horrid and detestable. . . . Whoever thinks that there is a God, and pretends formally to believe that He is just and good, must suppose that there is such a thing as Justice and Injustice, Truth and Falsehood, Right and Wrong, according to which he pronounces that God is Just, Righteous, and True. If the mere Will, Decree, or Law of God be said absolutely to constitute Right and Wrong, then are these latter words of no signification at all. For thus, if each part of a contradiction were affirmed for truth by the Supreme Power, they would consequently become true. Thus, if one person were decreed to suffer for another's fault, the sentence would be just and equitable ; and thus, in the same manner, if arbitrarily, and without reason, some beings were destined to endure perpetual ill, and others, as constantly to enjoy good, this would also pass under the same denomination. But to say of anything that it is just or unjust on such a foundation as this, is to say nothing, or to speak without a meaning. SHAFTESBURY's *Enquiry concerning Virtue,* b. 1. sect. 2.
† A prayer of Rev. Henry Ierson.

will in which we aim earnestly at the best possible conduct
is the only one in which Moral Intuitions are clearly heard.
The one faculty of the soul only works freely when its corresponding wheel meets it truly and turns readily.   Every
man's memory will supply instances wherein the solution of
some moral problem seemed to him impossible so long as he
presented it to his mind in the formula " What are my utmost
rights in the matter?"   " How little need I do in conscience
to benefit my neighbour?"   But all difficulty disappeared
when at the feet of the Father of Lights he asked " What is
my highest duty in the case ?   How much can I do to benefit
my brother and please my God?"

Our second question has now been answered.   The Moral
Law has been found in the Intuitions of the Human Mind.
These Intuitions are natural, but they are also revealed.   Our
Creator wrought them into the texture of our souls to form
the ground-work of our thoughts, and made it our duty first
to examine and then to erect upon them by reflection a true
Science of Morals.   But He also continually aids us in such
study, and He increases this aid in the ratio of our obedience.
Thus Moral Intuitions are both Human and Divine, and the
paradoxes in their nature are thereby solved.   All that in
them is Human Reflection is fallible, open to all the errors
of false logic and the inevitable imperfection of inaccurate
language.*   All that in them is Divine Inspiration is capable
of indefinite approach to infallibility in proportion as we
defecate our souls of the gross atmosphere which dims and
distorts the light of Heaven.†

---

* Δεῖν γὰρ περὶ αὐτὰ ἕν γέ τι τούτων διαπράξασθαι, ἢ μαθεῖν ὅπη ἔχει ἢ εὑρεῖν,
ἢ εἰ ταῦτα ἀδύνατον τὸν γοῦν βέλτιστον τῶν ἀνθρωπίνων λόγων λαβόντα καὶ δυσ-
εξελεγκτότατον, ἐπὶ τούτον ὀχούμενον, ὥς περ ἐπὶ σχεδίας κινδυνεύοντα διαπλεῦσαι
τὸν βίον, εἰ μή τις δύναιτο ἀσφαλέστερον καὶ ἀκινδυνότερον ἐπὶ βεβαιοτέρου ὀχήματος
ἢ λόγου θείου τινὸς διαπορευθέναι.—ΦΑΙΔΩΝ.

† "Human reason is feeble, and may be deceived ; but true faith cannot be
deceived."—Thomas à Kempis, c. xviii.

CHAPTER III.

THAT THE MORAL LAW CAN BE OBEYED.

~~~~~~~~~

" WHAT are thou?" saith Epictetus. " A living soul chained to a decaying carcase." — MARCUS ANTONINUS, *Medit.* b. iv.

" Oh, wretched man that I am! who shall deliver me from this body of death?

" With the mind *I myself* serve the law of God, but with the flesh the law of sin. . . . . The creature itself also shall be delivered from the bondage of corruption into the glorious liberty of the sons of God. . . . . For I am persuaded that neither death nor life, nor angels, nor principalities, nor powers, nor things present, nor things to come, nor height nor depth, nor any other creature, shall be able to separate us from the love of God. — *Romans,* vii. and viii., v. 24., *et seq.*

THE Senses of man inform him of Phenomena; they represent to him the appearances of things. The Understanding of man regulates and orders the impressions conveyed by his Senses, and combines them in the identity of consciousness.

The world of Phenomena, revealed to us by the Senses, and apprehended by the Understanding, is governed by a fixed mechanism of laws, producing an unbroken chain of causes and effects.

Man, as an inhabitant of this phenomenal or sensible world (*Homo phenomenon*), is subject to the mechanism and necessity of the laws which govern it.

But neither the Senses nor the Understanding can reveal to us " things in themselves," the substances beneath all appearances, the unknown noumena which must underlie all phenomena, and which cannot again be phenomena.*

The pure Reason of man alone enables him to cogitate the existence of this supersensible world of noumena. It supplies the Intuitions which enable him to predicate it, and disjoins the sensible and supersensible systems.

Of the nature and laws of this world of noumena it is impossible that we should know anything; the very grounds on which we predicate its existence being the necessity for somewhat below that which our senses can reveal as affecting them. Nevertheless, having assumed its existence, we perceive that it must contain the last ground of the world of

---

* " Of things absolutely or in themselves we know nothing, or know them only as incognizable ; and we become aware of their incomprehensible existence only as this is indirectly revealed to us through certain qualities related to our faculties of knowledge. . . . All that we know is therefore phænomenal, phænomenal of the unknown."—*Discussions on Philosophy by* SIR W. HAMILTON, p. 608., Appendix.

phenomena, and that all appearances in this world must hang, ultimately, on causations in the former; though how it is possible that the one should step forth into the other we cannot understand. Now, man is not only, as we have said, an inhabitant of this sensible world, a *Homo phenomenon* existing in time and space; he is also, in virtue of his immediate consciousness, without any modification of his sensory (the consciousness of the noumenal " I " at the basis of his nature), a member of the supersensible world—*Homo noumenon.* Man, therefore, has a twofold station, and the exercise of his powers is thereby regulated by a twofold set of laws. As an inhabitant of the sensible world, he is a mere link in the chain of causes and effects, and his actions are locked up in mechanic laws; which, had he no other rank, would ensue exactly according to the physical impulses given by instincts and solicitations in the sensory. But, as an inhabitant of the supersensible world, his position is among the causalities which, taking rise therein, are the ultimate grounds of phenomena. It is manifest that in this rank he is far above the reach of the physical impulses originating in the sensory; and it concerns us now to discover what his actions would be were they only regulated by the laws of his being as a *Homo noumenon;* as we have already seen what they would be were he only a *Homo phenomenon.**

We may solve the problem popularly by mere reference to the fact, that there is no man, howsoever abandoned and crime-stained, who, on the picture of a life of justice, truth, and purity being presented to his mind, does not feel in his heart that he would be just, pure, and true, IF there were not in his lower nature certain temptations to the contrary.

---

* This whole doctrine of Freedom is purely Kantian. I am well aware that, as regards Kant's doctrine of noumena and phenomena, various modifications have been proposed, if they have not superseded it. It would lead me far beyond the limits of this book to review, however succinctly, the opinions on this matter of Fichte, Schelling, and Hegel, and their respective followers, and still further to point out the bearing of such opinions on the doctrine of Freedom. For all the purposes of Morals, for the doctrines of freedom, and the veracity of our consciousness of necessary moral truths, I venture to affirm that the Kantian philosophy contains the largest portion of intellectual truth which has yet been vouchsafed to man ; and that whatever modifications it may hereafter undergo, or additions receive, it will ever supply the corner-stones of a sound " metaphysic of ethics." Even now it seems to be reassuming the ascendancy over Hegel's stupendous example of *verbal* dialectics.

These temptations of the sensory set aside, he inevitably conceives of himself as preferring the law of virtue to the no
longer attractive vice. "To the honour of human nature be
it admitted," says Schiller, "no man can sink so low as to
prefer the bad only because it is bad; but every one would
prefer the good because it is good, if it did not contingently
exclude the agreeable, and include the disagreeable."* Nor
can this spontaneous choice of good, when the temptation to
evil is excluded, be treated as a mere prudent bargain, whereby
the man, having no longer any pleasure to seek in vice, might
desire to obtain whatsoever hitherto despised pleasure might
be found in virtue. *Our* pleasure and gain in virtue cannot
offer any allurements to the Most High, and yet without
hesitation the worst of men believe that He (having no
temptations of a lower nature) *must* prefer the holy law for
its own intrinsic right. Thus, the commonest fact of the
intuitive feeling and belief of mankind will show us, that
the noumenal being, when conceived of separately from the
phenomenal, is conceived of as necessarily choosing the Right
for its proper worth.

The philosophical proof of the same fact has been given by
Kant, and is briefly this: —

Will is that kind of causality which is attributed to living
agents in so far as they are possessed of reason; and Freedom
is such a property of that causality as enables them to
originate events independently of foreign determining causes.
This freedom of will must practically belong to every being
who can only act under the idea Freedom. All laws must
bind him which are corollaries from the idea of Freedom,
just as much as if it could be speculatively proved that he were
free. Now, the Will cogitated us free and self-legislative, and
as one of the self-legislative wills belonging to all intelligents
in the universe, must, in legislating for itself, choose such
law only as is fit for law universal, its maxims must be
such as it would desire all other self-legislative wills to adopt;

---

* *Philosophic and Æsthetic Letters.* The Hegesiac branch of the Cyrenaic sect,
with the easy good nature of professed voluptuaries, affirmed "that all faults
are to be pardoned because no one commits them voluntarily, but is led by the
suggestion of some passion; . . . and that, instead of hating the offender,
we ought to teach him his duty."—DIOG. LAERT. *Aristip.*

and there is contradiction and absurdity in taking that for its private law which it cannot so contemplate as fit for universal adoption. But it will be found, on examination, that every law fit for law universal is the Moral Law, and it only. If we try a thousand cases, as, for example, whether breach of contract, lying, theft, murder, selfishness, could be things fit for law universal to permit, we clearly see that in each instance positive absurdity is evolved. Thus it is manifest that every intelligent who is free is thereby self-legislative; that, as self-legislative, he must contemplate himself as universally legislative; and that, as universally legislative, he can only choose for law that law which is Moral.*

The Free Man, therefore — the *Homo noumenon* — is, *as such*, purely moral.†

Of the twofold condition of man we now perceive the consequence.

In the sensible world, and so far as he is subjected to its mechanic laws, he is a slave, a mere machine, acted on by instincts within and sensations from without, impinging on his sensory.

In the supersensible world he is free, not governed by mechanic but by moral laws, of which he is to himself the lawgiver.

And as this supersensible world is the background and *substans* of the phenomenal world, whose laws (though incomprehensibly to us) it coacts, the man, in his character of an inhabitant of the supersensible world, is capable of co-

---

* See Kant's Grundlegung der Sitten.

† This truth, that it is the man himself who is always faithful to the Moral Law, explains the grand Stoical doctrine so often misunderstood, that " Virtue consists in living according to Nature." The " Nature " according to which *we* are to live is this higher nature, the very self of self, the *Homo noumenon*, which can alone legislate to the whole man that one law fit for law universal. To live according to *this* nature, to reduce the lower self, the *Homo phenomenon*, to obedience to it is indeed virtue — the only possible virtue of every intelligent creature. Nor did the Stoics fail to perceive, that this higher nature in us has the same law as the nature of God and of all other free beings in the universe. " The end," said they, " which we ought to propose to ourselves, is to live according to nature — that is, according to the virtue which our own nature prescribes to us, — doing nothing which the Common Law of All forbids ; which law is Right Reason, spread everywhere, and is the same which is in Zeus, and by which He governs the world. In this consists the virtue and the happiness of the happy man, that he rules all his actions in such a manner that they produce harmony between the Daimon which resides in every man, and the Will of Him who governs the universe."—Diog. Laert. *Zeno.*

acting himself in his phenomenal nature, and breaking in
upon the chain of instincts and solicitations of the sensory,
whereby, if only a *Homo phenomenon*, he would be totally
enslaved.

Thus, as has been so often said, there is a woof of Freedom
worked into the warp of Necessity, and the texture of human
life presents the alternations of each. Nay, more, it actually
presents the woof and warp in the very colours which *à priori*
we proved must respectively belong to them. The freedom
of the " spirit lusting against the flesh" constantly assumes
the hues of justice and purity; and the "flesh lusting
against the spirit" equally constantly bears those of selfishness and sensuality. Nor can we conceive of the reversal
of this order, and think of the free *Homo noumenon* working
on his lower self for evil, nor this lower self on him for
good.

All the great features of our moral position are explicable
by this system without recourse being had to doctrines so
unsupported by evidence as that of a pre-existent state, or so
injurious to the Divine Justice as that of Original Sin. When
we have admitted that our lower natures are enchained in
the concatenation of impulses and solicitations, we have
admitted all that is needful to account for the existence of
human transgression without any impeachment of the holiness
of our Creator. In making this lower nature, God has not
made an *evil* thing. It is not a rational free agent choosing
wrong for wrong's own sake as the higher nature chooses the
right; it is a mere animal, a slave of impulse, a being (so
far as morals are concerned) perfectly idiotic, having no choice
at all, but following blindly the guidance of its instincts, regardless of moral distinctions. To call such nature "evil,
corrupt, totally depraved " is the same absurdity as to apply
similar terms to the weights and pulleys of a gymnasium.
The strength, the virtue, of the true self is acquired solely
by its resistance and coaction of the gravitation of the lower
nature.

And, as I have already demonstrated (see Chap. I.), this
Virtue is the noblest End which it is possible for the finite
creature to attain. He cannot be holy as the Infinite is

holy, namely, through that very infinitude by which His
power, wisdom, and felicity are absolute and beyond possibility of increase.   Man as a finite creature must have
been either a brute, or have occupied the station he actually holds as a being capable of virtue, and *therefore* capable also of being *not* virtuous.   He must have had such
instincts prompting him to break the law if he were to be
made capable of a moral obedience to the law, — *i. e.*, of virtue.
Instead of an evil nature, this lower nature of ours is the
necessary postulate of all our virtue, the machinery without
which our moral life would be at a standstill for ever.   Its
immense power, the awful woes which ensue from it when
the strength of the righteous self is not exerted, and the great
weight of the lower, falls, crushing all before it to destruction,
— this tremendous power is but evidence how glorious is the
strength which the Maker purposes shall be acquired by the
resisting Soul.

Moral Evil, then, philosophically considered, is simply the
weakness, the non-exertion, of the *Homo noumenon.*   It is
not a *positive* thing at all.   It is not a choice of vice by the
higher self, for that self can by the very necessity of its nature
legislate only the universal Moral Law.   It is not a choice of
vice by the *lower* self, for that self is by its nature un-moral,
un-free, and incapable of determining its choice with any
reference to moral distinctions ; but solely according to its instincts, and their solicitations.   Moral evil, therefore, is a mere
negation, the *absence* of virtue, of the strength, the valour of
the higher self, by which it ought to execute that law which
it always Wills, and overcome the *vis inertiæ* opposed to it
by the lower self.

Some confusion has arisen on this subject from superficial
observation of the fact, that in some persons the weight of
the lower instincts is very great compared with what it is in
others ; and we thence popularly distinguish between what
are called faults of Strength and of Weakness.   The first we
conceive of as arising from the extreme violence of the instinctive propensity which outweighs the resistance of the
higher self ; though this last is by no means indifferent to its
law of right, or overcome without a struggle.   On the other

hand, we stigmatise as faults of Weakness those which a man falls into with very small prehension on the side of his instincts, which, nevertheless, small as it is, is able to outweigh the still feebler Will of right opposed to it. These distinctions are practically extremely useful; but of course theoretically they both resolve themselves into *that* weakness of the higher self which permits it to yield to the instincts of the lower, be their weight trifling or enormous.

So far, then, from attributing the sins of our race to the " Fall" of our ancestor a hundred and eighty generations past*,

---

* Among the theories which have been invented to account for the existence of physical and moral evil in the creation of a benevolent Almighty Being, none are more widely spread than those of a " Fall," and its corollary, " Original Sin." In ages of darkness and barbarism, when the world seemed to be retrograding rather than advancing in virtue and happiness, when the " fresh fuel thrown on the hearth of civilisation' seemed, to superficial observation, to have quenched its fires for ever, in truth at *all* times, before the slow progress of our race had advanced far enough to give assurance of its reality, it was natural for the most pious minds to imagine that such as they beheld it, could not be the condition God had designed originally for the life of man; and that some rude shock must at some period have disturbed for ever its "unstable equilibrium" of innocence and happiness. The vision of a Golden Age was conjured up by the ineradicable propensity of the human heart to forget the sorrows and magnify the joys of the Past, which it beholds always through its own natural hues of beauty and love, too often dispelled from the broad day-light of the Present. But over this Paradise of the Morning Land a fatal change had passed; and to account for it fresh myths arose not less in accordance with the rudimentary philosophy of the times. The absolute unity and solipotence of God is a doctrine which even now is but little recognised; and the existence of an Ahrimanes, a Serpent-devil, who could mar His creation and pervert His creatures, was the most obvious hypothesis to account for the frustration of His designs. And this frustration the Enemy must (it was thought) have accomplished by inducing the commission of some sin sufficiently enormous to account for its immense consequences. All suffering was supposed to be directly penal. Some great primal Sin, then, must have merited the great evil Death. That the sin of the parents of the race could incur the punishment of all their descendants was not questioned by men accustomed to the barbarous jurisprudence of the East, wherein a whole family were, as a matter of course, involved in the penalty of the treason of its chief. The revelations of geology, that Death existed for unknown millenniums ere sin or sinful man arose upon our planet were then unimagined; nor was importance attached to the teaching of analogy, that the human body must share in the conditions of decay and change belonging to all material substances. It was assumed almost as an axiom, that "only by sin came death." What was the sin which incurred such a penalty? The Persians, in whose creed the existence of an Evil principle bore so large a part, supposed that the great crime consisted in the acknowledgment of *him* as their Creator, instead of Ormuzd, by Meschia and Meschiane, the parents of mankind (*Zend Avesta, Boundehesch.*). The Hebrews, on the other hand, conceived that it was the acquirement by Adam and Eve of that Knowledge of good and evil which all rational free agents partake, in a degree, with God, and which distinguishes them from the brutes. " That Ignorance " (says MACKAY, *Progress of the Intellect*, b. i., p. 437.) " should be an essential condition of innocence and happiness, is a superficial inference easily made from the frequent

H

—so far from supposing ourselves "born children of the wrath"
of the all-loving God,—so far from deeming that we are laden

abuse of reason." The act of disobedience, then, by which man became as
"one of the Elohim, knowing good and evil," or, philosophically speaking,
became properly a Man, and not an animal devoid of moral nature, was the act
of the Fall. Yet how he could be guilty of disobedience before he had any idea
of good and evil, or why God planted the Tree of Knowledge if He wished
him not to eat it, or forbade him to eat if He wished to have rational creatures; and why God should give an arbitrary command whose infraction was
to cause such dire results, and how the eating of a fruit could convey those
Intuitions of the pure Reason which constitute the knowledge of good and
evil; all these and innumerable similar difficulties the labours of thousands
of commentators have failed to explain. Next to accounting for the existence of Death (which appears to have been its primary significance), the
history in Genesis was supposed to account for the prevalence of human
transgressions. By a strange perversion of reasoning the imaginary difficulty of accounting for the sinfulness of every child of man was thought to be
got rid of by attributing it to an inheritance of corruption from the sin of the
first man who yet was supposed to have issued most directly of all from his
Creator's hands. Yet if Adam, having no Original Sin, could yet break the only
law he received, it seems that Original Sin is nowise needed to account for
the sins of any of his descendants. Nor is the matter at all cleared up by
following the pedigree of evil up to the Fall of the Angels. If "Lucifer,
Son of the Morning," could sin in Heaven, it was easy for Adam to sin in
Eden, and easier still for each of his children to sin in such a world as this. A
just consideration of the necessary condition of all finite free agents explains at once why, in making us capable of virtue, God inevitably made us
capable of vice. Our imperfection and peccability are no mysteries at all.
But that we should inherit a corrupted nature from our ancestor, or that
his sin and ours should have been induced by the temptations of an Evil
Being left at large to exercise quasi-godlike powers to the perversion of
souls, these would, indeed, be "mysteries" enough to obscure the radiance
of Religion itself.

Such as it is, however, the doctrine of Original Sin was partially adopted
by some of the early rabbins. From a corrupted father, they affirm, could
only proceed corrupted offspring. The *propensity* of mankind to evil they call
jetzirah raah and admit as fully as do Christians ; but the doctrine of *imputed guilt*, — of the mass of mankind being predestined to eternal misery as
a punishment for the sins of Adam and Eve,—this they reject with horror.
Maimonides maintains (*More Neboth.*, p. 1., c. xxxix.) "that it is not easier to conceive how a man should be born with sin or with virtue, than to comprehend
how he should be born a skilful master in any art or science." That circum-
cision procured the remission of Original Sin, though affirmed by Gregory the
Great (*Moral. Job.*, xiii.) and St. Augustine (*De Civit.*, c. xvii.), is denied by
Justin Martyr (c. *Tryph.*), Irenæus (b. iv. c. iii.), Chrysostom (*Hom.* xxxix.),
and Jerome (in *Ep. ad Galat.*), who all affirm that it was only the sign of the
Jewish covenant Josephus and Philo found in the doctrine of a Pre-existent state the same natural substitute for that of Original Sin which it
has afforded many Christians down to Soames Jenyns and Dr. Beecher.
Mahometans hold to Original Sin, with the singular explanation that the
souls of all men literally existed in Adam, whose back was stroked by God
in the plain of Dahia, whereon the whole human race came forth in the
shape of ants. "And the Lord took them to witness against themselves,
saying, Am I not your Lord?" (*Koran*, c. vii.) After which they returned
into the loins of their ancestor. Jesus and Mary alone, of all the human
race, they affirm to have been born without Original Sin, and Mahomet to have
had it pulled out of his heart by the archangel Gabriel. In the Christian
Church it would appear that St. Paul's doctrine (*Rom.* v. 12.) was not controverted till the time of Origen. This great man, — whom St. Jerome says

with "imputed" or "inherited" guilt even before the first dawn of our moral consciousness or moral freedom, — so far from

(*Ep.* xxix.) the Bishops of Italy and Egypt persecuted, " because they could not endure the splendour of his merits;" but of whose followers the same saint afterwards boasted (*Apol. adv. Ruf.*) that he had obtained the banishment— Origen held the pre-existence of human souls, and therefore maintained that it was with our own, and not our ancestor's, guilt that we are born tainted.   One of his followers, John, Bishop of Jerusalem, afforded protection to the Irishman Pelagius, who, with Celestius the Briton, had broached a new heresy at Rome and Carthage.   Mosheim remarks that these two monks were universally esteemed for their extraordinary piety and virtue.   Nevertheless, St. Jerome, who, with St. Augustine, had previously admitted these merits, no sooner heard of the heresies of Pelagius than he accused him of all manner of vices, including gluttony and intemperance, and, to leave him without excuse, added, " Nec recordatur stolidissimus et Scotorum pultibus prægravatus !" (In *Hier. prefat.*, lib. i. — "Neither let him be set down as stupid and unwieldy with Irish stirabout !") The doctrines whose maintenance thus singularly transformed a saint into a sinner, and made the divines of his day say "that a great star had fallen from heaven," were briefly these : 1st, That the sin of Adam was imputed to him alone, and not to his posterity ; and that we are born as pure as Adam came out of the hand of God. 2nd, That man is absolutely free and capable of attaining virtue without internal grace. 3rd, That infant baptism is not the seal of remission of sin, but the "mark of admittance to heaven." Pelagius defended these dogmas by urging that an act, to be sinful, must be voluntary, and, to be voluntary, there must be power to resist it." He was acquitted of heresy by the Synod of Jerusalem, A.D. 415, and by the Council of Diospolis; but that of Carthage, in A.D. 416, condemned him, whereon he and Celestius appealed to Pope Zosimus, who pronounced their opinions orthodox. St. Augustine and the African Church, however, induced Zosimus to change his mind, and the Pelagians were persecuted both by him and the emperors, insomuch that the sect was extinguished.   In the controversies of succeeding ages respecting predestination, the doctrine of Original Sin was sometimes involved ; but it does not appear to have formed a special ground of dispute till after the Reformation, when several heresies on the subject were broached by De la Place, Pajou, Papin, and others, and condemned by councils, as may be seen in Mosheim (cent. xvi.).   From the condemnation of the doctrine of Le Cene by the French Synod in Holland, in the eighteenth century, it would appear that the dogma had received no assent within the pale of the larger churches.   It is admitted by all Romanists, forms a fundamental of Calvinism, and is even involved in the Five Articles of the Arminians, the third of which asserts that "man, in consequence of his natural corruption, is incapable of thinking or doing any good thing."   This doctrine of "*total* depravity" is that of Original Sin carried to its furthest extreme. Bishop Tomline endeavours to claim the honour of moderation for the Church of England on this subject. He says (*Refut. Calvinism*, p. 280.) : "There are Christians who assert that Adam's nature was not corrupted by the Fall, and there are others who assert that it produced so complete a change in his own nature and that of all his posterity, that God's rational creatures are now a mere mass of corruption, susceptible of no amendment by their voluntary efforts. But the Church of England, keeping clear of both extremes, declares that the nature of Adam was greatly impaired and corrupted by his transgression, and that he transmitted this weak and depraved nature to every individual of his descendants ; but it does not say that the moral powers of man are entirely destroyed." Whether this be indeed the orthodox doctrine, or whether Scott is nearer to it in affirming that "man is an unmixed and incorrigible mass of hopeless depravity," it matters little to the present discussion to inquire. A vast *degree* of guilt, pollution, and depravity is acknowledged by all Christian churches to be our inheritance from Adam ; and there seems justice in the remark of Mrs.

reviling, as "totally depraved," or "grievously corrupted," the glorious natures which God and God alone has given us, — a truer philosophy teaches us that what we *are* is the condition chosen for us by Infinite Love and Wisdom to give us the power to attain the highest end possible for a Finite Creature. It teaches us that, instead of being cursed by our Maker with a nature *totally* depraved, there is *nothing* in our natures not placed there for the express purpose of producing our everlasting approach to goodness and to God. It teaches us that we are enchained to no "inherited corruption,"—that our lower nature alone is enchained to its instincts, which are animal indeed and un-moral, but no way corrupt or depraved; but that true Self is free, an originating cause in the world of realities, and not only not depraved, but essentially and necessarily Righteous, willing the holy law and that only.

Such I believe to be (in a far-off, shadowy way) the true explanation of the great mystery of Human Freedom. It were idle to talk of it as complete and satisfactory; but it is much if it leave us the conviction that larger knowledge of the condition and laws of the supersensible world might enable us to account philosophically for that which appears

Hannah More, that the doctrine is logically involved in the scheme of the Atonement. " Genuine Christianity," says the respectable old lady in her *Practical Piety,* " can never be engrafted on any other stock than the apostacy of man The design to reinstate beings who have *not* fallen, to propose restoration without a previous loss, is altogether an incongruity, which would seem too palpable to require refutation, did we not so frequently see the doctrine of redemption maintained by those who deny that man was in a state to require redemption." On one point only it is needful to notice variance of Christians on this subject; namely, on the question whether Original Sin be *inherent* or *imputed.* That it is inherent appears to be the older and more popular doctrine. Bishop Hampden says (*Bampt. Lect.* v.) that " St. Augustine maintained the transmission of the *material* element of corruption from Adam, and that all the Fathers founded their whole doctrinal system on the principles of materialism." Malebranche works out the idea on the ground of the known transmission of hereditary qualities, and, as Foxton remarks, would in our day have assumed a " criminal brain," transmitted by the old Adam to his posterity. This may be presumed to be the orthodox doctrine of the Church of England, as the Ninth Article states decisively that " Original Sin is the fault and corruption of the nature of every man that naturally is engendered of the offspring of Adam. And this *infection of nature* doth remain," &c. The doctrine of *imputed* Original Sin has not, however, lacked numerous supporters. It teaches that there was a Covenant of Works always existing between the Creator and His creatures, that Adam was our " federal head," and " in his fall we sinned all." His sin, therefore, is *imputed* to each of his posterity, not as an infection of nature, but as a curse earned in the person of our progenitor, whose obedience, it is sometimes hinted, would have entitled us to immortal felicity. This doctrine appears to be a very complete counterpart of that of " imputed righteousness."

at first sight to be more than a Mystery,— a Contradiction. The Philosophical doctrine of Necessity (I am not now speaking of the Theological), the doctrine of the necessary enchainment of action with action, thought with thought, seems to meet the Intuition of Freedom breast to breast. In the dread combat the fall of one or other appears inevitable, and while all our hopes are with Freedom, all the chances of victory seem with Fate. If, then, an alliance be, we will not say probable, but *possible*, we ought to rejoice in such prospect of escape, and even in strictest logic are called upon to accept such possibility as sufficient. For, let it be remembered, the Intuition of Freedom, though wholly unsupported, is itself nothing short of proof. We are conscious that we are Free, that every intelligent being is necessarily Free. The truth assumes the position of an axiom in our minds. We cannot conceive it to be otherwise; for, let us talk ourselves never so much into fatalism, we still retain the conviction that there are things open to our choice, and that Virtue is to be honoured and Crime to be punished. An Intuition of this clearness and universality is as strong presumption of truth as any chain of argument could afford; and there are indeed very few truths of which we have equally valid demonstration. If, then, it be POSSIBLE that such Intuition be reconcileable by our theory with the deductions from other Intuitions which result in necessity, then that which is possible ought to be accepted as *probable*, because it is *more than probable* that both the doctrines it reconciles are true, and if so, the choice can only lie between different hypotheses to reconcile them, and we can scarcely frame any other hypothesis than this of the two worlds, sensible and supersensible, which also may be demonstrated on its own grounds. The answer therefore, to the Philosophical Fatalist is this:—It is true that, as a member of the sensible world, I am subject to the Necessity of its fixed mechanic laws. But this world revealed to the senses cannot be all in all; beneath its Appearances there must be somewhat *substans*,—there must be reality for the ultimate ground of what *may* be only phantasmagoria played off before the senses. In this supersensible world must lie the Causes ultimately governing the world of Appearances. I cannot tell *how*, because I know nothing of that higher

world; but it must be so that the Shadow is governed by the
Substance. Now, I am conscious that I belong to this Supersensible as well as to the Sensible World. There is that in me
—nay, *I myself* am—somewhat the senses can never perceive.
Beneath and behind all receptive faculties I am conscious of
something altogether distinct from them. I myself therefore
am an Entity in the world wherein lie the ultimate Causes of
phenomena What are the laws and mode of action of these
Causes I do not know; but this I do know, that I am conscious that I am a Cause. Such Consciousness is its own
warrant till it can be shown that it is impossible. But this
can never be done, for we can prove no negative in a world unknown. Therefore I am legitimately entitled to put faith in this
Consciousness of Freedom, and to consider my proper self—my
Will — as one of the Causalities having their rise in the supersensible world, and thence descending into action (I know not
how) among the things of sense. The bounds to which this
power of Causation belonging to me extends are the bounds
of my Responsibility. I am not *Fortunate,* but *Virtuous,* if
within these limits my actions correspond to the Moral Law;
I am not *Unlucky,* but *Wicked,* if they deviate from it."

But the more purely philosophical difficulty of reconciling
Necessity with Freedom exhausts but a part of this tremendous subject, which Milton deemed the highest for the debate
of angels. The Freedom of man seems immeshed in other
chains beside those of the mechanical necessity of the physical
world.   Over all the Causes in the world of noumena there
is One great First Cause, the Absolute Lord of all things
sensible and supersensible. He is not only Omnipotent, but
Solipotent ; it is not only beneath His control, but by His
Power, that anything is done throughout the universe. This
Absolute Lord originates and directs the whole mechanical
sequence of causes and effects in the world of phenomena.
It is by Him that the starry clusters revolve in the unimaginable periods of their stupendous cycles,—by Him that the in-
fusorial animalculæ move the viewless cilia of their infinitesimal forms,—by Him that man rises in the joy of youth from
his cradle, and is brought down in reluctant age to his tomb.
The necessary sequence of the phenomenal world, the whole

Laws of Nature, are the sequence appointed, and the laws upheld, by God alone.

And in the world of noumena must He not reign equally supreme? Whatever *that* is which is the ultimate ground of our being, and wherein our power of Causation exists, must it not be precisely as much enchained by His ever-immanent Omnipotence as are the physical laws whereby are regulated our stature and our longevity? It must be admitted that it is difficult to conceive how it can be otherwise. Yet, that we are really Free, really agents in the world of Causations, the believer in God ought to be the last to doubt. The Atheist might perchance be satisfied to think our Intuition of Freedom a delusion; but it is impossible to deem it so while we own that we have a Maker, and that He. is just. The Theist Fatalist is a Devil-worshipper. He believes that the Creator of man endued him with a conscience commanding one class of actions and forbidding another; that not only this conscience, but Providence, here and hereafter, will reward and punish according to his obedience; and yet that he *cannot* obey! Nay (climax of cruelty and deception!), this Almighty Fiend has deluded his poor victim all his life long into the conviction that he *is* free, giving him a consciousness of it entwined in the very roots of his being!

I hold that the Truth and the Justice of God are both pledged to the reality of human Freedom. If He be True and Just, He could neither have given us the Intuition of Freedom, nor rewarded and punished us according to our deeds, were we *not* Free. Therefore, however incomprehensibly to us, we must believe that in that unknown, supersensible world our higher natures do hold under God a real, originating power of causation, and that there is no illusion in the belief that this causation descends into the sensible world, and takes place therein not phantasmally, but actually.

Mixed up with the doctrine of Theological Necessity drawn from the Omnipotence of God is that of Predestination, involving also His Omniscience. It is here that the theoretic error, commonly harmless in the cool brain of the philosopher, becomes actively virulent, when fired by the fever of the fanatic who embraces a doctrine of which it may be truly said, that

it unites every idea derogatory to the character of God and every principle destructive of the morality of man.*

* A sketch of the history of this doctrine, and of the various forms it has assumed will justify my observation, and may not be out of place here.

The first disputes known to have occurred on the subject of Predestination commenced in the fifth century, when some monks of Adumetum maintained "that God not only predestinated the wicked to eternal punishment, but also to the guilt and transgression for which they are punished." This was strenuously opposed by St. Augustine and the Councils of Arles and Lyons. Basnage, who supposes there may have been Predestinarians from the days of Paul, thinks that this sect never reached maturity. The semi-Pelagians, like the Pelagians, denied Predestination *in toto*, and were reckoned in consequence no less heretical. The question among the orthodox was not whether God did predestine men some to heaven and some to hell; but whether He did so *arbitrarily* of His mere will and pleasure, or because He *foresaw* the actions by which they would deserve one or the other. To the latter opinion adhered Chrysostom, the majority of the Greek and a few of the Latin Fathers. To the doctrine of Arbitrary Predestination belonged Augustine, Jerome, Thomas Aquinas, and nearly all the Latin Church. In the ninth century the controversy was renewed by Godeschalcus, an "illustrious Saxon," whom Hincmar, Archbishop of Rheims, flogged into a recantation of the doctrine of Augustine and imprisoned for life, though his opinions were justified by the Councils of Valence (855), of Langres (859), and of Tousi (860.) These opinions were, "that God did not desire or will the salvation of all mankind, but that of the elect only." At the Reformation, while Zwingle and his followers adhered to the views of Chrysostom, Calvin, on the contrary, maintained "that the everlasting condition of mankind, in a future world, was determined from all eternity by the unchangeable order of the Deity, and that this absolute determination of His will was the only source of happiness and misery to every individual." This opinion, as we all know, found numberless adherents. The Lutherans, on the contrary, held that God's foreknowledge, and not His arbitrary will, was the cause of His Predestination; and Arminius and his followers went a step further, and affirmed "that God has *not* fixed the future state of mankind by an unconditional decree, but has determined to reward and punish men according to the use they make of their Freedom in keeping or rejecting the faith of Christ." These opinions of Arminius were strenuously opposed by Gomar, and referred to a great Synod at Dort in 1618, where the Supralapsarian Calvinists, who held "that from all eternity God had decreed the Fall of Adam, so that neither he nor any of the lost could avert their doom," were outvoted by the Sublapsarians, who condemned Arminius, but thought "that God had only permitted, and not absolutely predetermined, the Fall of Man." Meanwhile the Church of Rome, which asserts the *fact* of Predestination as an article of faith, but leaves the *motive* undecided, was disturbed by the war between the Jansenists and Jesuits. Molina, a Jesuit, published a book in 1588, in which he affirmed that Predestination was founded upon God's foreknowledge of the merits of the elect, to whom He accords grace of congruity; His "*scientia media*" enabling Him to foresee the future contingents arising from the nature and circumstances of His creatures. The book added many subtle distinctions between "Predestination to Grace" and "Predestination to Glory," "Grace Actual" and "Grace Efficacious," "Grace Preventing" and "Grace Co-operating," "Grace Concomitant" and "Grace of Sufficiency," all which profane quibbles on the mystery of the Divine aid have been immortalised in the *Lettres Provinciales.* But the Dominicans, who hated the Jesuits, and who especially adhered to the doctrines of Augustine and Aquinas, stirred up Clement VIII. to endless trials in the midst of which Jansenius wrote his famous unread book, upholding the Thomist or Augustine doctrine. Long and fierce was the war between the powerful, unscrupulous Jesuits and the ascetic, miracle-working Jansenists, illustrious by the names of Arnauld, Pascal, and Fénelon. At last the maltreated Jansenists

It has been argued that God, knowing all things from eternity, and ruling all things despotically, must have known and ruled from eternity the destiny, temporal and eternal, of

sunk into obscurity, and the victorious Molinists remained, much discredited by the contest.

Not a little strange is it to think that precisely similar disputes should have disturbed the followers of Mahomet. Sale informs us that the sect of Bash-arians believe man to be *absolutely* free, God exercising no control over him. The Kadarians hold " that injustice must not be attributed to God, but to man, who is free, and will be rewarded or punished as he uses his Freedom." The Ashàrians maintain " that God wills both good and evil, and *creates* an action, whenever a man wills it, ready for the man's *acquisition*." The Moderate Jabarians say, " that man has a power whereby he gains praise or blame, but which does not influence the action." The Orthodox hold "that God has predestined irrevocably every man's circumstances, faith, and eternal destiny." The Pure Jabarians affirm " that man can do nothing whatever, but produces all his actions of necessity, having neither choice nor will more than an inanimate object."

To return to the Protestants. The Divines of Saumur were dissatisfied with the Synod of Dort. Cameron and Amyraut, about 1634, broached a new doctrine, sometimes called Universalism, but more properly " Hypothetical Universalism; " for they believed that, " though God *desired* the happiness of all men, and made no decree against any, yet that millions would be lost because He does not grant them the *assistance* necessary to believing in Christ, though He does not *refuse* to them the power of believing." This farrago of contra-diction received the approbation of the Huguenots, and of many of the Dutch and even Genevese. At this time (says Mosheim, from whom we derive most of this information) "the Church of England resembled a ship tossed on a boisterous ocean." As it had not yet abandoned the Calvinistic doctrines of Predestination, King James gave his adherence to them by his emissaries in the Synod of Dort; and in the Conference of Divines at Hampton Court his opinions so pleased the bishops that Archbishop Whitgift said that " undoubtedly his Majesty spoke by the especial assistance of God's Spirit;" while Bancroft actually fell on his knees and returned thanks ! Nevertheless, no sooner had the English Solomon heard of the proceedings at Dort than he became con-verted to Arminianism, and persecuted Puritans and Calvinists for the rest of his reign. Laud also maintained the Arminian doctrines with vigour; but during the Commonwealth the extremest Calvinism was in the ascendancy with the Puritans and Independents. After the Restoration of Church and Crown, the Latitudinarians, headed by Tillotson, Patrick, and Burnet, endea-voured to introduce a more liberal system, in which the Athanasian Creed would have lost its position in the Liturgy; but, as Tayler tells us, the "hos-tility of the Lower House of Convocation was invincible, and the reforms fell to the ground." The Church of England sank into a lethargy, from which she was but partially aroused by the thunders from the pulpits of the Calvinist Whitfield and the Arminian Wesley; and the vast field of contention between the Tractarians and Evangelicals has not included any dogmas of the class of Predestination.

The Hindoo doctrine of Free-will is strikingly correct. Menu says: " All worlds are seated in the Divine Spirit; and He, no doubt, produces, by a chain of causes and effects consistent with Free-will, the connected series of acts per-formed by embodied souls." (*Institutes*, MENU, 12. 118.) Buddhism, the anti-thesis of Islam, holds to the absolute Freedom of man. " The main article of Buddhism (says Sir E. Tennent, *Christianity in Ceylon*) is that, neither in heaven nor on earth can a man escape from the consequences of his acts; that morals are, in their essence, productive causes, without the aid or intervention of any higher authority; hence, forgiveness and atonement are ideas unknown in the dogmas of Buddhism."

all his creatures. Consequently, that all our good and evil
deeds, and also their rewards and punishments, were mapped
out for us before our existence began; and that we can no
more be better or worse than was designed for us, than the
comets can choose a nearer perihelion or more distant aphelion
than the laws of matter fix in their path. Dark as this
doctrine would be in its simplicity, it is given yet a deeper
shade by its alliance with that of the Eternal Perdition of
the wicked. A pious mind revolts not merely from these
dreadful dogmas, but from the belief that any child of our
blessed Father has really *believed* such blasphemies against
Him; that it is possible that in this beautiful world men
in whose hearts their Maker's voice was ever whispering love
and mercy, have said " That some are born to honour and
some to dishonour, ' some (and they but a few) Elect to everlasting life,' some (and they the vast majority) predestined
to most grievous torments in soul and body in hell fire for
ever!"

The creed which can embrace such doctrines as these is
thereby destructive of both Ethics and Religion. Were the
boasted logic of Calvin really carried to its practical consequences, his disciples could recognise no *law*, for to the Elect
obedience is involuntary, and to the Reprobate impossible.
They could adore no *God;* for the character they ascribe to
the Creator is one which the nature the true God has given
them forces them to abhor. Nor could they even enjoy the
miserable hope of their own salvation amid the destruction
of their brethren. Do they say that the Divine Faithfulness is pledged in Scripture to their salvation? Even were
it found in the Gospel that God had sworn " A. B. shall be
saved," how will this secure him? " If it consist with Divine
Rectitude to consign to everlasting misery beings who have
come guilty and impotent from His hand, we beg to know
what interest we have in this rectitude, what pledge of good
it contains, or what evil can be imagined which may not be
its natural result? If justice and goodness, when stretched to
infinity, take such strange forms, why should not the Divine
Faithfulness transcend our poor ideas as well as Divine
Justice and Goodness, and why may not God, consistently

with this attribute, crush every hope which his Word has raised ?*

But with the hypothesis of the existence of an Eternal Hell the philosophic moralist, as I have already said, has nothing to do. Neither has he any concern with the question of the truth or falsehood of the exegesis of Scripture, on which particular rests the doctrine of Predestination to Good or Bad Works; but only with such arguments in its defence as theologians have drawn from the arsenal of reason. The Calvinist and the Mahometan alike ask us, " How is it possible that God, foreseeing all things, must not also fore-ordain them ? " It is this difficulty which the moralist is bound to meet.

In the first place, I apprehend this may be done by simply recalling that doctrine of the proper Eternity (not Immortality) of God, which, though broadly stated by Moses, has never yet been embodied in the Jewish or Christian creed. God is not the Being who " was, and is, and is to come : " He is the Eternal " I AM."† Time exists only for finite creatures whose thoughts present themselves separately and successively ; and by the rapidity or slowness of this succession the time which to one is long to another is short.‡ Eternity can never consist of finite parts ; it must be one and indivisible ; nor can the awful thoughts of God be successive, like ours ; but all events, past, present, and future, must appear, to the Infinite Mind, in one " perpetually instantaneous " view. § Our being is a ceaseless progression ; His an everlasting " Punctum stans." ‖   Now, Foreknowledge and Predestina-

* " The Moral Argument against Calvinism."—CHANNING'S *Works*, v. i., p. 171.

I must be permitted to record my conviction, that, whatever may be the more obvious sense of his words, nothing could have been further from the meaning of the large-hearted Paul than the doctrine of Predestination to damnation.

† The inscription over the Temple of Delphi was the one word " εῖ" (Thou art). Plutarch, in his treatise on it, considers it equivalent to εἰ ἑν (Thou art One), an assertion of the unity of God; "not in an aggregate sense as One thing, . . . but as a nature entire in its first principles."

‡ " Tempus item per se non est ; sed rebus ab ipsis
      Consequitur sensus, transactum quod sit in ævo,
      Tum quæ res instat, quid porro deinde sequatur."—LUCRETIUS.

§ See *Soames Jenyns' Disq.*, iv., *On the Nature of Time.* His error lies in the hypothesis that the soul of man can hereafter attain proper eternity. An immortal progress is all that is possible for the finite.

‖ The mystery of the creation of a world *in time* never found a more fitting

tion imply succession in time, and are possible only to beings existing successively, not instantly. God knows all things and rules all things NOW; He did not suddenly give forth the fiat when the earth was in one point of its revolution, or at a given date before the sun existed, " My servant Paul or Peter shall die at such a place." Thus, if Fore-ordination be reduced to Ordination, the difficulty of the Predestinarian is reduced to that of the Theological Necessitarian; namely, that of reconciling the Freedom of man with the Omnipotence of God. To this I have already given the only answer of which I believe it is capable: God's Truth and God's Justice are both pledged to us that we are really free, really causes in the world of noumena; and the stupendous nature of the gift of Freedom must not lead us to doubt that it is the actual as well as the grandest boon of Almighty Love.

But there is a sense in which we may say that God predestines us. The woof which our Free-will weaves is no less manifest to His eye from the beginning, than the warp which His immutable laws fix for it to work in. The whole tissue of our lives lies spread before Him in the everlasting Now which began for Him never. Thus, whatever may be the results of our Freedom, we may be sure He has for ever known them, and that *with that knowledge* has He given it to us. What, then, must follow, but that, whatever were His design in creating man (the species and the individual), He sees that ultimately that boon of Freedom will not counteract it? It is attributing to the All-wise nothing short of fatuity, to suppose that He has made one single creature for an end which end He sees the creature will never attain, and that precisely in consequence of a gift which He persists in bestowing on him. The Supralapsarians were quite logical when they affirmed, that if any man were to be damned, God must have made him for damnation.

But it is not a *Fiend* whose Intuitions we find in our hearts. In that sweet Voice there can we recognise aught that reveals its Speaker to be the ferocious Being who could destine his yet unborn creature to the immeasurable agony of everlasting

expression than that of the Hindoo: " Originally there was indeed Soul only; He thought, ' I will create worlds.' " — The *Veda* called *Aitareya Brahamans.*

Hell? Not so! From perfect Love, and Love only, did our Father create us. He made us, each and all, every man, every woman, every child, for *Virtue*, for endless growth in Goodness, endless increase in being, endless progress in Love and Joy, endless approximation to Himself!

" The END OF CREATION is the PERFECTING OF SOULS." And though the night of sin and sorrow be ever so dark and ever so long, yet the sun shall rise at last ; and though man may wander to the utmost verge of the wilderness of his iniquity, yet the Good Shepherd, rejoicing, shall bring the wanderer home, "*for He will seek till He find him.*"

So surely as God is Good must His design in creating each of us be Good : so surely as He is Wise must He know that no impediment can ultimately thwart that design for which He could call us into being. So surely as *God is God,* shall He at last " see all things that He hath made, and, behold! they shall be *very Good!* "

If the views now stated be correct, the Freedom of man is on this wise. As a *Homo phenomenon,* he is enchained in the concatenation of phenomenal causes and effects. As a *Homo noumenon,* he is himself an original cause, and, as such, descends as an agent into the world of sense. And this power of causation he holds from God, who vouchsafes to him a real Freedom within certain bounds. Yet God, who exists at once in the past, the present, and the future, when He created us saw (or rather *sees*) all that we are now, all that we shall be throughout our immortality. *Whatever* we are He saw it ere yet we had being in the World of Time and Space, and saw that it was not incompatible with the ultimate completion of His merciful designs. Thus, we enter on our glorious battle-field not only with the knowledge that God *wills* our virtue, and will make His outward Providence and His inward inspiration conspire to aid it, but also with the blessed faith that God *foresees* our virtue, and that sooner or later the victory *must* be won. There is no room for self-despair. We may fall again and again, and, bruised and wounded, debased in our own and all men's eyes, our heart's blood staining the dust, we may feel inclined to lie there hopelessly for ever, but this faith shall raise us up! God foresaw all our sin, but yet He made us! Yes, made us for that only End for which He could work — immortal Righteousness! The battle is fierce and cruel — it may last all our earthly life, and perchance for ages beyond; we may doom ourselves to groan beneath the burden of sin, and writhe beneath the lash of Retribution here and hereafter, till flesh and heart fail; but this Faith in God shall be the strength of our heart, while we know that His Love shall be our portion for ever.

Nor is it only for ourselves that this blessed Trust is precious. The fanatic may tell us in vain, that " the view of the misery of the damned will double the ardour of the love and gratitude of the saints in heaven, and they will be so much the more happy in the enjoyment of it." * It is not true! Even Calvin was not the " more happy " for the long tortures of Servetus. The heart of man, with all its " desperate wickedness," is the work of a God, not a Devil. Nor is it at its heavenly height, but at its lowest earthly degradation, that it can feel anything save pain at the torments of another. Men *think* that they think their brothers will be damned, and think that they themselves could enjoy the bliss of heaven, and behold it; but no man actually believes this. No man ever yet looked at his brother, and (*realising what Damnation means*) thought that he could —

> " Smile
> And doom be passed on him the while."

No man who had tasted a mother's love ever yet believed that it would —

> " Add to that mother's bliss to know
> The pangs her child must undergo."

Let us do justice to humanity. The removal of all fear for the future destiny of our fellow-creatures is the removal of a nightmare. It was not only while the thunder-cloud hung over our *own* heads, that it darkened our sky. Some natures are so hopeful and loving, that they never know fear of Hell for themselves. But it is when the lurid gloom has rolled utterly away from our horizon that we know how it

---

* Jonathan Edwards, quoted by Theodore Parker, *Theism, Atheism, and the Popular Theology.*

blackened the universe; and then only can we see the true splendour of the Sun throned, not " in clouds and darkness," but in a heaven of unshadowed light. Then only can we labour in confiding faith for all the sons of men, on whom no storm of destruction shall ever fall, but that blessed Sun shall rise alike " on the evil and on the good."

The limits of human freedom have now to be considered. These are of two kinds, one common to all men, the other peculiar to individuals; the first external, the second internal.

First. The freedom of all human beings is limited externally by what has been called the " Warp" of their destiny. In working out the tissue of our lives, we find ourselves from first to last immeshed on the right and left by a whole web of circumstances and events which have been arranged without consulting our inclinations. Necessarily we are given no choice whether we shall exist at all, or be born in this planet, or century, or country, or family; whether we shall be Caucasian or negro, the heir of a king or the child of a slave, beautiful and strong or deformed and blind, a man or a woman; all this, and all the vast chain of circumstances which hang from each of these alternatives, is decided for us. There are other circumstances of human life of which the limitations are less absolute. Though a man " cannot make one hair white or black, nor add one cubit to his stature," he can commonly do much to increase the powers of his body. Of his own health and longevity he is the guardian, and he may either destroy them or preserve them to their normal maximum, if no accident intervene, though not one moment beyond it. His worldly wealth and his knowledge he may or may not have opportunities of enlarging to an immense extent. In a word, every man's Freedom is externally limited by the force of all the circumstances in which he is placed, which circumstances are determined, both by the agency of natural laws, and of other free beings like himself.

Secondly. The freedom of some human beings is limited internally by the peculiarities of their organisation. These are of various classes: in the first, the limitation is absolute,

and there is no space left for Freedom at all.   In others there
is some Freedom, but its bounds are closer than in the normal
condition of the race.

There are beings to whom we must still concede humanity, who yet have utterly lost its crown of rationality,
or have never yet possessed it.   Of this class are maniacs,
idiots, infants, and dotards.   Here the loss of Freedom is absolute.   Next there is the class of savages, young children, half-
witted people, utterly uneducated persons, the intoxicated,
and those under excessive anguish or diseases of body affecting
the mind.   In all these there is a degree of responsibility, but
it is still imperfect.   Further, there are persons, not incapable
indeed of taking their part in daily life; but still of poor,
feeble, wavering minds, never grasping firmly the idea of duty,
but aiming at it blindly, if at all.   These persons are not
thoroughly self-conscious; and to them, " if they do not their
Master's will," but few can be the " stripes " He will apportion.

Finally, there is a class whom a modern school of philosophy has affirmed to exist, and whose position is at first
sight no less appalling than anomalous.*   It is said that there
are persons to whom vicious progenitors have bequeathed
such feeble powers for good, such furious passions for evil,
that to them virtue is *impossible*.   They are Moral Idiots,
though by no means Intellectual Idiots; the whole conscience
is suppressed in their nature, leaving only an intellectual,
affectional, and sensual being, clothed in the form of manhood,
but without its noblest distinction.   I shall not stop to consider the veracity of the philosophy which asserts *à priori* that
such things *may be,* nor yet sift the *à posteriori* evidence that
they *have been ;* neither shall I inquire into that portentous
class of phenomena which have doubtless given rise to the
notion of diabolic inspirations ;—the hallucinations of minds
otherwise morally well constituted, in which the unhappy
victims seem to be for a time continually inwardly prompted
to some special crime.   Let it be admitted that the existence
of Moral Idiotcy and Moral Mania, if not demonstrated, has

---

* See Combe on the Constitution of Man, p. 178., and Appendix, No. II

been shown to be possible. The moralist is not further concerned with them than to remark that, *if* they be found, they place their patients beyond the limits of his science; precisely as much as an intellectual idiot, maniac, or wild beast is irresponsible, so must be the man in whom conscience is utterly mute, or the freedom of the will annulled by diseased action of the brain. Human laws must punish as *mischievous* crimes committed under conditions which *morally* absolve the delinquent, but which conditions it would be frequently impossible for a human tribunal to take into consideration. But before the all-seeing God we may believe that such sins, though in *our* eyes " red like crimson," are in His as " white as wool." *

But having said thus much of the possibility that some human beings do not fall under the category of Responsible Moral Agents, it is necessary to remind the reader that, while this possibility ought to weigh in his judgment of his fellow-creatures, it can never apply to himself. The fact that he is able at any one moment to *question* whether he be morally responsible proves that at that moment he *is* so—Moral Idiotcy and Moral Mania can never be self-conscious. If a man can apprehend the Law he can obey it. He may indeed commit

---

* To some minds the idea of a moral idiot involves painful notions of the Creator. I may be permitted to remark that they rest on the false philosophy of the Eudaimonist. So long as we consider happiness as the great end of life, and virtue only its instrument, so long shall we find difficulties to solve in the mischiefs wrought by beings whom ignorance or fatuity renders irresponsible. To the Eudaimonist such mischief appears a final evil; and, as he is forbidden to attribute it to the irresponsible agent, he is driven to attribute it to God But the difficulty ceases when we perceive that the end of creation is the perfecting of souls, and that the production of happiness is altogether secondary thereto. Sin is now seen to be evil, not for the external mischief it produces, but for its own sake, as the most evil of all things. The outward act, be it ever so mischievous, is not *sin*—the Will constitutes the sin. Thus, when offences are committed by an irresponsible agent, God does not become the author of any sin; for sin is nothing but the conscious wilful delinquency of a free creature, and there is no sin without it, any more than in the ravages of the storm and flood. The *mischief* done takes its place along with the suffering which is necessary to the end of creation; and, when the Great Drama is further advanced, we shall understand the reason of what seems unaccountable in the one short scene we now behold. To ask further, why Moral Idiots should have been created, is equivalent to asking why there should be intellectual idiots, children dying in infancy, &c. We must deem their existence on earth motived by reasons which (while ignorant of all life beyond us) we may not guess. The children at a school marvel why a parent withdraws his son soon after entrance, or does not suffer him to learn with them; but it is all understood *at home.*

a crime under temporary mania, and afterwards recover and rightly absolve himself, but he can never say, "I am *now* doing no sin, for I am not in a Responsible State." And, again, —

We are by no means to conclude that every perverse reprobate we meet is a Moral Idiot. The thing (if it exist at all) must be the rarest as well as the saddest exception to humanity, and must be appreciated not by the frequency of sin, but by the absolute absence of all Virtue. The test must be, not "Does the man transgress continually?" but "Does he never show consciousness of Right and Wrong, never do a good act or repent of a bad one?"

"There are cases where individuals, from youth up, notwithstanding an education whereby others have been benefited, show so early a wickedness and persist in it up to man's estate, that one may be led to deem them innate villains; yet at the same time we so condemn them as if they continued as responsible as any other person." But this we do with justice; for we are compelled to believe "that everything arising from man's choice depended on a free causality at bottom, which causality impresses, from youth up, its character upon the phenomena; these phenomena do by their uniformity make a sequence in the physical system visible, but do not make the wicked quality of Will necessary; but rather such sequence follows the freely adopted evil and unchanging maxims which do therefore make him the more reprobate and the more blameworthy."*

Having thus discussed the Freedom of the Human Will, and its limits, necessary and contingent, I may remark, in conclusion, that as it is the most stupendous achievement of Almighty Power to have made a Free Creature, so the first duty of such a creature is the preservation of his Freedom.

It is indeed possible, and that without any logical quibbling, to resolve *all* duty into the struggle for that which Paul most philosophically denominated "the glorious Liberty of the sons of God." Strictly speaking, man is not Free to do Right *or* Wrong; he is only Free to do Right; when he does Wrong he is enslaved. The man himself, the inner Will, the

---

* Kant, Met. Ethics, On Freedom and Necessity.

Homo noumenon, always self-legislates the Right, and is interested therein by his moral sense of joy in its fufilment. It is he who, as a Free Cause, descends victoriously into the world of sense, bearing in his hand the Labarum of the Eternal Right. The lower man, the *Homo phenomenon*, alone can crave blindly for the Wrong; and, if successful, the true Man himself falls into the bondage of him whom he obeys, and becomes the Slave of his own lusts. Alas for him who deems that he can "assert his Freedom" by flinging to the winds that "sceptre of his kingdom which is a Right sceptre," and casting from his brows Humanity's sole and radiant crown! Even so did the Prodigal display his "Liberty" when he exchanged the heirship of his father's house for the task of the swineherd.

The duty of asserting our Freedom is commensurate with the whole of duty; for it is the assertion of the dominion of the Holy Will over the whole nature. Now, this (as I have remarked in Chap. I.) is only truly accomplished when there is some room for contest. When the requirements of the Eternal Law precisely coincide with those of the desires of our lower nature, we cannot be properly said to OBEY the Law (which implies the possibility of,—*i. e.* some motive for—disobedience); but only *not to disobey* it while we obey the dictates of our desires. Our conduct is then *innocent*, not *virtuous*; and it is the nature of our souls only to progress through Virtue, and not through Innocence. Amid innocent happiness they stand still, as they retrograde amid happiness which is not Innocent.* If we desire our souls to grow, to fulfil the design of their own and the world's creation, to approach nearer to God and Goodness, we must look to conquest over desires, to renunciation of Happiness as the sole means of growth. Hereafter, when I come to speak of the second great branch of Practical Morals—namely, that of Personal Duty, which is summed up in the axiom "Be ye perfect as your Father which is in heaven is perfect "—I shall

---

* To avoid continual circumlocutions, I class under the name Happiness both the Positive Happiness resulting from the fulfilment of our desires, *i. e.*, from pleasure; and the negative Happiness of escape from the counteraction of our desires, *i. e.*, from pain.

enlarge further on this topic.   It is enough at present to remark that what have been called " self-denial " and " self-
sacrifice " (or the denial and sacrifice of the desires of the
lower self) are the essential constituents of Virtue, the sole
manifestations of the true royalty of the pure Will; and that
even the errors of Asceticism, which would invent sacrifices
of Happiness in excess of the requirements of the Law, are a
less fatal heresy than that of the Eudaimonism which would
tread down all Virtue into a mere highway to Happiness.
The fact appears to be, that in the ordinary conditions of
humanity the demands made by Duty upon Happiness are
fully equal to our moral strength, and amply sufficient to afford
scope for our growth in Virtue.   But it would seem that there
are exceptions to this rule, and that God sees right sometimes
to try us by Pleasure as well as by Pain.   There are in the
lives of many of us periods when we occupy positions so singularly blessed, that nearly every duty coincides with our natural
desires, and the performance of it is unaccompanied by any
sacrifice, while Health, Wealth, and Love remove every thorn
from our paths.   Under these circumstances our trial is to
prevent our souls growing indolent and languid amid the Eden-
bowers of Innocent Happiness.   The waters of our spiritual
life are liable to become stagnant over such smooth, unbroken
beds, and stand in need of rocks and falls, or at least of spars
or pebbles, to freshen them by their resistance.   In cases like
these the duty of perfecting ourselves demands that we shall
find some opportunity to exercise our true Moral Freedom.   I
do not say that it demands of us to *exceed* the requirements of
the Moral Law; for the whole idea of Works of Supererogation
is essentially absurd.   It is the *same* Law which alone can
constitute any act a Duty, whether its application be social,
personal, or religious; and to exceed the requirements of
this Law is impossible, because it always requires of us to do
our very uttermost for the benefit of our neighbour and the
perfecting of our own souls.   But it is to *fulfil*, and not to
exceed the Law; to watch with unwearied care, lest our Happiness lead us into Moral Indifference and Unprogression, and
to seize with alacrity every opportunity to serve our fellow-
creatures, purify our hearts, and serve our God at the cost of

our inclinations.* But, beside this Universal Duty of Asserting our Freedom by giving to the true Will absolute dominion over the blind instincts of the lower nature, the duty into which, as I have said, all others may be resolved, there is also a Special Duty of Asserting our Freedom by resisting the encroachments of our fellow-creatures; and this concerns us only in our social capacity. Freedom is, in fact, of three sorts, — Moral, Personal, and Political.

By " Moral Freedom," I mean the Internal Freedom of the will over the lower nature, whereby the man *chooses* the Right and rejects the Wrong. This Moral Freedom our fellow-creatures have no *right* to limit, nor the slightest *power* to do so unless we abdicate it. This the Jesuit professes to do in favour of his superior, and he thereby commits, so far as in him lies, the suicide of his soul.

By Personal and Political Freedom, I mean the External Freedom belonging to a man; the first in his private capacity, the second as a member of the state. In such External Freedom lies the scope and domain wherein the Moral Free Will is to exert itself in the sensible world. Our Personal and Political Freedom our fellow-creatures have a *right* to limit only by the reservation of *their* equal Freedom. But they have often a *power* to rob us of one, or both. The slave is robbed of his Personal Freedom. Every person left without his voice in the state of which he is a member is robbed of his Political Freedom. The duty of both is to struggle for the entire possession of that domain given them by God for the exercise of their Moral Free Will. But while the deprivation of Personal Freedom constitutes such an incarceration of the soul as to justify violence for the recovery of that which is the whole scope given us for the work of our existence, the loss of Political Freedom shuts us out, on the contrary, from so

---

* " So needful is sacrifice to the health and hardihood of conscience, that if the occasions for it do not present themselves spontaneously in our lot, we must create them for ourselves; not reserving to ourselves those exercises of virtue which are constitutionally pleasant, but, on the contrary, esteeming the asperity of a duty as the reason why we should put our hand to it at once ; not acquiescing in the facility of wisely-adjusted habits, but accepting the ease of living well as the peremptory summons of God to live better. He is, in short, no true soldier of the Lord, nor worthy to bear the Christian armour, who, in service so high, will not make an hour's forced march of duty every day."— J. MARTINEAU, *Endeavours*, &c., i. 245.

small a portion of our rightful domain, that (while we remember that the end of our Freedom is the Perfecting of our souls) we shall frequently be called on not to relinquish, but to postpone, our struggle for our political rights to other duties more nearly affecting the great purpose of our existence.

I have now, I trust, elucidated sufficiently for the purpose of this work the five propositions which are included under the subject of this chapter; namely, —

1st. That the Human Will is Free.

2nd. That this Freedom, though involving present sin and suffering, is foreseen by God to result eventually in the Virtue of every creature endowed therewith.

3rd. That this Freedom is limited, necessarily and contingently, subjectively and objectively, righteously (by God through His laws and by our fellow-creatures claiming their equal rights) and unrighteously (by our fellow-creatures seizing *more* than their equal rights).

4th. That it is the essential character of all human duty to be an assertion of this Freedom, by giving practical dominion to the pure Will over the lower nature.

5th. That beside this universal assertion of Freedom, into which all human duty may be resolved, man has also a special duty of preserving his Moral Freedom without abdicating it to his fellow-creature, and of preserving his Personal and Political Freedom from the unrighteous invasions of his fellow-creatures.

CHAPTER IV.

WHY THE MORAL LAW SHOULD BE OBEYED.

~~~~~~~~~~

"A religious act, proceeding from selfish views in this world, or in the next, is declared to be concrete and interested. But an act performed with a knowledge of God, and without self-love, is called abstract and disinterested. He who frequently performs disinterested acts of religion, he sacrifices his own spirit by fixing it on the Spirit of God, and approaches the nature of that sole Divinity who shines by His own effulgence." — *Institutes of Menu*, 12. 89.

IN the last Chapter I endeavoured to demonstrate that the
pure Will, the true self of man, is by nature righteous,—self-
legislative of the only Universal Law, viz. the Moral, —
and that by this spontaneous autonomy would all his actions be
squared, were it not for his lower nature, which is by its constitution un-moral, neither righteous nor unrighteous, but
capable only of determining its choice by its instinctive propensities and the gratifications offered to them. Thus these
two are contrary one to another, "and the spirit lusteth
against the flesh, and the flesh against the spirit." In the
valour of the higher nature acquired by its victory over the
lower, in the *Virtue* of the tried and conquering soul, we look
for the glorious End of creation, the sublime result contemplated by Infinite Benevolence in calling man into existence
and fitting him with the complicated nature capable of de-
veloping that Virtue which alone can be the crown of finite
intelligences. The great practical problem of human life is
this: "How is the Moral Will to gain the victory over the un-
moral instincts, the *Homo noumenon* over the *Homo phenomenon*, Michael over the Evil One, Mithras over Hyle?"*

That this can ever be accomplished *absolutely*, either here
or hereafter, is a fond dream; for man must ever remain
finite, and short of infinity there is no perfection. Yet, even
if the gravitation of the lower nature should remain a fixed
quantity, the resisting force of the higher is indefinitely
susceptible of increase; and thus the holy Will may become
more and more completely dominant, world without end.

* I trust I shall not be supposed to hold the old worn-out heresy of the intrinsic *evil* of any part of the soul or body which the All-Good hath made.
This lower nature, which He has given as the necessary machinery of our
moral life, as the *weight* of the great timepiece, is precisely what it ought to
be, aye, and a beautiful nature too ! Καὶ τα κακῆς ὕλης βλαστημάτα χρηστὰ
καὶ ἐσθλα," cried even Zoroaster (Psel. 16., Cory, 278.) But when the weight
drags and overpowers the mainspring, the clock stops.

But how this force of the pure Will is to be maintained and
rendered victorious over the desires of the lower nature, is a
question which, though practically answered by the humblest
disciple of Virtue, is beyond the reach of philosophy to solve
in theory.   The Will itself resolves to be strong, and *thereby*
becomes so.   Such is the nature God has given to it.   We
can only constate the fact, and not explain it.

Nevertheless, it is of the utmost consequence that the Will,
thus asserting its sovereignty should do so on the one sole
true ground and motive; or, to speak more strictly, this
victory is only a real, and not a fallacious victory of the Will,
when it is gained purely by and for the Will's own self-
legislated holy law.   When any other motive is brought to
bear on the battle, when any banner is brought forward save
that of the Eternal Right, then the whole meaning and issue
of the contest is altered, and, whatever be the result, the true
free self can no longer claim the conqueror's crown.

For, let us put the case that a man relinquish the present
gratification of some intellectual, affectional, or sensual desire,
not from the consideration that it is *unlawful,* but that it
would be *imprudent,* and that by the postponement of this
gratification to-day he will have a larger gratification to-
morrow.   A superficial observer may cry, "*Io pæan!* The
victory is won — the unlawful action renounced!" But *what*
has won the victory ?   Is it the man himself, the holy Will
ordaining the Eternal Law ?   Not at all.   It is the lower
nature, instinctively and without any Moral Freedom, pursuing its gratification with whatever patience and cunning it
may possess.   The true self has not struck a blow in the
fight.   The man has not advanced one step towards Virtue.

Let us consider this more fully.

Happiness, or the gratification of the desires of our whole
being, is an end whose representation is the natural motive of
our instinctive actions.   To say that we do anything "to
make us happy," is universally understood to give an explanation of our conduct beyond which there is no need of
further inquiry.   And this of course it is perfectly fit, and
as it was intended by the Creator, should be the case, in all
our actions wherein moral distinctions do not intervene, and
concerning which the internal guide issues no mandates.

But, because this end of happiness is so obviously desirable, because in thousands of cases it is allowable, are we therefore to set it up as the ground of obedience to the law ?   To aim at the gratification of our desires, be it with ever so much prudence,* is only to add the foresight and caution of human intellect to the more straightforward pursuit of the brute. There is nothing *moral* in the case.   The beast has his appetites, which set before him, as desirable ends, his prey or his liberty, and he compasses the attainment of them with whatever cunning, patience, and strength he may possess. Man desires (equally instinctively) love, fame, knowledge, wealth, and he sets about their acquirement with greater cunning than the fox or the lion, postponing them, perhaps, till the end of life, for the sake of obtaining them more perfectly at last.   The difference is solely in the *degree* of human prudence, man's greater intellectual powers enabling him to take in a wider range of circumstances, and combine his measures better than the dog, even as the dog is wiser than the sheep. There is no one quality brought into play, in this prudent pursuit of happiness, which essentially distinguishes a moral agent.   Yet, if this be the only *virtue,* how idle is it to attribute to man the proud pre-eminence of a moral nature capable of approaching the divine !   Shall we get nearer to God by improving on the patience of the cat or the sagacity of the jackal ?

Again.   I have already referred to the distinction between that realm of noumena in which we are free causes, and that world of phenomena in which we are locked up in necessity. So far as our desires are concerned, they are the result of our original nature, modified by those circumstances of our past life which have passed beyond our recall.   So far as the solicitations which the external world offers to our desires, these also are independent of our choice.   If, then, we merely follow our desires to their gratification, where is our Freedom ?

* I use the word Prudence here and elsewhere in this Essay in its popular acceptation as that principle which teaches the preference of the greater future happiness over the lesser present one.   The old Moralists, however, gave to the Cardinal Virtue of Prudence a much wider sense.   Cumberland says, " Toutes les vertus sont renfermées comme dans leur source dans la Prudence qui dirige à rechercher la meilleure Fin par des moyens convenables." —*Les Loix de la Nature Expliquées par R. Cumberland, Evéque de Peterborough. Traduits du Latin par Barbeyrac,* p. 244.

It may be said that we exercise Freedom in prudently postponing present to future enjoyment. But this is fallacious, and no more true Freedom than that of the spider waiting till its prey be fairly entrapped. I wish not only for happiness, but for as *much* happiness as I can get. That is a part of my instinctive nature not dependent on my Will. If prudence, then, teach me that to obtain the greater happiness I must postpone the lesser, my determination to do so is decided by the same Necessity which would have urged me to snatch at the first gratification offered. That which determines me on one occasion to gratify my desires immediately, and on another to postpone doing so from a prudent regard to the future, is simply the preponderance of one or other Desire over one or other Hope or Fear. If I gratify my desire instantly, it is because it is stronger than my hopes or fears. If I forbear to do so (as a matter of prudence), it is because it is weaker. The vulture which dashes at its prey, and the fox which steals slowly up to it, are determined by precisely the same motives; their conduct is only modified by the greater or less degree of cunning with which Providence has endowed them.

But Moral Freedom must be something very different from all this; it must be the free choice of actions to which we are NOT determined by the instincts of the internal, nor the solicitations of the external, world ; it must be the *conquest* of the lower happiness-craving nature by the higher, self-legislating only the holy law.   Here alone are we free from the all-fettering chain of necessity ; here alone are our true selves the victors and masters, not the slaves of our own lusts.   So long, then, as we seek happiness as the aim of moral struggles (whether prudently or imprudently it matters nothing) we are not free, and consequently can have no ethical merit. The motive, therefore, which, if we are to be virtuous, must be the determining one of our Moral Freedom, cannot lie at all in the direction of happiness.

The law itself, the Eternal Right for right's own sake, that alone must be our motive, the spring of our resolution, the ground of our obedience.   Deep from our inmost souls comes forth the mandate, the bare and simple Law, claiming the command of our whole existence merely by its proper right, and disdaining alike to menace or to bribe!

Is this " a hard saying ? "   Are our hearts so base, that the summons of this grand, holy Law wakes no vibration through their thousand chords?   Is Happiness a sufficient aim for us, and Virtue not enough?   Is it a final reason for an act, that it makes us Happy, and no final reason that that act is Right? Blessed be the God who made us, it is not so !   Our natures, poor and weak though they be, *are* capable of that disinterested obedience to which they are called; nor have any teachers shown such ignorance of them as those who have tried to bribe us to Virtue.   So long as petty and selfish motives are urged, so long shall we stand by cold and indifferent.   Vainly are sent round, amid the mutineers of the passions, one subaltern after another, with promises and threats.   But when the true King comes forth, all unarmed and alone, and simply claims our allegiance, straightway the mutiny ceases — the rebels own their Lord.

It is the inculcation of this obedience to the law for the law's own sake which peculiarly distinguishes Intuitive Morals, and divides them from all moral and religious systems which set forth present or eternal happiness as the motives of Virtue.   The distinction is perfectly sharp, and of immense import.   There is a law to be obeyed, and it must needs be obeyed, either for its own sake or for some other reason.   The controversy involves no less than the whole existence of Virtue ; from *we* affirm that obedience from any other motive than the true one has neither Moral Freedom nor any moral characteristic whatever.

I shall presently consider more at length the systems opposed to this doctrine.   It is of importance now to develope a little further the true motive of Virtue.

Assuming that it is a bare Law which is to determine our actions, we perceive that this law will set forth its own proper Ends, having nothing in common with the end of our private Happiness set forth by the instincts of our lower nature.*   As subjects of the law, we are called on to pursue

---

* " The relation of an end to a duty may be contemplated in a twofold manner, either beginning with the end to assign the maxim of actions in harmony with duty, or beginning with the maxim to determine that end, which it is a duty incumbent on man to propose to himself.   Jurisprudence advances by the first method.   But morals strike into an opposite march.   Here we cannot commence with ends man may design, and from them determine and

the ends which it lays it upon us to seek; which ends, be it remembered, we are never to consider as the reason *why the law
exists,* as if it were a set of technical rules for the acquiring of
the art of Virtue;* consequently, we are not to do Right
that there may be a Heaven, for all the glory and sanctity of
celestial souls must depend on the fixity of the law, but we
are to say —

"Fiat Justitia, ruat Cælum."

Now, the ends which the Moral Law ordains us to seek
(as we shall discuss more fully in Practical Morals) are, 1st,
Our own Perfection; secondly, Our neighbour's Happiness.

And the results which would ensue from obedience to this
law (namely, primarily Virtue, and, secondarily, Happiness)
are precisely those which form the ends of our Creator's design
in bringing us and our world into existence.

Absolutely harmonious, then, are Ethics and Religion; for
both set before us the same ends in the same order of
sequence. Ethics tell us that we must pursue these ends
because it is Right to do so; Religion tells us that we must
pursue them because they are the ends of that Will which is
absolutely Righteous; and it adds the all-inspiriting assurance
that heaven and earth may pass away, but those Ends which
God hath willed can never fail of their accomplishment.

But this unity of Morals and Religion is not only in the
Ends they set forth, but in the Motives on which they claim
our obedience. Hitherto I have defined only those of true
Morals, because for many reasons it is necessary that we
should be able to divide them in *theory* from Religion. I now
turn to show that not only are their motives and ends in

---

statute the maxims he has to take, for in this latter case the ground of his
maxims would be experimental, which we know beget no obligation, the idea
duty and its categorical imperative taking rise in pure reason only. In this,
branch, then, the idea obligation must guide to ends which we ought to aim at,
and constitute maxims pointing to those ends, conformably to ethic laws. . . .
But because an act fixing an end is a practical principle, ordaining not a means
(which were a hypothetical commandment) but the end itself (*i. e.,* unconditionally), it follows that there is a categorical imperative of pure reason con-
necting the idea duty with that of an end in general." — KANT, *Met. of Ethics,*
ii. & iii.

   * The laws of numbers do not exist for the sake of making arithmeticians,
but by the study of those laws men become arithmeticians.

unison, but that Morality necessarily includes Religion, and
that the same Intuition which teaches us disinterested obedience to the Law because it is Right, teaches us also disinterested obedience to that Will which is Righteous.

I have said that Virtue consists in the valorous resolution
of the true self to assert its authority and uphold over our
whole nature its self-legislated law. This resolution of the
soul is an act of the greatest significance and solemnity ;
it is an act whose first performance is generally accompanied by effort sufficiently strong to leave durable impression on the memory. Many men can remember the
hour, the " fresh May-dawn" of the better life, when each
first said in his heart —

> " I *will* be wise,
> And just, and free, and mild, if in me lies
> Such power." *

But if the moral life thenceforth proceeded healthfully, the
hourly ratifications of the resolution required less and less
effort, till at last it became the " settled purpose of the soul."
Now, in such cases as this, unless the mind chance to be entangled either in a false theology, making God no god for
the heart, or in a false philosophy leaving no personal deity
at all, the natural consequence of Morality is Religion. When
we have learned by practising goodness to love it, we inevitably love infinite goodness — God is of necessity felt to be
the Father and Friend of the good — He is the judge who
watches us with approbation, the Sovereign beneath whose
banners we fight. No sooner do our hearts cease to condemn
us for any present desire to sin, than we instantly " have confidence towards God," and look to Him for aid in our holy
undertaking. Thus starting with Morality we arrive at Religion.

But this is rather the exceptional than the ordinary development of the human soul. In nine cases out of ten men start
with Religion and arrive through it at Morality. That solemn
resolution to obey the law of right has sprung from the view
of that law personified in God, and it is the mighty torrent

* Revolt of Islam.—Introd.

of the awakened religious sentiment which has borne down
the opposition of the lower nature.   It is the beauty of holiness contemplated in the All-holy which has won them, or
the remembrance of their offences contrasted with His long-
suffering love which has melted them.   And a blessed thing
it is for man that he should be susceptible of such religious
feelings whose warmth far exceeds all that he can give to
abstract law.   The strongest element in his nature is the
religious, which has engraved its name on every page of
his history, and set up its monuments over all the earth.
Volumes have been written on what may be called the
Physiology of Reformation and Regeneration; and so wonderful are these transformations of our nature, that it is small
marvel men have persisted in attributing to them a super-
natural origin.   But the truth appears to be what I have
stated;   namely, that in the conquest of the pure Will
over the desires, the victory is generally won and the scale
turned by the alliance of the pure Will with the religious sentiment.   The bare Law, our rightful sovereign, *may*, indeed,
and *ought*, to obtain our unqualified allegiance from the first;
and there are more minds than divines have reckoned upon
in whom this naked law does actually enforce its own right.
There are hundreds who are brought to the renunciation of
their sins, and the commencement of a true moral life, by the
mere comparison of themselves with the standard within them,
being, at the time (so far as their own consciousness goes),
altogether at a distance from God, and, perhaps, sceptical of
His existence.   But, on the other hand, there are thousands,
aye, millions, whose consciousness of God is clear and bright,
while that of the abstract Law is dim and confused.   In some
blessed moment the absolute Holiness of God blazes upon
their hearts.   In that personified law they first see what *are*
goodness, purity, and truth ; and by the same light they perceive all the hideousness of their evil passions, pollution, and
falsehood.   This sight of God's perfection produces love, which
is warmed still more by personal gratitude, and reaches its
climax where the soul recognises that God also loves *it*.   The
first result of Divine love is the desire to resemble, and to
please by resembling, the Object of our adoration.   Intuitively

we believe that God desires our Virtue, and is ready to aid it; intuitively we believe that He hears prayer.   Then we pray; and the lightning we have summoned comes down from heaven to " purge away our dross and take away all our tin."   The wondrous Palingenesia is accomplished !   Thence-forward the iron Moral Law binds our hearts, welded to the golden chain of piety towards Him who linked it around us at the first, and then drew it to Himself " with the cords of a man and the bands of love."

Be it remembered, however, first, that it is by no means *every* soul in which the resistance of the lower nature has been strong enough to make such contest and victory appreciable.   Secondly, that it is the wildest fanaticism to suppose that any moral Reformation or religious Regeneration can exclude future transgressions and future recurrence to fresh resolution and fresh repentance.   In more than one sense have the marvellous achievements of spiritual influence been mistaken for miracles.   But the imperfection of man remains the inevitable consequence of his finite condition. God inspires him, but he does not become *infallible;* God sanctifies him, but he does not become *impeccable.*

To return to the case of the man who is first awakened to moral life through Religion, and who thenceforth obeys the Moral Law *as* the Law of God.   Is there any contradiction here with what I asserted above; viz., that the resolution of man to obey the Moral Law is to be founded on the bare *right* of that law to command him?

Not so; for God, the true God, is the personified essential Law, and it is His right *as such* to command us that must be the determining motive of all acceptable service.*   Not on His greatness and power, not on His creating and preserving

---

* God, in giving us conscience, has implanted a principle within us which forbids us to prostrate ourselves before mere power.   Our Creator has, consequently, waived His own claims on our veneration and obedience any further than he discovers Himself to us in characters of benevolence, equity, and righteousness.   He rests His authority on the perfect coincidence of His will and government with those great principles of morality written in our souls.   He desires no worship but that which springs from our discernment of His rectitude and goodness.   He accepts no love but from those who can understand the nature and proofs of moral goodness.— *Channing's Works, People's edition,* b. i. p. 168.

K

benefits, not on His absolute mastery of our whole souls
and bodies, has He founded His claims to the obedience of
the creatures whom He has endowed with free rationality.
Were He as great and as powerful as He is, and *wicked* also,
the natures He has given us would forbid the worship of Him.
But He is the absolutely Good, the absolutely Holy. He
wrote the Moral Law in our hearts, *because it is His own,*—
the spontaneous law of a Perfect Will, unresisted by any lower
nature, and altogether complete and infinite. Thus, the pure
law which His finger traces on the fleshy tablets of our hearts
is at once simply the Moral Law and simply the Law of God.
In obeying it for its intrinsic right we may also obey Him for
His right founded on His identity with the Law. As we are
not to be Moral because it is Expedient, neither are we to be
Religious because God is Almighty. As we are not to be
Moral for sake of any End, neither are we to be Religious
for sake of any Reward. But in our heart of hearts we are
to swear obedience to the Pure Law, which we may, indeed,
in *thought* abstract from God, but which is impersonated in
Him alone.

Wherein lies now the difference between the Atheistic and
Theistic Moralist? The advantages are all on the side of the
Theist. Theoretically both admit that the law they find in
their hearts has absolute claim to their obedience. But to the
Atheist this law is an abstraction, — a holy and solemn and
beautiful Idea, but only an Idea, to which he gives no personality, nor, consequently, any of those sentiments which a
Person alone can call out. To the Theist the law has a
"habitation and a name." He impersonates it in that Being
to whom he traces every joy of his life, every lesson of his conscience, — the nearest, the kindest, the noblest of all Beings.
The Atheist may revere the law, but it is the Theist alone
who can love it.

This difference would subsist on the Atheist's own hypothesis, — that there be, in truth, no God; and that, consequently, his nature may be in complete and normal action
without piety. He must, however, admit that the personifi-
cation of the law in the Father and Judge of the Universe is
an *idea* (if, as he will have it, but a mistaken one) fraught

with, and filling the soul which receives it with, the energies
of love and confidence.*

But this Atheist's view of things is, in truth, an utterly
incomplete one.   There *is* a God; and man's nature, so far
from being entire without piety, is a mere mutilated fragment
of humanity till this keystone be added to the arch.   Speculations concerning what *would* be morals, *were* there no God,
may be useful, both in clearing our thoughts respecting the
reality of the Divine attributes, and also in teaching us to do
justice to those persons who, without consciously believing in
God, have yet practised virtue and loved that goodness which
He alone impersonates.   It is time to give over our bound-
less reprobation for Atheists like these, and reserve it for that
far direr sort who hate the character of the Holy One, and
so " choose darkness rather than light, *because their deeds are
evil.*"   The man whose intellect has been entangled in metaphysical subtleties till, in Pantheism or Atheism, he loses hold
of that personal God whose works and laws are still his delight, such a man is profoundly to be pitied.   His soul is like
the snow-clothed and sunless plains which stretch around the
poles.   While all the world beside is brightened by the orb
of day, over *his* frozen nature no sun arises to warm or cheer
through the long winter of his soul.   But this darkness is not
for ever; the morning shall yet break over every godless
heart, — a " day-spring from on high" arise over its desola-
tion, and *never* set again !   Not here, perhaps, not now, shall
the sleeping spirit awake to recognise the arms of love in
which it has been cradled all its life long; but " Death shall
illumine the Land of Dreams."   While we on earth are
speaking of " Shelley the Atheist," Shelley the Theist has
long ago learned in whose infinite Breast dwells that goodness
he loved so well.

But while pitying the Atheist's blindness to the Sun which
illumines our path, and doing justice to the strong Moral Will
which can keep him virtuous, without that piety which we
find to be Virtue's best ally, we yet must guard against de-
luding ourselves into the belief that his position is logically

* " The most agreeable reflection which it is possible for human imagination
to suggest, is that of genuine Theism."—HUME.

tenable. If, in a universe without a God, man could still be man, then, indeed, he might be perfectly moral, yet perfectly irreligious, as an orphan may be moral without filial piety. And this, to an honest Atheist, being subjectively true, such severance of morality and religion becomes *pro tempore* practicable for him, as a man who *believes* himself an orphan is morally in the same position as one whose parents are really dead. But to one who knows that there is a God, in whom the Moral Law is impersonated, there is no such irreligious morality allowable, any more than there is a morality without filial piety allowable to him who dwells beneath his parent's smile. The Theist *cannot* love the Holy Law without loving Him in whom it is impersonated; nor can he obey its behests of perfecting his own nature and returning gratitude for benefits, while he asks no grace from the enlightening Spirit, and returns no thanksgiving for infinite benedictions. The whole being of a man is fragmentary till he become religious. He is acephalous, monstrous—a temple without an altar; or rather (what Plutarch affirmed the world did not contain) a city without a temple. And as the inaction of any of the faculties or affections of humanity produces a dull, aching want, so the torpidity of the religious sentiment, being the very highest of our affections, entails after it the most woeful restless pain. We fly from one thing to another, to sensual pleasures, to earthly ambition, to knowledge; but the whole world offers no rest to the dove till it return to its ark. In human love we place, perhaps, our fondest hopes to satisfy our craving hearts. But not by such drops — the mere spray of the great Fountain— can our thirst be quenched. God, in His goodness, forbids that it should be so, till at last we find that He is himself—

> ———— "that One we seek
> When our blind, creeping souls explore
> Earth's desert cold and bleak.
> We seek for love, and find but woe,
> While He stands pitying by.
> We grieve o'er frailty, while we shrink
> From Infinite Purity.
> We mourn the absent—He is near;
> The dead—He liveth ever;
> The lost and fallen, the estranged,—
> The Eternal changeth never!"

WHY THE MORAL LAW SHOULD BE OBEYED. 133

On this whole subject I shall have much to say when I come to treat of Religious Duties as a branch of Practical Ethics. But before proceeding to any further investigation into the true motives of Morality, it was necessary to clear up all obscurity respecting their union with Religious Motives.

We *must*, then, love God for His own sake while we love the Law He impersonates for its own sanctity. There is no arbitrary choice. Religion is not a thing ulterior to Morality, to be dissevered from or amalgamated with it at pleasure. God and Goodness are identical. Our moral life and our religious life are indissolubly united. There is no Piety without Virtue, and (for him who believes in God) no true Virtue without Piety.

It is indeed true that in different constitutions the moral and religious elements develope themselves with very varied relative power, and it is even credible that in some the whole vigour of the latter never becomes manifest in this life.* Persons there are, of high moral attainments, full of reverence towards God, and anxious to perform all their duties towards Him, yet never, properly speaking, *loving* Him, never arriving at that culmination of Prayer where communion becomes conscious. This distinction has been much insisted on by religious writers of Pietist tendencies, and the line drawn between Spiritual and Unspiritual persons they have supposed to commence in the phenomena of Regeneration. Undoubtedly, when that wondrous change is strongly marked, the soul does commonly enter into spiritual relation with God simultaneously with, or rather antecedently to, its moral palingenesia. But, as I have said, these violent revulsions are not the invariable, or even perhaps the ordinary rule, of either spiritual or moral development. In a child properly trained, the commencement of true love to God, and the solemn adoption of the Moral Law are events unaccompanied by those throes which great previous errors entail on the New Birth. And though it must be thought that fresh spiritual life will always impart fresh activity to the moral, the converse will not invariably hold good. It may be long years before the best

* See some admirable remarks on this subject in J. J. Tayler's *Christian Aspects of Faith and Duty*, p. 45.

Reformed Moralist become truly Spiritual; his natural progress being stopped by a false creed or some similar cause. All the ordinary theories, then, on the subject seem to be one-sided. Some writers tell us that there is no Morality without Religion, and no Religion without strongly marked Regeneration. Others again insist, that the distinctions of Spiritual and Unspiritual natures are constitutional and indelible as those to which they liken them, of Feminine and Masculine. But the truth is, that Morality may exist in an Atheist without any Religion, and in a Theist with a Religion quite Unspiritual. Nor does Spiritual Religion necessarily involve a marked Regeneration. Nor, finally (and this is the most important), does it at all appear that the distinctions of Spiritual and Unspiritual are anything more than differences in the *Growth* of different souls. A very interesting chapter it would be in our psychology to trace the varied developments of Conscience and the Religious Sentiment in persons of different temperament and placed under different circumstances. But, I repeat, it seems to me a grievous practical error to teach that these distinctions are not to be utterly merged in the normal development of the soul; that we are not to hold out to every one the anticipation of the very highest spiritual communion as the natural landmark of his progress. It is impossible but that the infinite Father must mean all His children sooner or later consciously to enjoy the unutterable bliss of His present Love; and whether in this life we all succeed in obtaining it, or whether many of us know it only in a future world, still it is the birthright of all our race, and it ought to be also the recognised aspiration of all our hearts. Whenever we fail of this there is wrong *somewhere;* perhaps in some theoretic error, giving to us a God we cannot wholly love; perhaps in some practical callousness and indolence of our hearts resting satisfied with a little, instead of hungering after more.

Never, then, must man deem he is fulfilling the end of his being, while he is moral without Religion, or religious without Spirituality. Separate may be their sources, and unequal their strength; but the two streams must become confluent at last, and the clear waters from the celestial Fount of

Piety must mingle with the strong current of Virtuous Will to bear onward the soul to its perfection.*

But, just as pure Morality must be a disinterested thing, so must all pure Religion be disinterested. It is a mournful matter that this simple truth should need to be insisted on; that people should go about hunting for reasons and motives, hopes and fears, why we should love the All-lovely! After all, what is the deepest want of our hearts? Is it not " some One to Love?" Some Being who fulfils to the uttermost all our dreams of Goodness, some Being who will love us infinitely, immutably, eternally? Human friends, parent, child, wife, brother, fulfil our cravings in this respect very poorly and partially; yet we love *them* each for his own sake, and would deem it foulest insult to be told " we *ought* to love our mother, or she will disinherit us, our child that he may support our old age." Is it only a dowry a husband loves in his bride? or the strength of his arm which binds a wife to her husband? But if the poor love of earth can be disinterested, who shall dare to soil our Piety with threats and bribes? † Who shall say that a good *man* can be loved for his own sake, but not God, *He* is not good enough!

It is only in the disinterested Love and Obedience to God, and the Law He personifies, that human nature assumes its true dignity. So long as the Love of God is only the love of the favoured slave to a Master whom he believes to be cruel and unjust to his fellow-servants; so long as the Obedience to the Law is only a judicious bargain between penalties and gratifications, so long is man in a merely childish and animal condition; his Piety is rather canine love than human reverential adoration; his Morality is the obedience of a horse guided by the bridle and driven by the whip, not the loyalty of the Freeman to the Law of his "great city of the universe."

But it is disinterested Love and Obedience I am persuaded which *practically* (though commonly unconsciously) lie at the

* In Francis Newman's noble book, *The Soul*, this distinction of the Spiritual and Unspiritual is supposed to be indelible (see p. 141.). I cannot, without the utmost diffidence, put forth an opinion in opposition to that of one I so much revere.

† "Deus colitur et amatur. Non potest amor cum timore misceri."—SENECA, *Ep.* xlii.

bottom of nearly all the Religion and Virtue the world has
honoured. Now and then they break out in clear expression. The Hebrew cries, "Though He slay me yet will I
trust in Him." * The Roman, throwing open to doubt his
Immortality, adds, "But what will all this be to me? *I
shall have done my Duty!*" † Yet such manifestations of
the true foundations of Piety and Virtue are very rare. Few
indeed have been the *theoretic* divines or moralists who have
acknowledged them at all, much less made them the bases of
their systems; consequently their disciples, though imbued
perhaps with genuine love of God and goodness, accustom
themselves to set forth in their own minds as the proper
stimulants to Piety and Virtue, those motives of interest
which are in reality corrupting to and destructive of them
both.

The motive, then, of our Virtue must be simply this:
Reverence for the Moral Law as the Law of the Eternal
Right impersonated in the All-righteous God.

If our virtue have *this* motive, there is no fear that it will
confine itself to the mere outward Actions, which alone the
care of Health, Wealth, Reputation, or the like Eudaimonist
motives can demand of it. The Moral Law requires us to
feel the *Sentiments* which are Right no less than to do the
Actions of a corresponding character. If, then, we revere the
Law for its own sake, we shall obey it, as much in controlling the Sentiments or Inward Actions of our hearts, as in
controlling the outward deeds of our hands. As the subject
of these sentiments is a somewhat obscure one, some attempt
at explanation of it may be desirable.

---

* JOB, xiii. 15. There is a prayer of Ibn Zaffer, a Sicilian Arab of the 12th century, so sublime that I shall be pardoned for quoting it in connection with the
above. It begins thus : " O Thou who beholdest my state, and knowest that of
necessity I cannot do otherwise than be content with it, Thou from whom there
is neither refuge nor defence, let not Thy power and greatness suffer that he
whom Thou protectest should perish. But if it be Thy pleasure that he should
perish, behold me ready for whatever Thou mayest appoint. Every chastisement which cometh from Thee shall be sweet to me, excepting separation from
Thee."—*Solwân*, iv. It is little known how beautiful are many of the Moslem
prayers. That which is daily used by the Muezzins includes a sentence the
compendium of all prayer: "Thou art to me all that I desire ; make me to
Thee what Thou desirest, O Thou the most merciful of the merciful ! "
† Seneca.

The Science of Morals does not include necessarily a perfect system of Psychology; else were it beyond human attainment. The emotions and conditions of our intellectual, affectional, and sensual natures, are for ever receiving fresh classification and new nomenclature, and the very subtlest investigation fails to afford a thoroughly satisfactory result. But for the Moralist this is unnecessary. He observes and admits that the lower nature is by its constitution subject to sudden spontaneous Emotions of various kinds, which arise on their appropriate representation being made to the sensory. These Emotions, and the no less spontaneous Thoughts, called forth without any act of choice on our parts, cannot have a Moral character, for with regard to them we are not free agents. But, beside these *involuntary*, spontaneous thoughts and emotions, there are also an immense number of thoughts and emotions quite voluntary. When the outer world offers no interruption, we may force ourselves to Think at will on one matter or another; when the first sudden Emotion has passed, we may compel ourselves to Feel to some extent (and that is the extent of the Moral character of the feeling) as our Will ordains. Now, these *voluntary* Thoughts and prolonged Emotions which may be called " Sentiments" have (as I asserted at the opening of this book) a Moral character of Right and Wrong no less real than that of Actions. As an Act is eternally distinguished as Right or Wrong for a rational free agent to do, so a Sentiment is eternally distinguished as Right or Wrong for him to feel. The power of the Will is no less called upon to control those desires which would nourish thoughts and emotions of anger, till they became the Sentiment of malevolence, than it is called upon to control the desire which would make the hand strike the offender. The *whole* nature must be subdued by the Will to obedience to the Law. If the Thoughts be not pure, outward purity is the whiteness of the sepulchre; if the Feelings be not charitable, to give all our goods to feed the poor profiteth nothing.*

---

* In popular phraseology, these sentiments are confounded with the Will; and we talk of a " good will," or a " bad will" (benevolence or malevolence) to-towards a person. This is, of course, inadmissible in a scientific statement of

We may consider, in fact, that whenever the desires of
our lower nature clash with the requirements of the Eternal
Law, there are two actions of the Will necessary to achieve
the victory which constitutes Virtue. It must co-act the
outward bodily deed, and it must co-act the inward sentiment. The man must forgive his enemy in his heart as well
as in external manifestation ; he must feel Benevolence for
the poor as well as display Beneficence ; he must be Single-
hearted as well as Veracious ; he must be Pure in thought as
well as Chaste in deed ; he must love God as well as pay Him
outward homage.

Nay, in the co-action of the Sentiment lies in truth the
decision of the whole battle ; for if the sentiment be brought
into accordance with the Law, if the man be forgiving,
benevolent, single-hearted, pure, and pious, there is no
danger but that he will also be merciful, beneficent, veracious,
chaste, and reverent. But, on the other hand, it is perfectly
possible that he may outwardly show obedience to the Law,
may be externally merciful, beneficent, veracious, chaste, and
reverent, and yet may be inwardly implacable, malevolent,
double-minded, impure, and irreligious. Therefore, to control our Thoughts and Emotions at the very first moment that
the Will can reach them, to secure that the first spontaneous
impulse shall never pass into the condition of a Sentiment
until it has been brought into harmony with the Law, this is
the great work of the Moral life.

The Sentiments are, in fact, collaterally with the true
holy Will, the springs of our outward actions. Taking their
rise among the desires of our intellectual, affectional, and
sensual natures ; passing through the stage of spontaneous and

the case. The *true* Will is *always* benevolent and altogether righteous. It is
the weakness and failure of the true Will, under the temptations of the lower
nature, which produces malevolence and other evil sentiments.

How far Intuitive Morals are sundered in the doctrines of which we are now
treating from those of Eudaimonism may be seen by a reference to the following
passage in Bentham's *Introduction to the Principles of Morals*, p. 169. : " There
is no such thing as any sort of motive that is in itself a bad one. Let a man's
motive be ill-will; call it even malice, envy, cruelty—it is still a kind of Pleasure
that is his motive, the pleasure he takes at the thought of the pain which he sees
his adversary undergo. Now even this wretched pleasure taken by itself is
good : it may be faint; it may be short ; it must at any rate be impure ; yet
while it lasts, and before any bad consequences arrive, it is as good as any other
that is not more intense ! "

involuntary Thoughts and Emotions, they reach their full growth, and become the Sentiments of love, gratitude, veneration, and the like, or of hatred, malice, and contempt.   In the cold temperament, and under ordinary conditions, they continue as these Sentiments; in warmer natures, or under special excitement, they become Passions.   Now, the primary constitutional desires of our nature, and the spontaneous Thoughts and Emotions called forth in us by the objects presented to us by the external world, have no control over our actions, (or, at least when they do spasmodically affect the muscles of our limbs, we do not consider such motions as real actions;) but just at the point in which they enter under the dominion of the Will they simultaneously become practical. The sentiment, and, *à fortiori*, the sentiment risen to a passion, is a direct spring of action.   It stands for the time being as the representative of the whole lower nature.   If the true Will do not exert its supremacy, the Sentiment inevitably works its way.   If the true Will exert itself, it may enforce the outward Action without subduing the Sentiment, or it may both enforce the Action and subdue the Sentiment into harmony with the Law.   It is to be remarked, however, that the point in which the Sentiment passes from a blind, irresistible impulse into the dominion of the Will, is one of difficult appreciation.   We are of course bound to *endeavour* to co-act our thoughts and emotions from the first; but there is many a case in which we are called upon to perform the right Action before it is within our power to feel the right Sentiment.   In this, as in all other cases, the bounds of our Freedom are those of our responsibility; and if we cannot do more than we actually accomplish, that which we perform constitutes Virtue.

Thus, in speaking of a " Virtuous Action," we in fact use a figure of speech to imply an action in which both the pure Will (which is always in accordance with the Law), and the Sentiment (which may or may not be in accordance with it), have both been manifested; or (more properly still), we imply " an action in which the pure Will has been manifested in the totality of its authority over both the inward sentiment and outward deed."

Further, as the Pure Will, the true self of man, is *always* legislative of the Eternal Law, Virtue must consist, not in the mere feeble willing to do right, *if* no temptation of the lower nature intervene; but in the willing it *so strongly*, that the temptation be actually resisted, and the lower nature borne down.   Virtue cannot consist in *having* a higher nature irrevocably self-legislative of the Right, and interested therein by the Moral Sense of joy in its fulfilment; for no man can divest himself of this nature, which is his true Self.   Virtue must consist in giving to this glorious nature its domination over our whole being, over the sentiment of the heart and the action of the hand.   Therefore, when it is asked, whether a Will can be accounted Virtuous which does *not* manifest itself in action,—the answer is clear.   If the action be practicable for him, and the man, instead of performing it, merely feebly wishes it were to be done with less cost,—if he indolently say, " Be ye warmed and fed, while he gives not those things which are necessary," then he is guilty not of a particular *kind* of sin, but of that which is the *only* possible sin, the abdication of the practical authority of the Will over the lower nature.   " *All* immorality in actual life results from the collision of the Good with the Agreeable, of the Desires with the Reason."*   To call a man Virtuous who professes to Will to do Right, and never *does* that Right, though it lie in his power, is utter absurdity.   The same may be said of the worst created being in the universe, " He *would* do Right, *only* he prefers to do Wrong.

On the other hand, when a right action is physically impracticable to a man who has a Will to do it so strong that he would have accomplished it had it been within his power, and who has brought his Sentiment into full accordance with the duty (as, for example, when he feels entire benevolence towards his neighbour, and would give him bread if he had it to give), then, undoubtedly, such strong Will and right Sentiment are " counted to him for righteousness."   He has exercised such Moral Freedom as pertained to him in choosing the Right and bringing his Sentiment into harmony therewith.   It is no fault of his that his Personal Freedom does not extend to the ex-

* Philosophic and Æsthetic Letters of Schiller, p. 203.

ternal act which would manifest his Will and Sentiment. "All virtuous actions," says Confucius, "all duties which have been resolved beforehand, are *thereby* accomplished." That is to say, the Virtue is achieved when the Will has gained its victory.

I have now to the best of my ability defined what Virtue, according to Intuitive Morality, really is. I have affirmed that it is the " Voluntary and Disinterested Obedience of a Free Rational Intelligence to the Eternal Law." I have affirmed that such Disinterested Obedience must be motived solely by pure Love of God and Goodness, and must be carried out by the subordination of all our Sentiments as well as Actions, to that Law of Right which equally refers to them both.

From this System of Morals I turn to the other Ethical Schemes which prevail in the world, for the purpose of en- deavouring, by displaying the most glaring of their incon- sistencies, to give to Intuitive Morals the only demonstration which such axiomatic truths are able to receive, namely, the negative. I shall attempt (without venturing on any la- boured refutation of adverse systems) to prove simply, that absurdity is involved in every one which proposes, as a motive for the performance of duty, any other principle than that disinterested allegiance to the Law which is inculcated by Intuition. In the last Chapter I endeavoured to show the *philosophical fallacy* involved in all Moral Systems which pro- fess to be founded on the Experience of the Senses. I shall now attempt to show the *moral heresy* of all those which make any kind of Pleasure or Pain the motive of Virtue.

And, first, as a preliminary observation concerning them, I may remark, that they necessarily abandon the station of the ethical Law, and become *technical,* mere *Arts* to reach a given end. And so, indeed, Morals were long ago de- scribed as

" Ars bene beateque vivendi."*

---

* Henry More, Encheiridion Ethicum.

Thus, like every other art, the Art of being Blessed will
have a good method, and a better, and a best; and a bad
method, a worse, and a worst. We have quitted the region
of absolute, immutable, Necessary Truth, of Positive Right,
and its Negation, Wrong; and we may for the future study
the doctrine of chances, and invent " hedges " and " martin-
gales " to the best of our ability.

I have already stated, in Chapter I., that Happiness,
properly speaking, is the gratification of all the desires of our
compound nature, and that moral, intellectual, affectional,
and sensual pleasures are all to be considered as integers,
whose sum, when complete, would constitute perfect Happiness.* From this multiform nature of Happiness it has
arisen, that those Systems of Ethics which set it forth as the
proper motive of Virtue have differed immensely from one
another, according as the Happiness they respectively contemplated was thought of as consisting in the pleasures of
our Moral, or of our Intellectual, Affectional, and Sensual
natures; whether the pleasures were to be sought by the
virtuous man for his *own* enjoyment, or for the *general*
happiness of the community,

The pursuit of Virtue for the sake of its intrinsic, *i. e.*
Moral pleasure, I have already designated Euthumism.

The pursuit of Virtue for the sake of the extrinsic Affectional, Intellectual, and Sensual pleasure resulting from it
I have designated Eudaimonism.

Euthumism is of one kind only; for the individual can
only seek the intrinsic pleasure of Virtue for his *own* enjoy
ment thereof. Though (as Benevolence is a Virtue having

---

* " The Cyrenaic sect dissected eagerly the nature of that 'Ηδονή (Happiness)
they considered as the *summum Bonum*. They agreed it " consisted in the as-
semblage of all particular pleasures ;" but they placed the pleasures of the body
so far before those of the soul, that it appeared doubtful whether any intellectual or affectional pleasure should be accorded the name. They said that a
man might possibly receive pleasure from some propitious event occurring to
his country ; but not from either hope or memory. Wisdom, they said, was not
desirable for itself, but only for the advantages derivable from it (an opinion
which will be found broadly stated by Beattie in his *Essay on Truth*) ; and, so
far from admitting moral pleasures, they affirmed that 'no pleasure was to be
reckoned less a good because its cause was shameful.' The Hegesiac and An-
nicerian branches disputed whether friendship and beneficence were goods,
i. e., pleasures ; and whether we do well to maintain them when they can no
longer maintain us."— DIOG. LAERT. *Aristip.*

its intrinsic pleasure), he will reflectively desire that his fellow-creatures should also enjoy the happiness of Virtue, yet *their* joy cannot become *his* primary end; his desire of it is for his *own* Moral pleasure in such desire.

Eudaimonism, on the contrary, is of two most distinct kinds. That which I have called Public Eudaimonism sets forth the intellectual, affectional, and sensual pleasures of all mankind as the proper object of the Virtue of each individual. Private Eudaimonism sets forth the same pleasures of the individual himself as the proper object of his Virtue.

These two latter systems are commonly confounded under the name of "Utilitarian Ethics." Their principles, as I have stated them, will be seen to be wide asunder; yet there are few of the advocates of either who have not endeavoured to stand on the grounds of both, and even to borrow elevation from those of the Euthumist. Thus, by appealing alternately to philanthropy and to a gross and a refined selfishness, they suit the purpose of the moment, and prevent their scheme from deviating too far from the Intuitive Conscience of mankind. It may be remarked, also, that the Private Eudaimonists insist more particularly on the Pleasures of a Future Life, and in the exposition of them necessarily approach nearer to the Euthumists.

I shall now discuss the three systems which have arisen from the different views of Happiness, each contemplating it as the proper motive of Virtue; namely, 1st, Euthumism; 2nd, Public Eudaimonism; and, 3rd, Private Eudaimonism. This done, I shall add a short analysis of an Ethical Scheme of an opposite kind — namely, the Law of Honour.

1st. Euthumism. This system, as I have said, sets forth the Moral Pleasure, the peace and cheerfulness of mind, and applause of conscience enjoyed in Virtue as the proper motive for its practice. Conversely, it sets forth as the dissuadent from Vice, the pain of remorse, the inward uneasiness and self-contempt which belong to it.

Democritus appears to have been the first who gave clear

utterance to this doctrine, maintaining that Εὐθυμία was the
proper End of human actions, and sharply distinguishing it
from the Ἡδονή proposed as such by Aristippus.* The
claims of a " *mens conscia recti* " to be the " *Summum bonum*,"
occupied, as is well known, a large portion of the subsequent
disputes of the Epicureans, Cynics, Stoics, and Academics,
and were eagerly argued by Cicero, and even down to the
time of Boethius. Many of these sects, however, and in
particular the Stoics, though maintaining that Virtue alone
was sufficient for Happiness (that is, that the inward joy of
Virtue was enough to constitute Happiness in the midst of
torments), yet by no means set forth that Happiness as the
sole motive of Virtue. They held, on the contrary, the
noblest ideas of "living according to Nature," that is, as
Chrysippus explained it, according to the " Nature of the
universe, the common Law of all, which is the right reason
spread everywhere, the same by which Jupiter governs the
world ; " and that *both* Virtue and Happiness consisted in so
regulating our actions that they should produce harmony
between the Spirit in each of us, and the Will of Him who
rules the universe." † There is little or no trace of Euthumism in the Jewish or Christian Scriptures, or (to my
knowledge) in the sacred books of the Brahmins, Buddhists,
or Parsees. The ethical problems argued by the mediæval

"The end of our actions is Εὐθυμία, not such as can be confounded with
Ἡδονή, as some have falsely understood ; but that which places the mind in a
state of perfect peace ; so that, being constantly satisfied, it is troubled neither
by fear nor superstition, or by any other passion. This state is the true state
of the soul."—Diog. Laert. *Democritus.*

† Diog. Laert. *Zeno.* The precise nature of the pleasure which Epicurus
made the end of our actions is a matter of considerable obscurity. The following passage would seem to class him as a Euthumist : " The virtues have nothing
to make them desirable by themselves, but from the pleasure which results from
their acquisition. But it is only Virtue which is inseparable from pleasure ; all
the other things which are attached to it are but evanescent accidents." (Diog.
Laert. *Epicurus.*) If Epicurus meant that any intellectual, affectional, or sensual pleasure was inseparable from Virtue he was absurdly mistaken. Is it not
more probable that he meant that moral pleasure which is intrinsic in it ? Adam
Smith (*Theory of the Moral Sentiments*, p. 441. *et seq.*) gives a long analysis of
the doctrines of Epicurus, who as he affirms starts with the assumption that bodily
pleasure and pain are the sole *ultimate* objects of desire and aversion, but per-
ceiving that those of the mind (*founded* on hope and fear for those of the body)
are more vivid and durable, teaches that these are to be primarily considered.
I confess I cannot find Smith's authority for attributing these definite views to
Epicurus.

schoolmen do not, so far as I am aware, embrace the subject in question. The doctrine was revived, however, in the seventeenth century, and, besides blending with more or less distinctness with the views of a vast number of lesser moralists, it reckons among its professed adherents no less names than Henry More and Bishop Cumberland.* Euthumism, philosophically considered, will be found to affix itself most properly on the doctrine of the " Moral Sense " laid down by Shaftesbury as the origin of our *knowledge* of moral distinctions ; which, if it *were*, it would naturally follow that it must afford also the right *motive* of Virtue. Hutcheson, also, still more distinctly stated that this Moral Pleasure in Virtue (which both he and Shaftesbury likened to the æsthetic Pleasure in Beauty) was the true grounds of our choice.† To this Balguy replied, " that to make the rectitude of moral actions depend upon instinct, and, in proportion to the warmth and strength of the Moral Sense, rise and fall like spirits in a thermometer, is depreciating the most sacred thing in the world, and almost exposing it to ridicule."‡ And Whewell has shown very neatly that the doctrine of the Moral Sense as the foundation of Morals must always fail, whether understood as meaning a sense like that of Beauty, (which may or may not be merely a modification of the agreeable), or a sense like those of touch or taste (which no one can fairly maintain that any of our moral perceptions really resemble). §

But, though neither the true source of our *Knowledge* of Moral Distinctions, nor yet the right *Motive* why we are to choose the Good, this Moral Sense of Pleasure in Virtue and Pain in Vice is a psychological fact demanding the investigation of the Moralist.   Moreover, the error of allowing our moral choice to be decided by a regard to the pure joy of Virtue or awful pangs of self-condemnation, is an error so

---

* Sharrock appears to have been the first English moralist by whom it was clearly stated. See his Ὑπόθεσις ἠθική,, published in 1660. Cumberland held that "the Common Good is the Sovereign Law," and that the Pleasure we feel in Benevolence and Piety, is the right Motive for being Benevolent and Pious. See *Les Lois de la Nature Expliquées. Traduits par* BARBEYRAC, p. 42., and Chap. v.
† Inquiry into the Ideas of Beauty and Virtue.
‡ Inquiry concerning Virtue, 1726.
§ Whewell, Hist. Moral Phil. in Eng.

venial in comparison of other moral heresies, and so easily to
be confounded with a truer principle of Morals, that it is
particularly necessary to warn generous natures against it.
" It is quite beyond the grasp of human thought," says Kant,
" to explain how Reason can be practical; how the mere
Morality of the Law, independently of every object man can
be interested in, can itself beget an interest which is purely
Ethical; how a naked thought, containing in it nothing
of the sensory, can bring forth an emotion of pleasure or
pain. Reason thus appears to have a causality of a peculiar
kind of its own, a power of begetting a feeling of *amenity* in
the discharge of duty; and this power of the Reason to
attach an interest of its own to the performance of its behests was undoubtedly necessary for beings like ourselves,
affected by sensitive excitements totally different in kind
from the causal laws of Reason." This is the Internal (as
all Nature is the External) system of Rewards and Punishments wherewith our Father guides his children towards the
blessed end of their creation, and upholds the *Justitia rectoria* of the universe. Unconsciously, this Sense of Pleasure
in a Virtuous Act, the thought of the peace of conscience
which will follow it, or the dread of remorse for its neglect,
must *mingle* with our motives. But we can never be permitted consciously to exhibit them to ourselves as the ground
of our resolution to obey the Law. That Law is not valid
for man *because it interests him*, but it interests him *because
it has validity for him* — because it springs from his true
being, his proper self. The interest he feels is an Effect,
not a Cause; a Contingency, not a Necessity. Were he to
obey the Law merely from this Interest, it would not be
Free Self-legislation (autonomy), but (heteronomy) subser-
vience of the Pure Will to a lower faculty — a Sense of Pleasure. And practically we may perceive that all manner of
mischiefs and absurdities must arise if a man set forth Moral
Pleasure as the determinator of his Will. For, in the first
place, one who should systematically set about acting for the
applause of his conscience would naturally listen with unbounded self-gratulation to such applause, for which he would
soon begin to substitute the voice of his own spiritual pride.
A man who should say, " I will do this act of self-denial to

enjoy to-night the approbation of my conscience," would at night, in all probability, endeavour to solicit such applause, which the error of his motive had forfeited. It is difficult to imagine what moral disorders might not arise from persistence in such a system. On the other hand, if, instead of the future approbation of his conscience, it is the present momentary instinct of Moral Pleasure to which he consciously yields, the man will not only enervate and degrade his higher nature from the Stoic dignity which belongs to it, to the mere "good nature" of a moral Sybarite, he will also find his guide forsake him at the entrance of all the more rugged and thorny of the paths of Virtue. There appear to be many acts commanded by the Moral Law, in whose performance the best of men feel a Pain far in excess of the Pleasure derived from the Moral Sense of the performance of duty. For example, the punishment of a criminal, the reproof of a child, the renunciation of an unworthy friend, the bearing witness against a parent; would it not be absurd to represent the *Pleasure* to be taken in such acts as the proper motive for their performance?

Thus, the maxim of Euthumism " Be virtuous for the sake of the Moral Pleasure of Virtue," may be pronounced false.

2nd. Public Eudaimonism sets forth, both as the ground of our knowledge of Virtue and the motive for our practice of it, " The Greatest Happiness of the Greatest Number." This Happiness, as Paley understood it, is composed of Pleasures to be estimated only by their Intensity and Duration ; or, as Bentham added, by their Certainty, Propinquity, Fecundity, and Purity (a freedom from admixture of evil).* It is, as I have before remarked, with Pleasures of the *lower* nature, with intellectual, affectional, and sensual Pleasures, that this system and that of Private Eudaimonism properly concern themselves.

Though Paley has counted the Moral Pleasure of Virtue as among the integers of the Happiness he sets forth as our proper end, no Public or Private Eudaimonist can be permitted in logic to make such claim. The Public Eudaimonist professes to found his *knowledge* of Right and Wrong on the ascertained results

* BENTHAM, *Introd. Principles of Morals*, p. 51.

of actions, and to reduce his Morals to an inductive science
founded on ascertained facts. The inward Joy of Virtue must
be confessed to be a thing wholly inappreciable by the profoundest Statistician. He may construct tables of the health
and sickness, wealth and poverty of the community; but of
the self-applause of Virtue and the hidden pangs of Remorse
he cannot possibly take account. And as to the Private Eudaimonist, " if he were to found his ethical science on his
own experience, and say, " *I* find both a Moral Pleasure intrinsic in Virtue, and a Sensual Pleasure extrinsic to but re-
sultant from it, and I will pursue it for the sake of both,"
he also would act illogically. If he make the *Moral* Pleasure
of a good action his aim, he cannot at the same time aim at
that exterior reward, to place which before him as an End
would wholly prevent the enjoyment of the Moral Pleasure.
The true pure Will is not to be cheated into bestowing its
own peculiar joy. Conscience knows very well whether a
man have aimed at any external reward here or hereafter, for
his action, and if he have done so she leaves him to felicitate
himself in the enjoyment or anticipation of it. But *her* joy
he tastes not, that is reserved for him who disinterestedly
obeys her mandates. Nay, it is only when an action is in the
highest possible degree disinterested that this true Moral Pleasure is felt. Eudaimonists confound *Affectional* with *Moral*
Pleasures when they imagine they enjoy the latter for an
action done from motives of interest. Let us suppose a case
of a simple kind. A. (in accordance with the dictates of
Paley) does an act of charity to B., aiming thereby to
enjoy a Moral Pleasure, to gain the gratitude of B., and
to increase his own chance of everlasting Happiness   What
is the result? He does gain the gratitude of B. and feels in
the belief of it a pleasure which he mistakes for the Moral
Pleasure of benevolence. It is no such thing. It is an *Affectional* Pleasure, perfectly innocent and natural, but having
nothing in common with the approbation of conscience. But
let him, on the contrary, have so managed his charity that B.
has no knowledge of his benefactor, and let him be entirely
free from all thought of buying the rewards of heaven. What
will he now feel? He receives no gratitude, he entertains
no new hope; but his inmost soul glows with the conscious-

ness that he has done Right for the Right's own sake; he feels a throb of joy, not having its origin in any gratified desire, but swelling up from the very depths of his being where dwells the true Self of Self whose law he has obeyed.   His Moral Sense enjoys its highest gratification.

In refuting erroneous systems it is not our business to concern ourselves with the illogical divagations of their adherents. In treating, therefore, of Public and subsequently of Private Eudaimonism, I shall assume that they confine their objects to the Pleasures of Intellect, Affection, and Sense, entering a protest against any disciple of either scheme making use of arguments drawn from Euthumism, and observing, that even if he be permitted to do so, that system has been refuted in the last pages.

Public Eudaimonism, then, as I have said, sets forth as the end of Virtue, "the Greatest Happiness of the Greatest Number." * Let it be granted, for argument sake, that the calculable Happiness resulting from actions can determine their Virtue (although all experience teaches that resulting Happiness is not calculable, and that the Virtue must at least be one of the items determining the resulting Happiness).   On the Utilitarian's own assumption, what sort of a motive for Virtue can be his end of "the Greatest Happiness of the Greatest Number ? "

In the first place, this doctrine distinctly sets forth, as I have said, the *Happiness* of mankind as the highest of all

---

* This celebrated formula Bentham borrowed from Priestley.   Public Eudaimonism, however, as I have described it, is not Benthamry   It must not be supposed that Bentham taught that this end of the " Greatest Happiness of the Greatest Number " was to be pursued by the Individual disinterestedly.   His whole system may be summed up in the following passage in the *Deontology*, (p. 17).   " What is Happiness ?   It is the possession of Pleasure, with the exemption from Pain.   What is Virtue ?   It is that which most contributes to Happiness, that which Maximises Pleasures and Minimises Pains.   The first law of nature is to wish our own happiness ; and the united voices of Prudence and Efficient Benevolence [the two sole Virtues in his system] add, Seek the Happiness of others,—seek your own happiness in the Happiness of others."— So far is he from admitting of Disinterested Virtue, that he affirms that if a man give up a larger pleasure of his own for a smaller one of his neighbours his action by diminishing the general amount of Happiness becomes one, not of Virtue, but of *Folly*."—(*Deon.*, p. 191).   If we may judge from indications in the late literature of the subject, these views of Bentham's have been considerably modified and given a more generous extension by his living followers.   I wish it to be understood that Public Eudaimonism, as I have above defined it, cannot properly be reckoned as the system of Bentham, who personally approached much nearer to Private Eudaimonism.

aims, the acknowledged end of human existence; that is
simply the sum of the pleasures of our intellectual, affectional, and sensual natures, which pleasures are calculable
only by their intensity, duration, certainty, propinquity,
fecundity, and freedom from admixture of pain.*

But whatever be in truth this wondrous multiform nature
of man, is he, after all, capable of nothing nobler, nothing
purer, no higher conception, no more exalted aspiration, than
that same *Happiness?*   What think you, reader?   I can but
appeal to your consciousness; how seems it to you?   Is
" Excelsior " a " *strange* device?"   Build yourself up in
thought a " Palace of Art" like Tennyson's, a " Palace of
the Senses" like Vathek's.   People them with the Affections
in all their brightest forms; dream that Pain and Sorrow,
Poverty and Death, are banished from the earth, and all the
human race as *happy* as yourself; then roll out the glowing
panorama into Eternity, and say, is it complete?   Methinks
there are few who will say " Yes!"

There comes from the very heart of humanity an echo to the
exclamation of Antoninus, " There is something more worthy
of goodness and truth than to save or be saved."†   At first
outset of existence we are all of one language and one speech.
We cry, " Let us build us up a Tower of Pleasure which shall
reach to heaven."   But God confounds our presumption, and
after we have wandered over the wilderness of life, we gaze
and marvel in old age at the ruins of the Titan ambition of
our youth.   There lie, burnt out and cold, the walls of the
Senses, once so strong that they hid the Inner Soul; there
lie the shattered sculptures of the Intellect; but the pure
gold of the Affections we find it not—it is molten and lost.

There are very few who think that *Sensual* pleasures can
fill their souls, even when gilded over by all the refinements
of art.   I do not mean to undervalue such enjoyments; they
are far greater than sour fanatics would have us believe.   To
be surrounded by beauty, music, perfume; to luxuriate in

---

* In Jeremy Bentham's strange book the *Table of the Springs of Action,* he
classes all the possible interests of humanity as follows:— 1st. Interest of the
Palate.—2. Sexual Interests.—3. Interest of the Senses.—4. Of the Purse.—
5. Of the Sceptre.—6. Of the Spying-glass.—7. Of the Closet.—8. Of the
Trumpet.—9. Of the Altar.—10. Of the Heart.—11. Of the Gall-bladder.—
12. Of the Pillow.—13. Of Existence.

† Medit. b. vii.

glorious gardens and dwell in stately chambers where the ear
meets no discords, the eye no vulgar forms, no jarring colours;
to find the wheels of our animal life glide over the smooth rails
laid down by Civilization and Wealth—all this is no mean
matter.   It is a *great Happiness*, let philosophers and senti-
mentalists say what they will.   The Eye and Ear of man are
the two most perfect of the physical works of God on our
planet; and their highest gratifications, so far from being trifles,
are things for which we are bound to return fervent thanks.
The Senses are *much*, but they are not *enough*; the lowest
Vitellius among us dreams of something more.

The *Affections* are not enough.   There are some who doubt
this, because among human desires the gratification of our
desire for Love is the one most rarely tasted, and the disap-
pointments we experience we are always inclined to attribute
to some individual failing rather than to the inevitable conditions of human imperfection.   But the truth is, that human
Love would *never* satisfy our infinite longings.   Rousseau
said well, " Ce que les créatures peuvent occuper du cœur
humain est si peu de chose, que quand on croit l'avoir rempli
d'eux, il est encore vide.   Il faut un objet infini pour le
remplir."

The *Intellect* is not enough.   Knowledge comes nearer to
Happiness in minds which have once awakened to its joy
than either the pleasures of the Senses, which are less pure
and exalted, or those of the Affections, which are less within
our own reach less calm in the enjoyment, and less secure
from loss.   But in truth the glorious thirst after Knowledge
never finds its life-long draught sweet enough, if it merge not
into the still nobler " Thirst after Righteousness," and add to
Knowledge Virtue, and to Virtue Religion.   It is the Moral
and Religious views of the subjects opened to us by Science
which give them their true grandeur and interest.   History
and Statistics only acquire their meaning when we trace in
them the progress which Providence works out for our race,
and when we deduce from them the proper means of accele-
rating that progress.   Exact Science is cold till it wring from
us the cry of the sage of old—

" Geometry is the praise of God !"

The earth is an illegible tablet till our enlightened eye
learns to read on its rocks the record that —

> " The Power which made the gold.
> The iron, the coal, and the stone,
> To be man's Cyclop servants
> Till the earth's great work is done,
> That Power in prescience builded,
> In the twilight dawn of Time,
> Like mother for her unborn child,
> Our cradle world sublime."

And Astronomy — how is that possible without Religion?
Methinks those still and awful heavens would paralyse us
with their silence, did no voice in our hearts make them all
resonant with their Creator's glory!   The stars glittering in
the wintry sky would freeze our souls could we never
deem them

> " The thousand eyes of God."

True Knowledge, then, is a sacred thing — sacred in this life
and in the next!*   It is the celestial food on which our souls
have grown to their full stature, and it is ours for ever.   When
the miser's wealth shall pass away from his grasp, — when the
proud man's coronet shall tarnish on his coffin-lid in the
vault, — when Affection itself shall be all transformed, amid
new relationships, — even then shall Knowledge be the wealth,
the honour, and the love of the new-risen soul.

Happiness, then, distinct from Virtue and Religion — a
mere heap of sensual, affectional, and intellectual pleasures, —
is not enough to satisfy our aspirations.   We may pile Pelion
on Ossa, and Ossa on Olympus, but the throne of the Im-
mortals will never be scaled by such a ladder.   Most of us,
as we advance to middle life, begin to feel this ; unless, indeed,
keen want, or pain, or sorrow have left us few pleasures,
whose insufficiency we might experience.   Of course the
more luscious our banquet has been, the more hastily we
have snatched at the joys (especially at the grosser joys)
of earth, the sooner are we satiated.   The *thorough* Sensual-

---

* "To desire therefore and covet after Truth, those truths more especially which
respect the divine nature, is to aspire to be partakers of that nature itself, and to
profess that all our studies and acquirements are devoted to the acquisition of
holiness, is an employment more truly religious than any external purification,
or mere service of the temple can be."— PLUTARCH, *Of Isis and Osiris, β.*

ist becomes worn out; while he who has partaken more
moderately, and with greater refinement, of the pleasures in
his reach, grows only indifferent.   On nearly all thinking men
and women there comes down, sooner or later, a November
of the Soul; not tempestuous, not frozen, but clouded, chill,
colourless, unhopeful.   We do not desire this thing or the
other; but, " 'mid enjoyment languish for desire," we cry with
Festus, —

> " It is the one great grief of life
>   To feel all feelings die."

That is to say, it is the one great grief of the prosperous, the
healthy, the beloved.   The joys they crave are theirs; but
while they taste them leanness enters into their souls.   Thus
the paradox comes true, that the more pleasures we possess
the fewer we enjoy ; the nearer we approach to happiness the
further we recede from it.   Dives may pity the sores of
Lazarus, and Lazarus pity the rich man sickening at his
luxurious board.

But if that cumulation of intellectual, affectional, and sensual pleasures which Eudaimonists set forth as constituting
Happiness, be not enough to satisfy the aspirations of the humblest heart, is it not a pitiful thing to set it up as the sole
goal of humanity, the only Aim of all our struggles, the
one end proposed by Omnipotence in the creation of the universe ?   It seems to me that we insult our nature when we
measure its swelling flood by a Nilometer like this, and that
we derogate from the character of God when we deem that
He has said to it, " Hitherto shalt thou come, and no further."

And again.   Could we succeed in reconciling our thoughts
to this low destiny, had we heart and enthusiasm to work for
the pauper child of Time and Pleasure, as for the royal heir
of Immortality and Virtue, even then what sort of moral
system could we logically follow ?   We find, indeed, that the
personal virtue of each of our neighbours does contribute to
the happiness of the community ; and so we may, in a collateral
way, countenance the same, and add to the donation of a loaf
a tract on Temperance, while we insert a good word for honesty
as decidedly " the best policy " into an exhortation to sanitary
reform.   Whether treating such tremendous things as the
Eternal Law and the relationship of a child of clay to the

Lord of the Heavens, in this sort of subservient convenient way, will ever produce much effect, I must, however, be allowed to doubt. When we attempt to dam up the torrent of Passion with the mud of Prudence, we must expect that when the waters rise a little our wretched dam will be washed away. In weak or stagnant characters — people with a great deal of fear, or people with very little passion — prudence has its effect. It will prevent men from breaking ground in a new vice or larger crime than usual; and there are also, perhaps, some calculating souls who are capable of making up their lives as sagaciously as a black-leg does his betting-book; and as they find " Morality " to be the best, or, at all events, the longest-winded horse in the field, they lay their schemes in consequence. But persons so judicious as these are the rare exceptions, even if they exist at all, amongst us. Health and respectability *in futuro* are, no doubt, very sweet sugar-plums to promise to the child, if he will consent to relinquish his play just at present. But human nature cries, " A bird in hand is worth two in the bush," — " I will enjoy my play now, and run my chance of the sugar-plum by and bye." Present Pleasure will always lure the majority of mankind more than future Reward, and present Passion plead more powerfully than the fear of future Chastisement.

Again I repeat it. Those who have endeavoured to bribe man to Virtue or menace him away from Vice, have shown the profoundest ignorance of his nature.

But if we may reasonably fear that our efforts to promote the general Morality of mankind as a matter of Prudence will produce very little effect, what will become of our *own* Personal Virtue if we set forth as the aim of our existence only, "the Greatest Happiness of the Greatest Number?"

True, in doing this we start with the real and most important Virtue of Benevolence; a Virtue which may be considered to include a third part of all human duty. But man is not *only* a Social being; he is also a free rational Personality, and a Creature of God. Beside his Social duties, he must therefore have Personal duties and Religious duties. Now, I ask, where are we to find a motive for the performance of these, if the sole End of existence be the promotion of the Greatest Happiness of the Greatest Number? Where are we to find restraints for our passions when they prompt us to be gluttonous, intemperate, unchaste, indolent, ignorant and irreligious ? Living in a social state, it is an event of daily occurrence that our Personal Virtue comes into competition with the immediate Happiness of our fellow-creatures. On what grounds may we refuse to degrade ourselves for them, if their Happiness be our only aim ?

It is true that Eudaimonists, foreseeing this question, have attempted with some plausibility to answer it thus. Their theory, they allege, includes the construction of certain General rules, which general Rules are all in favour of Personal Virtue ; for this reason, that each man's Personal Virtue is in *general* more conducive than Vice to the Happiness of the community. Accordingly they affirm, that when my Virtue and my neighbour's Happiness clash together, I am bound to preserve my own Virtue, because experience has shown that *on the whole* it tends more to public Happiness that I should do so. This is so important a doctrine that it deserves consideration.

No sooner has Paley laid down the grand principle of his system, "Whatever is Expedient is Right," than he proceeds (as he thinks) to guard against its malapplication by arguing that nothing is expedient which produces along with *Particular* good consequences *General* bad ones, and that thi*s is done by the violation of any useful general rule. "You cannot," says he, "permit one action and forbid another without showing a difference between them. Consequently, the same sort of actions must be generally permitted or generally forbidden. Where, therefore, the general permission of them would be pernicious, it becomes necessary to lay down and support the rule which generally forbids them." *

Now, let the number of experienced consequences of actions be ever so great, it must be admitted that the Inductions we draw therefrom can, at the utmost, be only provisional, and subject to revision should new facts be brought in to bear in an opposite scale. For example: In Europe we all think that we have experienced that Monogamy and Mono-andry are general rules conducive to the Happiness of

---

* Moral Phil. b. ii., cc. vi. vii.

mankind. But the votes of the millions of the East are in favour of Polygamy, and even Englishmen have been obliged to confess that Polyandry "works well" among the Buddhists. It is questioned whether the true Eudaimonist would be open to conviction on this matter and satisfy himself with a decimal share in a wife, supposing ample statistics could be procured proving the "Expediency" of the practice?

Further, from experience the rules induced must be not only Provisional, but Partial. The lax term "General" misleads us. A Moral Rule must be either *universal* and open to *no* exception, or, properly speaking, no rule at all.* Each case of Morals stands alone; for no two circumstances of human life precisely resemble one another, and the inductions made from ninety-nine can at the utmost only afford an analogical presumption for the hundredth; which presumption may be altogether overbalanced by the fresh circumstances of the particular case, leading us to anticipate an opposite result. Ninety-nine times' experience may show me that lying produces more mischief than good†; but on the hundredth occasion the expected good result may be immediate and immense and the contingent mischief apparently completely guarded against. It is false logic to pretend that our General Inductions can here be pushed a step beyond the last experiment. Thus, the Experimentalist's conclusions that "Monogamy conduces to Happiness," may possibly require revision from the consideration of new facts, and the conclusion that "Lying does more harm than good" may be quite remodelled by the fortunate discovery of so prudent a kind of falsification as shall obviate the mischief and leave the advantage. No doubt can remain on the mind of any

* "Principles of self-love contain general rules for adapting means to an end, and so are merely theoretic or technical principles; *e. g.*, how he who would like to eat bread has to construct a mill. But no practical principle founded on them can be necessary or of catholic extent; for when the Will acts from maxims of Self-Love, the determination of choice is based on feelings in the sensory; and it is uncertain that these feelings are universal, not even certain that they are unalterable in respect to the same external objects."—KANT, *Analytic of Principles*, p. 95.

† See *Whewell*, p. 211., answered in *Westminster Review*, No. iv. p. 364. The reviewer rightly justifies Bentham, inasmuch as his system by no means contemplated the continual private formation of an ethical code, but the construction of a broad and universal one for all mankind, based on the whole experience of the world. But even this must be provisional.

student of Paley that this would have been his own line of argument, "*If* we can only prove that a lie be expedient, then it becomes a duty to lie." As he says himself of the rule (which if any rule may do so may surely claim to be general) "Do not do evil that good may come," that it is "salutary, *for the most part*, the advantage *seldom* compensating for the violation of the rule." So to do evil is *sometimes* salutary, and does now and then compensate for disregarding even the Eudaimonist's last resource — a General Rule!

But if this principle of general rules cannot be logically grafted on Experimentalism, or, when so grafted, cannot be carried to the decision of those precise cases most requiring solution, then it appears that the ground on which the Public Eudaimonism sought to erect Personal Virtue is taken from under his feet. If each individual case is to stand on its own merits, and I am bound to balance continually between my personal truth, self-improvement, purity, and self-reverence against the intellectual, affectional, and sensual pleasures of my neighbours, it is clear enough what would become of my own soul. Postponing its interests to my fellow-creatures' pleasures I must sink for ever lower and lower. Thus Public Eudaimonism involves the absurdity that the true motive for the Virtue of All entails the destruction of the Virtue of Each!

2nd. Private Eudaimonism. There are several formulas, in which this system (the lowest, but the most logical of Moral heresies) is embodied. Rutherforth puts it thus, "Every man's Happiness is the ultimate end which Reason teaches him to pursue, and the constant and uniform practice of Virtue towards all mankind becomes our duty; *when* Revelation has informed us that God will make us *finally happy in a life after this*."* Paley (who properly belongs to this school, but endeavours frequently to seat himself on the corners of the stools of Moral and Public Eudaimonism), Paley, the standard Moralist of England, defines Virtue thus, "Virtue is the doing good to mankind in obedience to the will of God, and for the

---

* *Essay on the Nature and Obligations of Virtue*, 1744, quoted by Whewell, who asks, "How does our obedience to God on this view differ from obedience to an arbitrary tyrant?"

sake of Everlasting Happiness.   According to which definition
the good of mankind is the subject; the will of God the rule;
and *Everlasting Happiness the motive of Virtue.*"*

But though these two Moralists make *Everlasting* Happiness
the professed motive of Virtue, they by no means are sufficiently
illogical to exclude from their calculation the transitory pleasures of this world.   It is our *whole* Happiness, here and hereafter, which this school set forth as the aim of Virtue, and
embody in the sagacious apophthegms " Honesty is the best
Policy ;" " Be good, and you will go to heaven.   Do not be
bad, or you will be damned."

Nothing can be more intelligible than all this.   Certain
actions are perceived to have certain results in this world,
and are predicted to have the same in a far greater degree in
the next.   These results, therefore, are assumed to afford the
proper motives for the performance of the actions.   This is
very logical, and the more so that we may observe : — 1st.
That the results in question are undeniably really good and
desirable.   2nd. That there is every reason for confidence that
under the government of God they will take place with absolute adaptation to the actions.   3rd. That it may seem that
God *having* attached Rewards to Virtue, and Punishments to
Vice, *means* us to be determined thereby in our choice of the
one and rejection of the other.   I am not aware that this
latter argument has ever been strongly put forward in defence
of Private Eudaimonism ; but to me it seems the best plea
it can urge.   However, I hope to show it to be utterly
fallacious.

Happiness is a Real End, a Positive Good.   It may indeed
be treated by us sometimes as the means to warm and soften
human hearts and so prepare them for Virtue ; and it is
quite possible that it is as such it is bestowed by God † who
alone can righly estimate its infinitesimal smallness compared with the glorious realm of Virtue of which man is the
heir.   But still I apprehend that, deduction made of its power

---

* Moral Phil. b. i., c. vii.
† " I am, furthermore, well convinced that this life is not the land of enjoyment, but of labour and toil ; and that every joy is granted us but to strengthen
us for further exertion."— FICHTE.

to promote Virtue, Happiness is a true end in itself, and that the law of benevolence commands us to make our neighbour Happy when it is out of our power to conduce to his Virtue.

It is a Good — a *Bonum-in-se.* But, if my reader have gone with me hitherto, he will concede that it is not the *Ultimate* Good, the *Summum* Bonum, — *that* is, Virtue. Now, Morality, or obedience to certain rules of conduct, has two results. *One* is the production of that gratification of our desires which we call Happiness; *another* is the production of that condition of the soul which we call Virtue.

But if Virtue be the *Summum Bonum,* and Happiness only an inferior Good, it appears that, if we are to practise Morality for any end, we must in reason practise it for its *highest* result, namely, the production of the Virtuous condition of, Soul. The man who pursues an opposite course, and obeys the Law to obtain Happiness, is like one who observes the rules of hygienics not to preserve his health, but for the sake of avarice. What Health is to the price of medicine, Virtue is to Happiness. Thus at the outset Private Eudaimonism is in error by setting forth as the end of Morality that which at best is only its secondary result.

But in truth this mistake, and the more radical logical one, exposed in the last Chapter, of assuming that any rules of conduct which could be called Moral are deducible from the principle of " Every one for himself,"—these mistakes, I say, are trifling in comparison of the sacramental error of the system, that of affirming *that any conduct pursued only for the sake of our own Happiness can be Virtuous at all.*

I am aware that all argument on this line must appear to Eudaimonists a begging of the question at issue. They affirm that Virtue *is* the judicious pursuit of Happiness. I affirm that its essence lies in the renunciation of Happiness, in the postponement of the gratification of all our intellectual, affectional, and sensual desires now and for ever to the Eternal Law. Of these two opinions one must be the true and the other grossly erroneous, but both assume positions so fundamental, that nothing but Intuition can be called in to decide between the true axiom and the fallacious aphorism; there is no *proving* the axiom. Yet it seems to me, that if there be any one truth which Intuition does teach us more clearly than another, it is precisely this one,—that Virtue to be Virtue must be disinterested. The moment we picture any species of Reward becoming the bait of our Morality, that moment we see the holy flame of Virtue annihilated in the noxious gas. A man cannot be Virtuous who is honest, because it is "good policy," beneficent from love of approbation, pious for the sake of heaven. All this is Prudence not Virtue, Selfishness not Self-sacrifice. If he be honest for sake of policy, would he be *dis*honest, if it could be proved that it were more politic? If he would *not*, then he is not really honest from policy, but from some deeper principle thrust into the background of his consciousness. If he *would*, then is it not foulest mockery to call that honesty Virtuous which only waits a bribe to become dishonest?

But there are many Eudaimonists who will be ready to acknowledge that a prudent postponement of our happiness in *this* world cannot constitute virtue. But wherefore do they say we are to postpone it? Not for *present* pleasure or pain, that would be base; but for that anticipation of *future* pleasure or pain which we call Hope and Fear. And this, not for the Hope and Fear of this world, which are still admitted to be base motives; but for Hope and Fear extended one step beyond the tomb — the Hope of Heaven and Fear of Hell. This demands consideration.*

" If, through Hope merely of reward or Fear of punishment, the creature be incited to do the good he hates, or restrained from doing the ill to which he is not otherwise in the least degree averse, there is in this case no virtue or goodness whatever. There is no more of Rectitude, Piety, or Sanctity in a creature thus reformed, than there is meekness or gentleness in a tiger strongly chained, or Innocence and Sobriety in a monkey under the discipline of the whip. . . . The greater submission caused through this sole motive is only the lower and more abject servitude, and implies the greater wretchedness and meanness in the creature who has those passions of self-love so predominant, and is in his temper so vicious and defective. . . . What the fear of *future* punishment and hope of future reward, added to this belief (in the existence of God), may further contribute towards Virtue, we have now to consider. . . . Neither this hope nor fear can possibly be of the kind called Good Affections, such as are acknowledged the springs of all actions truly good. Neither can this hope or fear, as above intimated, consist in reality with Virtue, if it either stands as *essential* to any moral performance, or as a *considerable motive* to any act of which some better affection ought alone to have been a sufficient cause. It may be considered withal, that in this sort of discipline the principle of Self-love, which is naturally so prevailing in us, being no way moderated or restrained, but rather improved and made stronger every day by the exercise of the passions in a subject of more extended self-interest, there may be reason to apprehend lest the temper of this kind should extend itself in general through all the parts of life; for, if

"It is the creed of the human race," says Parker; "that the soul of a man never dies." Thus much Intuition teaches all nations and even all individuals, with exceptions so few as only to prove the rule. On this basis the collateral Intuition of Justice erects the scheme of a State of Rewards and a State of Punishments. The small glimpse which from our distant position we can obtain of the great drama of a human life, leaves on us the impression (whose veracity I am not concerned to question) that Justice is not meted completely in this world. Accordingly, having a consciousness that there is another and immortal existence before us, we almost inevitably conclude that it will be the stage whereon the final act of the tragedy will take place, and the perfect Justice be accomplished. Nearly all traditional creeds have embodied this Intuitive view of the case, and given us mythical representations of a heaven and a hell suited to the peculiar genius of each creed. It is noticeable, however, that till the *Moral* element be somewhat developed in the nation, the future state is not thus converted into one of rewards and punishments, but is simply a prolongation of this life, with such slight amendment of circumstances as the short-sighted Hope of the savage might dictate.*

the habit be such as to occasion in every particular a stricter attention to self-good and private interest, it must insensibly diminish the affections towards the interests of society, and introduce a certain narrowness of spirit, which (as some pretend) is peculiarly observable in the devout persons and zealots of almost every religious persuasion. This, too, must be confessed, that if it be true Piety to love God for his own sake, the over-solicitous regard to private good expected from Him must of necessity prove a diminution of Piety."—SHAFTES-BURY, *Characteristics*, vol. ii. p. 38. 39.

* Such are the "Happy Hunting Grounds" of the Red Indian; *Innis na n'oge* (the Isle of Youth), the Paradise of the Pagan Irish; the submarine Eden of the Greenlander (luxurious with abundant fires and salt-fish); and in general the ideal heavens of the barbarous tribes of Africa and America. None of these have the *pendant* of a Hell. The creeds which have taught future rewards and punishments are Brahminism, Buddhism, Zoroastrianism, the old Egyptian creed Jovism, Odinism, Druidism, Christianity, and Islam. The earlier Judaism is quite anomalous in its mixture of morality and secularism. Warburton was absurd to try to deduce evidence of *special* Divine instruction from a defect; but the singularity is not less remarkable, as showing the extraordinary force of theocratic pragmatism in the Hebrew mind. Antigonus of Socho, whose disciple Sadok founded the sect of the Sadducees, left only one grand dogma, that "Goodness must be done for its own sake, and not from hope of reward." This is a principle utterly at variance with Mosaism, which continually sets forth abundant harvests as rewards, and plague, pestilence, famine, and "the noisome beast," not to speak of cutaneous disorders, as punishments (*e.g.*, *Deut.* xxviii. 27.).

On the other hand, those creeds which admit the doctrine
of future Rewards and Punishments, seem to have carried
out so natural an anticipation far beyond the limits of reason.
It can hardly be ONLY the balancing of the account of these
poor three score years and ten which is to occupy the million
millenniums of eternity. Retribution is a great thing, for it
is the behest of the everlasting Law; but Virtue is a greater
far, for it is the Result and Accomplishment of the Law.
God, then, who works ever for the greatest ends, must have
made our souls for some further purpose than to be ground
down throughout all Eternity in the tremendous mill of Retribution. Some Bread of Life must come forth at last from
the Punishment, some glorious Work remains for us to do
after the Reward of the rest—if Bed of Rest the universe
contain.

There seems, indeed, to be an error still more fundamental
in this doctrine of Future Rewards and Punishments, to
which I have already briefly adverted in the First Chapter.
We possess, it is true, an Intuition that there is in the
Eternal Law such a principle as Retribution, that is, that the
infraction of the Law *ought* to entail suffering on the offender
proportioned to his guilt; and with the utmost confidence we
rightly expect to see that in this life or the next the Judge
of All will inflict this Retribution; that is to say, He will
add Pain or deduct Happiness in proportion to all guilt.
This is plain and undisputed so far as the doctrine of *Punishment* is concerned; but have we any corresponding Intuition
regarding what is so commonly classed as its natural and
equally valid converse, the doctrine of *Rewards?* It seems
to me that, while the infraction of the Law constitutes Guilt,
which *ought* to be punished, the fulfilment of the Law which
constitutes Virtue, has no corresponding claim to Reward,
being only the fulfilment of that which we are *bound* to fulfil.
I think that Intuition does not warrant us to say that " Virtue
has a *Right* to Happiness" in the same sense that " Sin has a
Right to Unhappiness." If this be so, to speak of future
Reward is obviously improper. The fact seems to be, that
the Justice of God requires that He should inflict propor-
tionate Unhappiness on all sin; *which done*, His Justice has

no further work, but leaves room for His Benevolence.   Now
Benevolence requires that Happiness should be bestowed on
every sentient being; therefore, so soon as the claims of Divine
Justice are satisfied, we may be sure that the Divine Benevolence always steps in and bestows Happiness.   But this is
a Free Gift, not a Reward; God indeed *does Right* when He
inflicts Unhappiness, and Right when He bestows Happiness.
But we *have a Right* only to Justice, not to Benevolence; to
the Unhappiness, not to the Happiness; to Punishment, not
to Reward.   The doctrine, then, of future Rewards and
Punishments as commonly understood, does not fulfil our
Intuitions.   It is not altogether a false, but it is an imperfect,
one-sided doctrine.   Doubtless there *is* Retribution beyond
the grave, and doubtless there, as well as here, we are " secure
to be as blest as we can bear," as happy as is compatible with
and will be justified by our progress in Virtue ; but, judging
from every evidence accessible to us, we are forced to conclude that the end of Creation is the *Perfecting*, and not
merely the Rewarding and Punishing of Souls.   Further, a
common error respecting a future happy state is, that therein
the souls of the blessed will be impeccable.   This notion I
have already controverted in Chapter I.   I endeavoured
there to demonstrate that even the Almighty could only
make a finite being incapable of Sin by making it incapable
of Virtue.   The miracle of making a creature at once Imperfect (*i. e.* bounded in knowledge and strength), and Perfect (*i. e.* unbounded in Moral Wisdom and Virtue), would
be equal to that of making a geometrical figure which should
be at once a circle and a triangle.

To return—if the Immortal Life be something more than
everlasting Punishment or never-ending Reward,—if it be an
eternal approximation to Perfection carried on through Trial,
through Virtue and Happiness, ever imperfect though ever
increasing—if, in a word, the future worlds of our habitation
be only higher schools than this,—then the idea of doing Right
for the *Rewards* of a Future Life becomes obviously absurd.
We are not *paid* with pleasures hereafter for doing our own
work now ; we are only *fed* with them in both worlds by our
Master, precisely to enable us to do it.   What a pitiful life it

were with no other aim than the week-day bread and water, and the Sunday's richer meal at last!

But in truth this doctrine of the Hope of Heaven being the true Motive of Virtue is (at least in theory) just as destructive of Virtue as that which makes the rewards of this life — health, wealth, or reputation,— the motive of it. Well says brave Kingsley —

> " Is selfishness for time a sin,
> Stretched out into eternity, celestial prudence ? "

If to act for a small reward cannot be virtuous, to act for a large one can certainly merit no more.* To be bribed by a guinea is surely no better than to be bribed by a penny. To be deterred from ruin by fear of transportation for life, is no more noble than to be deterred by fear of twenty-four hours in prison. There is no use multiplying illustrations. He who can think that Virtue is the doing right for *pay*, may think himself very judicious to leave his pay in the savings-bank now and come into a fortune all at once by and bye; but he who thinks that Virtue is the doing right for Right's own sake, cannot possibly draw a distinction between small bribes and large ones, — a reward to be given to-day, a reward to be given in eternity.

In practice, however, it is only fair to remark, that the doing right for the sake of Heaven is a far less debasing and injurious principle than that of doing right from motives of earthly prudence. Into our visions of that future world *some* thoughts of God and goodness must, perforce, intermingle even with the lowest imagining. Thus, the man who uses the formula, " Do Right for the sake of Heaven," may *possibly* mean the same as he who says, " Do Right to become

---

* It is perfectly horrible to read the heresies which have been put forth on these topics by divines of illustrious reputation. Surely Waterland's Defence of Trinitarianism was hardly so good as to shelter a doctrine like the following : " To be just or grateful so far as is consistent with our temporal interest, and no farther, has no more moral good than paying a debt for our present ease, or in order to be trusted again ; *and the being further just and grateful without future prospects has as much of Moral Virtue in it as folly or indiscretion has;* so that, the Deity once set aside, it is a demonstration there could be no Morality at all." Methinks the controversies of the Homoousion and the Filioque hardly touched us all so closely as this doctrine that disinterested justice and gratitude are *folly;* yet Waterland and Rutherforth and Paley are no heretics, " all honourable men ! " See also Robert Hall's *Modern Infidelity*, p. 20.

Virtuous," or " Do Right to enjoy a closer union with God."
In such cases he only falls into the error of proposing the End
of morality as our aim, instead of its Law as our rule.   Yet
the mistake is rarely so innocuous as this, and Heaven means
to most men a great deal else beside Virtue and Divine communion.   That world of endless progress is thought of as a
" Rest "— a rest, not so much from the importunities of the
lower passions, as from pain and worldly trouble.   Others go
beyond these negative hopes, and look for all manner of splendours and pleasures* ; insomuch that they actually relinquish
them here for the purpose of obtaining the same things more
permanently hereafter ; and, in the hope that God will

" Give Humility a coach-and-six,"

they renounce the vanities of the world !

But whether more or less gross or spiritual be our conceptions of a future state, to act for the sake of it is a false
principle, whose effects can only be more or less injurious.
As I have so often repeated, the true Freedom and glory of
man is his Obedience to that Law which he finds in his heart,
and so far as he seeks an End instead of obeying that Law, so
far he derogates from the prerogatives of his higher nature.

Nevertheless, it cannot be denied that the belief in Immortal Progress is of vast value.   Such belief, and that in an
ever-present God, may be called the two wings of human
Virtue; without which it is a tremendous task for it to support
itself over the miry paths of life.   I look on the advantages
of a faith in Immortality to be twofold.   First, it cuts the
knot of the world, and gives to our apprehension a God whose
Providence need no longer perplex us, and whose immeasurable and never-ending goodness blazes ever brighter before
our contemplating souls.   Secondly, it gives an importance
to Personal Progress, which we can hardly attribute to it so
long as we deem it is to be arrested for ever by death.   The

---

* I have even heard of instances in which, fully to excite the cupidity of
children, they had been encouraged to picture to themselves the gratification of
all their appetites.   Light, and jewels, and music, golden harps, and cities with
gates of pearl, offer no attractions to the infant ; so it must be lured with toys
and dainties.   The reader will doubtless smile, but he might rather sigh, to be
informed that a mother once told me that she " found it necessary to allow her
child to expect *pork-chops* in Heaven !"   This is Eudaimonism in caricature.

M 3

man who does not believe in Immortality may be, and often
actually is, more Virtuous than his neighbour; and it is quite
certain that his Virtue is of far purer character than that
which bargains for Heaven as its pay.   But his task is a very
hard one — a task without a result, — and his road a dreary
one, unenlightened even by the distant dawn of

> " That great world of light which lies
> Behind all human destinies."

We can scarcely do him better service than by leading him
to trust that Intuition of Immortality which is written in the
heart of the human race by that Hand which writes no false-
hoods.

But, if the attainment of Heaven be no true motive for the
pursuit of Virtue, surely I may be held excused from de-
nouncing that practice of holding out the fear of Hell wherewith many fill up the measure of moral degradation ?   Here
it is vain to suppose that the Fear is that of an Immortality of
Sin and banishment from God, as we are sometimes told the
Hope of Heaven is that of an Immortality of Virtue and
union with Him.   The mind which sinks to the debasement
of clutching at any Fear, is already below the level wherein
Sin and estrangement from God are terrors.   They are the
lot of such a mind at the moment you hold them forth as
threats.   You are foretelling a disease in which the patient is
writhing.   Nor is the *continuance* of the malady likely to
alarm him ; for, from the first, he has had it in his power to
" wash and be clean."   It is his weakness of *Will* alone which
hinders him from saying, " I will arise and go to my Father ; "
and, unless you can strengthen that Will by some different
motive, it is idle to threaten it with its own persistence.

No !   Tell the sinner of a burning abyss and torturing
fiends, gnashing teeth and deathless worms, and if in the
nineteenth century he believe the dream of Dante, and yet
escape a madhouse, then you will have had the triumph of
making him — what ? — Virtuous?   Not so : only a Vicious
Coward.

To be determined by any motive except the intrinsic
Right of an action detracts the Virtue from its performance ;

but to be determined by Fear is to be moved by the very
basest principle in our nature — a principle having no one
element of good in it, and degrading the wretched soul which
stoops under it to the rank of a self-despised coward.   I
doubt not, also, that of two men, each longing to commit a
sin, he who refrains solely from fear is more vicious than h
who actually commits it.   The latter at least retains some
manhood, some courage, which, turned hereafter to a better
cause, may lead him far on the right road ; but he who consciously recognises the turpitude of an action, who believes
that his gracious Creator abhors it, who feels that his passion
is not so strong but that he can completely curb it ; and who
yet cannot find in his heart one spurn of hatred for the sin,
one spark of love to God — but only Fear — base, selfish,
hound-like Fear — is not that man *vicious ?*   To love and
choose Evil is Vice.   Does it lessen its viciousness to be,
furthermore, a dastard ?

But, it is asked, " If all this be true, if Virtue cannot
be the offspring of either Hope or Fear, how comes it that
God has attached Rewards and Punishments to Virtue and
Vice by His visible Providence on earth, and (according to
universal consent) in the next world also ?   Does not this
fact prove that He *means* us to be determined by Hope and
Fear ?

I answer, it proves nothing of the kind.   It proves and
brings home to our doubting souls the great truth that
" there is a God who judgeth the earth," who holds the
Justitia rectoria of the universe He has made, and who will
fulfil to the uttermost the claims of Justice.   It proves the
truth that there is a Father for ever watching over His
children, " hedging up their way with thorns," when they
wander too far, and with a father's — aye, a mother's — love
planting in that path every innocent joy which will not im-
pede their progress.   By these punishments God reminds us
of Himself and His Law ; He vindicates His Justice, and He
sets bounds to iniquities which, without such checks, misused
Freedom would extend till they had desolated the world.   By
the Joys He grants us He shows His endless love, He wins
our hearts to Himself, and strengthens us for moral exertion.

But how does all this prove that He means us to be spurred by Pain and lured by Pleasure to the performance of Duty? A mother punishes her child when he disobeys her commands, and gives him every joy at her bestowal which she thinks innoxious; but does that mother mean that her child shall always obey her *for Fear* of her chastisement, or love her *for Hope* of the gifts she bestows? Even human love puts to shame the pseudo-piety which professes to love God because He will pay our wretched alloy with everlasting Paradise. And, even if human love were not perfectly disinterested, we might still be assured that God would never design to move us by degrading principles. He it is who has taught us to love Goodness for its own sake, and to stand self-condemned when we would take that heavenly bride to our bosoms merely for her Dowry — aye even, or for her Beauty. The highest, the purest aspirations of our nature are precisely those which we may with greatest certainty trace to our Maker's teaching; nor is it possible that we can ever conceive of a Moral Principle which shall be higher than He intends His children to follow. The parasite of an earthly despot can only please his master by *pretending* disinterested attachment to his person, and disclaiming hopes of court-advancement or fears of banishment; and God, who infinitely deserves all the adoration of our souls, will *He* be satisfied by our mercenary love?

Men strive to excite our hopes of Heaven and fears of Hell as stimulants of Piety and Virtue. Methinks they would do better to teach us how to thrust out from our hearts every selfish thought, and purify our Love, so that it may dare to meet the Eye which now beholds all its baseness, shallowness, and hypocrisy.*

---

* If any one desire to obtain a full idea of Private Eudaimonism, let him read Waterland's third Sermon, *On the Nature and Kinds of Self-Love.* The following extracts will convey some notion of it:—

" Self-love, directed to, and pursuing what is, on the whole, and in the last, result of things, absolutely best for us, is innocent and good; and every deviation from this is culpable and vicious. Be a thing ever so good otherwise, yet if it be not so likewise with respect to *ourselves*, first or last, it loses all its influence upon us, and cannot be the object of a rational and deliberate choice. It might seem, perhaps, reasonable in the nature of the thing (if we may be allowed to put an impossible case) for a man to submit to die and to be eternally extinct or miserable for saving of many thousand souls, because this is preferring a public to a

4th. Beside Euthumism and Public and Private Eudaimonism, I have remarked that there exists a fourth popular
Scheme of Ethics of an entirely different principle; and though
only of a supplementary character, and hardly recognised as
a Moral System, yet of immense practical influence in the
world. I speak of the Law of Honour, the great but im-

private interest, the whole to a part. And yet this is what no one could de-
liberately chose while he has a principle of self-love remaining; neither could it
be reasonably expected of him. The wisest course for any man to take is to secure
an interest in the life to come. This is certainly, upon the whole and in the last
result, absolutely best for him. He may love himself in this instance as highly
and as tenderly as he pleases. All virtue and piety are thus resolvable into a
principle of self-love. It is what Scripture itself, in other words, resolves them
into, by founding them upon faith in God's promises and hope of things unseen.
In this way it may be rightly said that there is no such thing as disinterested
virtue. It is with reference to ourselves, and for our own sakes, that we love
even God himself : ' We love Him because He first loved us ;' that is, because
we love ourselves. He is our sovereign good, our prime felicity. Some divines
of the mystic way, not distinguishing between esteem and love, pretend that God
is to be loved for His own sake only, for His own intrinsic excellency and perfections. But this is a difference rather in words than in things. We do love
God for His own sake when we love Him not for any low regards or little
sinister ends ; when we love Him as being infinitely more lovely, that is, infinitely more *able to make us happy* than all things beside. And yet this is loving
Him for our own sakes and with regard to ourselves, who have our happiness in
Him, so amiable and kind a Being. And when we are said to love God above
all things, the meaning strictly is, that we prefer Him, not before ourselves (who
pretend not to be the objects of our own happiness), but before all other objects
which might be supposed to contribute anything towards our happiness. It
may be said, perhaps, that we may be conceived to love God with a love of good-
will, as when we wish that His name may be exalted and His laws observed, and
that we ought to wish for this in the first place, even before our own happiness, and
without any regard to it. But these fine-spun notions, however they may appear
in theory, and carry a resemblance of the most resigned devotion and most exalted piety, yet are, I am afraid, much too high for practice, and perhaps hardly
reconcileable with the reason and nature of things. It is utterly impracticable
for any reasonable creature having a principle of self-love to act at all without
some motive—that is, without a view to his *own good*, present or future. And,
however a man may pretend to abstract from all self-regards, and to fix his
aims, wishes, and desires upon God's glory, yet among all that seeming dis-
regard to his own welfare, this thought will perpetually steal in, that the further
he runs off from self the more impossible will it be for him to fail of being
happy. To deny ourselves any gratification, without an equivalent either in
hand or in prospect, is unnatural and unreasonable. It is refusing happiness formally considered as such, and is, therefore, neither a rational nor indeed a possible choice. For the like reasons, it is natural for us to endeavour after a
speedy deliverance from any present uneasiness by all proper methods; and all
are proper which do not in their consequences, here or hereafter, tend to involve
us in more or greater. No man can be moved to submit to anything painful
but in order to avoid something more painful. What man in his senses would
choose to be uneasy so much as for a moment without a valuable consideration
for it, or to prevent the suffering of something worse? "

If any justification be needed for the publication of this Essay, I conceive that
it will be amply supplied by the above quotation from a writer who has been
patiently suffered to occupy for a century the position of one of the standard
orthodox divines of England.

perfect brilliant struck off the pure diamond of the perfect
Moral Law.

The history of the formation of the Law of Honour, could
we trace it accurately, would be a most singular chapter in
the progress of humanity.   What more remarkable sight can
we have presented to us than that of a vast number of the
higher classes of society neglecting entirely the study of the
Eternal Law of the universe, whose axioms God Himself has
deigned to teach them, and yet not only studying, but obeying
with most punctilious and self-sacrificing submission, a set of
Canons of Honour derived from the obscure Intuitions of ages
of barbarism — ages whose civil legislation is utterly derided
by the very same individuals ?

A thousand years ago, in the midnight of the ages, Europe
had well nigh forgotten the Intuitive Morality of the philosophers of Greece and Rome.   That Voice in the heart of
man, always so " still and small," was scarce audible amid the
fierce clamour of the robber tribes, disputing the plunder of
the world.   The cord with which the cruel Theodoric
crushed the brain of Boethius seemed also to have crushed
out of the human mind the sublime " Consolations of Philosophy."   The Church, whose office it should have been to
perpetuate the Traditional Morals of the Gospel, became
utterly false to her charge, and preached, instead of a " Sermon on the Mount," a Parænesis of St. Pacian.   The noble
voices of Seneca and Antoninus chanted no longer their magnanimous strophes in Nature's own sonorous major ; but celi-
bate monks whined out in dreary minor their doleful *misereres.*
Nor was this all.   The corner-stone which Christ Himself had
laid for His Church, the " Love of God and Man," was by
these false builders thrust from its place, and supplanted by a
formalism such as never disgraced the teaching of Buddh or
Menu, Zoroaster or Mahomet. *

* St. Eligius, in the seventh century, thus defined Christian morals : " He is
a good Christian who comes frequently to church, who presents an oblation that
it may be offered to God on the altar, who does not taste the fruits of his land
till he has consecrated a part of them to God, who can repeat the Creed and the
Lord's Prayer.   Redeem your souls from punishment while it is in your power,
offer presents and tithes to churches, light candles in holy places as much as
you can afford, come more frequently to church, implore the protection of the
saints.   For if you observe these things, you may come with security at the

In piteous dilemma were the consciences of men, while on one side stood the Priest preaching for Virtue, the prostration of soul and body to his corrupt Church; and, on the other, the Knight exalting the courage of the brute into the glory of the disciple of Jesus of Nazareth.

In this night of the world the yet unquenched spark of Intuition lighted up suddenly the sole Lamp of those dreary ages — Chivalry ; chivalry, the golden crest of the iron-clad time, which even now surges up glorious to the eye of memory over the vast battle-field of mediæval Europe. Through the roar of that ceaseless warfare, 'mid the cry of the trampled Serf, the tortured Jew, the slaughtered Saracen, there come to us, clear and sweet, the trumpet-voices of Bayard and Du Guesclin, of the Black Prince and the Cid.

I envy not the Moralist who could treat disdainfully of Chivalry. It was a marvellous principle that which could make of plighted Faith a Law to the most lawless, of Protection to Weakness a Pride to the most ferocious. While the Church taught that Personal Duty consisted in scourgings and fastings, and Social Duty in the slaughter of Moslems and burning of Jews, Chivalry roused up a man to reverence himself through his own courage and truth, and to treat the weakest of his fellow-creatures with generosity and courtesy. True, it did not teach all Morality, perhaps not half of the Moral Law; and how far its principles, as we find them in romance and myth, were ever practically brought into action, it is difficult to decide. Still, so far as it went, Chivalry was the best thing then in the world, its motives the purest, its ideal the highest.

But the electric light flamed forth but fitfully and at length almost died out in that cold, grey dawn before our glorious

Day of Judgment to say, ' Give unto us, Lord, for we have given unto Thee.' " —(MOSHEIM, *Cent.* vii. c. iii.)   Thus the "good Christian " of St. Eligius may be a liar, robber, perjurer, assassin, and adulterer ; but still, if he have paid his tithes, lighted sufficient candles, and attended frequently at Mass, he may confidently claim the Paradise he has *purchased* from God !   Well may Hallam remark " Whether the superstition of these dark ages had actually passed that point when it becomes more injurious to public morals and the welfare of society than the entire absence of all religious notions, is a very complex question, on which I would by no means pronounce an affirmative decision."—*Middle Ages,* c. ix.

century arose.   As Enthusiasm and Faith faded away an
extraordinary modification of Chivalry took place.   Of the
numerous virtues it had inculcated, a selection was made, and a
Common Law of Honour thence gradually compiled.   Active
physical Courage was still accorded the highest rank, but it
was no longer required to display itself in Quixotic enter-
prises for the relief of oppressed individuals or nations.   The
Vaudois might be persecuted, or the " poor widow " robbed
by her "adversary;" but the " Man of Honour " or the
" Honourable House " had no need to listen to their cry.   A
Duel, or a War of Policy, had become the proper fields for
valour.   The Breach of a Promise was still held to be dishonourable, but exceptions were made to the rule.   If a vow
were made to a Wife at the altar of God, its violation entailed
but trivial discredit.   The Lie of the Gambler consigned him
indeed to eternal disgrace, but that of the Seducer was almost a jest.   To defraud a wealthy gentleman of the price of
a horse was decided to be in the highest degree shameful; but
to ruin a dozen over-trustful tradesmen by dishonest debts
was qualified only as "extravagant."   Not to follow further
the delicate intricacies of this singular code, let it suffice to
say that the man whom it would still recognise as "honourable" might, without any derogation from that character, be
cruel, profligate, and voluptuous, lost in debt, a gambler,
drunkard, adulterer, and blasphemer.

Of recent years there has been a strong tendency to soften
the worse features of this system.   To profane the Holiest
Name in passion or in jest is now felt (at least in England) to
be an offence against good manners; drunkenness is recognised as degrading; to provoke the unoffending is known to
be ungentlemanlike; duelling under ordinary circumstances
stands condemned.   But there is yet much room for progress
in this direction, many Virtues to be recognised as Virtues,
many Vices to be condemned as Vices, before the Law of
Honour can be brought into conformity with the Moral Law,
and the general Conscience of Society be applied to its proper
use of supplying the deficiencies of individual neglected Consciences.   In particular, the absurd difference between the
male and female Codes of Honour must be done away with.

The lie which would disgrace the Man must not be treated
as venial in the Woman.   The unchastity which is the
Woman's irretrievable dishonour must not be without shame
for the partner of her sin.   The cowardice which would
bring ignominy to the Man must not be *taught* to the woman
as the proper ornament of her sex.*

Finally, whether it be the masculine or feminine Code
of Honour which is instilled into the young, it must, I think,
be admitted that we are in the habit of giving it far too much
prominence in their education *as a Law resting on the opinion
of others*.   This defect is not inherent in the system.   The
true principle of Honour is before all a principle of *Self-
reverence*, of a man's own private respect for himself as he
knows himself in his heart, and in this light it is a grand and
noble branch of the highest Morality.   But the moment the
"opinion of the world" is brought in as a motive, the transcendental character of the principle is lost, and Private Eudaimonism takes its place.   Recurring to its true character,
the Law of Honour, when duly enlarged and rectified, becomes
highly valuable.   We perceive that, amid all its aberrations
and imperfections, it has been the truest voice of Intuition,
amid the lamentations of the believer in "total depravity,"—
and the bargaining of the expediency-seeking Experimentalist.
While the one represented Virtue as a Nun and the other as
a Shopwoman, the Law of Honour drew her as a Queen;
—faulty perhaps, but freeborn and royal.   Much service has
this Law done to the world; it has made popular modes of
thinking and acting far nobler than those inculcated from
many a pulpit; and the result is patent, that many a "publican
and sinner," many an opera-frequenting, betting, gambling
man of the world, is a far safer person with whom to transact
business than the Pharisee who talks most feelingly of the
"frailties of our fallen nature."   I would far rather that son
of mine should take for his manual the "Broad Stone of
Honour," than "Paley's Moral Philosophy."

In reality it was impossible that a system should have ob-

* Antisthenes insisted on the identity of nature between male and female
virtue.   (See *Diog. Laert.* in Ant.)   The Virtue of Courage is given its high
place because without it we can have no security for any other Virtue.   How
does this hold less of a woman than a man?

tained so greatly in the world, had it not embodied a great
truth as well as propagated many errors. Now this the Law
of Honour actually did accomplish. When Religion itself de-
scended to be the nurse of prudent selfishness, and to set forth
Heaven and Hell as the sole motives of Virtue, it stepped in
with the manly appeal, " Before *all that* be Honourable; respect yourself, your word, your reputation; be fearless!"
This is the inner sense of the whole code, and it is a noble
one. The man who is thoroughly Honourable, even according to its imperfect definition, has in him the materials of a
hero. That soul which amid excesses of passion and even of
vice can yet retain *some* noble principle, and be a law to itself
while regardless of earthly laws; that soul which can thus
retain its self-reverence, will ere long bow to the whole law of
its nature, and devote its not unpractised energies to the holy
cause of Virtue and of God. But, on the other hand, the
man who is *not* honourable, whatever may be his other moral
and religious pretensions, is *not* virtuous; nay, he fails in so
high and peremptory a Law of Virtue that all his other merits
are utterly nugatory. I do not say there is no hope for him who
will lie and cringe, and play the spy and the poltroon — God
forbid that I should say it ! There is Hope, a sure and certain Hope, for all. No child of God can ever fall so utterly
prostrate but that his Father's arm shall be strong enough to
raise him up. But this I say. No faults are so ruinous as
disgraceful faults, none so polluting to the whole soul, none so
difficult of eradication.

The Law of Honour, then, merits to be re-integrated into
the Moral Law as a principle in itself pure and high, setting
forth a true branch of Morals on its proper ground of a Law,
and not as means to an End. But, before it can be thus re-
integrated, it must undergo vast corrections, additions, and
emendations. Nor must we forget that, while those Virtues
which concern Truth and Courage claim peculiarly the title
of Honourable, and those Vices of Falsehood, Duplicity,
Cowardice, and Baseness the name of Dishonourable ; yet,
nevertheless, *all* Virtue, be it ever so mild or simple, deserves
reverence ; *all* Vice, be it ever so blazoned and audacious,
merits only contempt.

There never was deed of hero or of patriot *so* "honourable" as when the scourged and crucified Son of the Carpenter cried in his agony and shame, "Father, forgive them, for they know not what they do."

Returning from the contemplation of the lowness of aim common to all the forms of Eudaimonism and of the incompleteness and errors of the Law of Honour, how magnificent seems the grand and holy doctrine of true Intuitive Morality! Do Right for the Right's own sake — love God and Goodness *because* they are Good! The soul seems to awake from death at such archangel's call as this, and mortal man puts on his rightful Immortality. The Prodigal grovels no longer, seeking for Happiness amid the husks of Pleasure; but, "coming to himself," he arises and goes to his Father, heedless if it be but as the lowest of His servants, he may yet dwell beneath that Father's smile. Hope and Fear for this life or the next, mercenary bargaining and labour of eye-service for lure of Honour, all are at an end; he, is a Free-man, and Free shall be the oblation of his soul and body, the Reasonable, Holy, and Acceptable Sacrifice.

There is nothing of *excitement* about this bare and naked thought of duty to be performed for its own sake — it is a calm and solemn thing : no Houri-form beckoning us to Paradise; but a giant's cold strong hand laid on our heads and urging us ever onward through an endless road : no sound of "harp and tabret" bidding us to the dance; but the trumpet's clarion-call to battle.

Oh, Living Soul! wilt thou follow that mighty Hand, and obey that summons of the trumpet? Perchance thou hast reached life's solemn noon, and with the bright hues of thy morning have faded away the beautiful aspirations of thy youth. Doubtless thou hast often struggled for the Right; but, weary with frequent overthrows, thou criest, "This also is vanity." But think again, Oh Soul, whose sun shall never set! have no poor and selfish ambitions mingled with those

struggles, and *made* them vanity? have no theologic dogmas, from which thy maturer reason revolts, been blended
with thy truer principle? Hast thou nourished no extravagant hope of becoming suddenly sinless, or of heaping up
with an hour's labour a mountain of benefits on thy race?
Surely some mistake like these lies at the root of all moral
discouragement. But mark —

Pure Morals forbid all base and selfish motives, — all hap-
piness-seeking, fame-seeking, love-seeking, — in this world
or the next, as motives of Virtue. Pure Morals rest not on
any traditional dogma, — on history, on philology, on criticism,
— but on those Intuitions, clear as the axioms of Geometry,
which thine own soul finds in its depths, and knows to be
necessary truths, which, short of madness, it cannot disbelieve.

Pure Morals offer no panacea to cure in a moment all
the diseases of the human heart, and transform the sinner into
the saint. They teach that the passions, which are the necessary machinery of our moral life, are not to be miraculously
annihilated, but by slow and unwearying endeavour to be
brought into obedience to the Holy Will; while to fall and
rise again many a time in the path of Virtue is the inevitable
lot of every pilgrim therein.

Pure Morals teach that the power of man to conduce to
his brother's virtue is only one of the thousand agencies by
which God works for the same end; and ill does it become
us to be offended at the failure of our puny efforts while He
persists in sending down, with unwearied love, his rain of
mercies on the heads of the just and unjust.

Again, the disappointment commonly felt of the aspirations
of youth after Goodness seem traceable, in a great measure,
to the narrow and sordid views of life and human destiny
with which our minds are early chilled and contracted. It is
not often, perhaps, that any of us stand still for an hour on
the hill-tops of Thought, to take in an extended view of our
earthly road. We usually move on restlessly with our eyes
bent on the few thorns or flowers either immediately within our
grasp, or but a few paces in advance. Now and then, however, some accident of the road, perchance some milestone
anniversary, causes us to pause and count over the many we

have passed, the few which may yet remain. Then it is that
the breadth and clearness of our Moral Sight, the brightness
and grandeur of our view of the Design of Creation, becomes
of the utmost importance. If this world seem to us but a
" Vale of Tears," a scene of disappointed hopes, severed affections, and quenched aspirations; if we believe that we are
intended to pass through it, disdaining and rejecting even the
few pleasures it may offer, and only by so doing hope to pass
unscathed by the fiery pit which yawns beside its bourne;
then, indeed, a comprehensive view of life is calculated to
produce a degree of terror, which, according to the vividness
of our realisation of its truth, may lead to fanaticism or madness. Or, if our existence here seem only a stormy and most
uncertain passage to a dead haven of calm, wherein no further
progress can take place, what room is there for joy, what
reason is there in our unutterable longings after the Infinite?
But if, on the other hand, we hold a nobler philosophy, how
different seems the glorious perspective, stretching out for
ever beyond the stars! Heirs of Immortal Progress, whose
title thereto is the Will of Omnipotence, whose security
thereof is the Immutability of God, we stand on this "pinnacle of time" as young eagles spreading their pinions for
the sky. There is no Fear for us, for the Wings of the
Great Parent are ready to bear us up whensoever we
falter. We see that His world is a blessed place, filled
with tokens of God's Love, and affording us more space
than we shall ever fill for virtuous deeds. Our hearts
burn within us, when for a moment the vision rises before
our sight of what we might make our life even here upon
earth. Faintly can any words picture that vision!

A life of *Benevolence*, in which every word of our lips, every
work of our hands, had been a contribution to human Virtue
or human Happiness: — a life in which, ever wider and
warmer through its three score years and ten, had grown our
pure, unwavering, Godlike Love, till we had spread the
same Philanthropy through a thousand hearts ere we passed
away from earth to love yet better still our brethren in the
sky.

A life of *Personal Virtue*, in which every evil disposition had

N

been trampled down, every noble sentiment called forth and
strengthened; a life in which, leaving day by day further
behind us the pollutions of sin, we had also ascended daily
to fresh heights of purity, till self-conquest, unceasingly
achieved, became continually more secure and more complete,
and at last —

> " The lordly Will o'er its subject powers
> Like a throned God prevailed,"

and we could look back upon the great task of earth, and
say, " It is finished ! "

A life of *Religion*, in which the delight in God's presence,
the reverence for His moral attributes, the desire to obey
His Will, and the consciousness of His everlasting love, had
grown continually clearer and stronger, and of which Prayer,
deepest and intensest, had been the very heart and nucleus,
till we had found God drawing ever nearer to us as we drew
near to Him, and vouchsafing to us that communion whose bliss
no human speech may ever tell; the dawning of that day of
adoration which shall grow brighter and brighter still, while
all the clusters of the suns fade out and die.

And, turning from our own destiny, from the endless
career opened to our Benevolence, our Personal Virtue, and
our Piety, we take in a yet broader view, and behold
the whole Universe of God mapped out in one stupendous
Plan of Love. In the abyss of the past eternity we see the
Creator for ever designing, and for ever accomplishing the
supremest End at which Infinite Justice and Goodness could
aim, and absolute Wisdom and Power bring to pass. For
this End, for the Virtue of all finite Intelligences, we behold
Him building up millions of starry abodes, and peopling them
with Immortal Spirits clothed in garbs of flesh, and endowed
with that Moral Freedom whose bestowal was the highest
boon of Omnipotence. As ages of milleniums roll away, we
see a double Progress working through all the realms of
space—a Progress of each race and of each individual. Slowly
and securely, though with many an apparent retrogression,
does each world-family become better, wiser, nobler, happier.
Slowly and securely, though with many a grievous back-
sliding, each living soul grows up to Virtue. Nor pauses

that awful march for a moment, even in the death of the
being or the cataclysm of the world.   Over all Death and
Change reigns that Almighty Changeless Will which has
decreed the holiness and happiness of every Spirit He hath
made.   Through the gates of the grave, and on the ruins of
worlds, shall those spirits climb, higher and yet higher
through the infinite ages, nearer and yet nearer to Goodness
and to God.

Such views as *these* of human destiny have nothing in them
of terror, nothing in them to send us into a monastery or a
madhouse, nothing to repel us back from our contemplation
of them into the pitiful round of worldly pleasures.   The
heart which throbs not at their grandeur, which leaps not
with exultation at their glory, beats not in human breast.
Virtue has but to be seen to claim our adoration.   But it is
not the feeble words of our fellow-sinner which can give Her
to our sight.   That must be the Intuition of our own Souls.
Neither will it suffice to take in once, in one ecstatic glance,
the glorious Design of Creation.   That must be gazed upon
and pondered hour by hour, till we gain from it courage and
patience to fulfil the life-long labour by which it must be accomplished.

And now, O deathless Spirit of Man, wilt thou begin thine
everlasting Task?—the Task which thou shalt for ever
fulfil, yet never through the cycles of thine Immortality complete.   Wilt thou " be Perfect, even as thy Father, who is
in heaven is Perfect?"

Answer it, I pray thee, to thine own heart, not hastily, in
momentary enthusiasm; not thoughtlessly, forgetful that along
that interminable ascent grows many and many a thorn of
Self-sacrifice, nay, that it is all spread with thorns; but calmly,
reasonably, devoutly, as becomes the greatest of all human
decisions, answer it,—

"SHALL I BE GOOD, AND DO GOOD, BECAUSE IT IS RIGHT?"

THE END.

For EU product safety concerns, contact us at Calle de José Abascal, 56–1°,
28003 Madrid, Spain or eugpsr@cambridge.org.